Bryant, Sir Arthur
The fire and the rose

DATE DUE			

THE FIRE AND
THE ROSE

Sir Arthur Bryant

THE FIRE AND
THE ROSE

Doubleday & Company, Inc., Garden City, New York

1966

Library of Congress Catalog Card Number 66-20505
Introduction Copyright © 1965 by Sir Arthur Bryant
Text Copyright © 1965 by Sir Arthur Bryant
All Rights Reserved
Printed in the United States of America

Why should we celebrate
These dead men more than the dying?
It is not to ring the bell backward
Nor is it an incantation
To summon the spectre of a Rose.
We cannot revive old factions
We cannot restore old policies
Or follow an antique drum.
These men, and those who opposed them
And those whom they opposed
Accept the constitution of silence
And are folded in a single party.
Whatever we inherit from the fortunate
We have taken from the defeated
What they had to leave us—a symbol:
A symbol perfected in death.
And all shall be well and . . .
All manner of thing shall be well
When the tongues of flames are in-folded
Into the crowned knot of fire
And the fire and the rose are one.

                              T. S. Eliot

Introduction

My old friend and master, G. M. Trevelyan, always held that narrative was the essential basis of the historian's craft. For though, apart from his initial task of research, a writer of history has other and, perhaps, more important functions—of analysis, interpretation and judgment—man is a creature of time, and, history is the record of what time does to him and of what he does with time. There are moments—T. S. Eliot called them "timeless moments"—when the history of a nation, and sometimes of mankind itself, turns on what, in a few hours, days or weeks, men make of the time given them. Such a moment occurred over England during the summer of 1940; another "in the hundred days that changed the world" at Petrograd in 1917. And the historian of such moments has, first and foremost, to use the instrument of narrative; to practise the chronicler's art.

Having sometimes essayed that art, I have taken from the detailed mass of political, economic, social, legal, religious, literary and architectural history in which they are embedded, nine accounts of decisive events in which men were pitted against time and one another. To give them unity and set them in the wider context of continuing time I have partly re-written all but one of them. All were contests of will in which the contenders staked their all, including life. Three occurred in the Middle Ages—the duel between Henry II and Becket that ended in the latter's martyrdom, the miraculous victory of an outnumbered army at Crécy, and the rising of a despairing peasantry who, turning against their rulers the weapon which had enabled them to triumph on the battlefields of France, were only stayed by the courage of a young king from destroying

7

the realm of which they were part. In a 17th-century interlude I have described how another king was saved—and with him the English monarchy—by the loyalty and devotion of a handful of his poorest subjects.

My remaining narratives are drawn from the great conflict in which for more than twenty years, much of the time single-handed, Britain contended against the dynamic power of Revolutionary and Napoleonic France. They tell how, in the midst of a life and death struggle for national survival, the hard-driven, ill-used seamen of the Royal Navy won redress from intolerable wrongs; how their hero, Nelson, at the Nile and Trafalgar "revolutionised"—to quote Conrad—"not the strategy or tactics of sea-warfare but the very conception of victory itself "; how a British army, in a near disastrous retreat to the sea, saved at the eleventh hour its own and its commander's honour; and how another army, in the epic holding-action of Waterloo, thwarted the final throw of the greatest conqueror of all time.

Through these widely diversified chronicles runs a common thread—of the greatness of the human spirit and its capacity to transcend disaster. Someone said of the British people that their spiritual home was the last ditch. It was certainly there that the protagonists in all these contests found themselves. Their common theme is how men, who had reached the point of no return, faced death for something they felt to be greater than themselves. And because victors and vanquished are now, in T. S. Eliot's words, "folded in a single party"—that of the grave and history—I have chosen my title from his poem, *Little Gidding*, which I quote on a previous page. For it is not the victors' triumph over their adversaries that matters to-day but their victory over themselves.

Save in a few cases I have omitted reference notes since these are contained in the works in which they first appeared and which are listed at the end of this volume.

ARTHUR BRYANT

April, 1965

Contents

To Dick O'Connor
who in
the Western Desert,
when Britain stood alone,
took Time by the forelock

Part One

CHAPTER I

The Holy Blissful Martyr

"From every shire's end
Of Engeland to Canterbury they wend
The holy blissful martyr for to seek. . . ."

Chaucer

HIGH AMONG THE founders of the world of ideas and institutions we inherit was the king who eight hundred years ago created a framework for the Common Law. To his contemporaries the first Plantagenet was, like Napoleon, a terrifying phenomenon. At the core of his being lay a daemonic energy. This ruthless, formidable man, with his bullet head, sandy, close-cropped hair and hoarse cracked voice, who ascended the throne of England at twenty-one and died before he was forty-seven, was always on the move, always imposing his will, always ordaining. His restless vitality drove both his wife and children to rebellion; slaving far into the night over the business of an empire that stretched from the Cheviots to the Pyrenees, and constantly travelling from place to place, he never wasted a moment or tolerated the least delay. Beneath his urbane manner and hail-fellow good humour ran the diabolical temper of the Angevins; there were times when he tore off his clothes in rage and gnawed the straw from his mattresses. All who opposed him were met with unrelenting, unscrupulous resolution.

Yet those who worked with Henry II loved him. The praises of his judges and Exchequer officials were based on more than flattery. For his devotion to their common task—the creation of order in his kingdom's affairs—was the consuming passion of his life.

Above all, he sought to make his rule endure. It is this that constitutes his claim to greatness. The supreme object of his crowded, stormy life was to create institutions that could pre-serve his inheritance after his death from the disintegrating forces that threaten all emergent societies. He used the prerogative to bring the whole system of freehold tenure under national law. By making the smaller landowner's right to his property depend-ent on royal instead of feudal courts, he struck at the root of the great lord's power over his military tenants. And he dealt a death-blow to trial-by-battle and private war. Selfish, crafty, unscrupulous, the great lawyer-king wielded the sword of justice "for the punishment of evil-doers and the maintenance of peace and quiet for honest men". His judges made his remedies avail-able in every corner of the realm. With the precedents they en-shrined in their judgments they little by little created a common law for all England. They established the same system for north, south, east and west, for town and country, for Norman, English-man and Welshman. They nationalised, as it were, the Law.

Henry's achievement was far in advance of his age. By the end of his reign there was no major offence against the public peace which could not bring the offender within range of a royal writ. Henceforward whoever gave law to England was to have a machinery by which it could be enforced—against the strong as well as the weak. The professional judges Henry trained, the courts in which they sat, the writs they devised to meet popular needs, and the judgments they left behind to guide their successors, helped to ensure that justice should be done even in the royal absence or in the reign of a weak or unjust sovereign. By making the Common Law the permanent embodiment of a righteous king sitting in judgment, the great Angevin established the English habit of obedience to law which has been the strongest of all the forces making for the nation's peaceful continuity and progress.

Yet, in trying to subject every part of the nation's life to the

Law, the great Plantagenet fell foul of the one Power which in that age no prince could safely challenge. Wherever in western Europe man turned his eyes, he was confronted by the majesty of the Church. He could not read a book that churchmen had not written and copied by hand; unless he was a churchman trained by churchmen, he almost certainly could not read at all. Everything he did was blessed or cursed, approved or disapproved, explained and solemnised by the Church. He was baptised by it, married by it, buried by it. He went into battle calling on its saints to aid his arms; he sought a cure for his ills at its martyrs' shrines or in its holy waters and wells; he made his oaths on its sacred relics. Its superstitions, often touchingly beautiful, were part of his daily life. He prayed before the painted images of its saints and angels for help, comfort and forgiveness. The bells rang, and the familiar gargoyles grinned from the village church tower to guard him from demon or storm; he brought his corn to be blessed at its altars, and, repeating its hallowed Latin incantations, danced round his apple trees to make them fruitful. The very oxen of the fields, he believed, knelt in the byres on Christmas night in remembrance of the manger birth.

The Church not only dominated men's minds and imaginations. It enjoyed immense wealth. In an age when most people lived in huts little bigger or cleaner than pigsties, the Church's buildings towered above the landscape and blazed with colour and jewels. And it commanded in every country a host, not of warriors, but of men and women disciplined to its service. They ranged from scarlet-robed cardinals and mitred archbishops to humble parish-clerks, bellringers and church-sweepers—members of the Minor Orders, as they were called; from judges, lawyers and physicians to the poor ragged students who begged and sang their way along the roads of Europe to hear the Church's famous doctors lecture on theology and canon law in its cathedral schools and universities. In its heyday in the twelfth and thirteenth centuries, it has been reckoned, one out of every thirty adult males was a cleric of some kind.

To the pope or bishop of Rome, as Christ's vicar on earth, lay

an appeal from every man and woman in Orders. A system of
ecclesiastical or canon law, derived from early Christian and
Roman practice and constantly added to, provided the machinery
—meticulous, bureaucratic, authoritative—for enforcing papal
control over all clerics. For by the twelfth century the Roman
Church had won for its members almost complete exemption
from the processes of secular criminal law. If a cleric—even a
poor ragamuffin student—committed a murder, burglary or
other breach of the peace, it claimed the exclusive right to try and
punish him. And as the canon law forbade the use of mutilation
and the death sentence, and as the keeping of prisons was costly,
it relied for punishment mainly on penance and spiritual penalties.
Any malefactor who could read or mumble over a Latin text
from the Bible—the test of clerical status—and so claim "benefit
of clergy," could escape the king's judges. The worst that could
befall him was a fine or brotherly scourging or, in the last resort,
defrocking, in which case he remained free to repeat his offence.

Thus Henry II, seeking to establish a common law for all
Englishmen, was confronted by ecclesiastical privileges incom-
patible with his object. The Church's punishments were far too
light to maintain order in a violent and unpoliced age. To the
king's orderly and autocratic mind it was intolerable that episcopal tenants-in-chief should have the right to appeal over his head
to foreign courts and leave the realm to advance their suits
against him. It seemed equally so that papal legates, over whose
appointment he had no control, should exercise judicial powers
inside his dominions and constrain, by threats of excommunication and suspension, those who were his vassals and ministers.

For the Church sheltered so many beneath its ample cloak that
it formed a complete sub-section of humanity. Had a majority of
clerics been what they were supposed to be—and the best were—
its claim to immunity from national Law would have been
reasonable enough. But most of them were merely ordinary men
in clerical dress leading clerical lives. Their leaders—though a
few were saints and many men of ability and learning—were as
given to pomp and luxury as the lay lords by whose side they

presided over realm and neighbourhood. They entertained in halls off plate of gold and silver, wore jewels, rings and costly garments, kept fine horses, hounds, hawks and armies of retainers, and travelled with magnificent cortèges. Monks, who in theory had withdrawn from the world to mortify the flesh and exalt the spirit, lived in a manner at startling variance, not only with their own professions, but with the poverty-stricken life of the countryside around them. Other churchmen not in regular orders did not even trouble to wear the outward garb of piety, but went about, like the fashionable chaplains of the feudal magnates, with curled hair, pointed beards and effeminate clothes or, like secular canons in non-monastic cathedrals, in fine linen instead of sheepskin. And some, though mostly in minor orders, were knaves and malefactors, as dangerous to the public peace as any other criminals. In Worcestershire, in the early part of Henry II's reign, one of them raped a girl and then murdered her father; another, a canon of Bedford, slew a knight at Dunstable and, after being acquitted in the teeth of the evidence by the bishop's court, insulted a royal judge who had been sent to investigate the matter. It was such men that Henry II wished to bring under the Common Law.

He proceeded with great caution. As in his attacks on the powers of feudal magnates and their franchises he relied on subtly disguised and harmless-looking legal devices to bring the ecclesiastical courts under his control before anyone could realise what was happening. In this he was aided by the man he made his chancellor and who showed almost as small respect as he for clerical claims which conflicted with the needs of royal revenue and justice. It was characteristic of Henry's freedom from the prejudices of his age that this favourite counsellor was the son of a London merchant. Thomas Becket at the time of Henry's accession was archdeacon of Canterbury and the primate's legal adviser. Dark, handsome, and immensely tall, with a great hooked beak and wonderful vitality, this brilliant ecclesiastical lawyer became the young king's inseparable companion. As chancellor and keeper of the great seal he was loaded with gifts and favours; the wood-chopper, the contemptuous nobles called him after his homely origin. His wealth, splendour and vast train of retainers became the talk of England and France. The very bits of his horses' harness were made of silver. When in 1158 he went on an embassy to Paris to negotiate a marriage between his master's son and the French king's daughter, he rode on a magnificent charger, preceded by hundreds of knights and liveried choristers and with richly-caparisoned pack-horses ridden by monkeys in silks and velvets. A year later he led the royal army in Aquitaine and captured the city of Cahors, unseating a French champion in open tournament.

In 1162, wishing to have a loyal and subservient ecclesiastical collaborator, the king raised this low-born clerk to the supreme office of archbishop of Canterbury. With his aid, he felt, he would be able to bring the practice of every court in the land into line with the principles of law and order he was seeking to enforce. Brushing aside opposition, he induced the monastery chapter of Christ Church, Canterbury, to elect Becket to the vacant see, though he was not even ordained a priest until the day before his consecration as head of the English Church.

In doing so, however, the king made a grave miscalculation. For Becket, who received his sacred office with reluctance, had no sooner accepted it than, at the age of forty-five, he completely changed his way of life. The most resplendently arrayed and attended man in England, who had taken the field at the head of seven hundred of his own knights, worn the long-embroidered sleeves of a baron and once told his sovereign that his royal cloak was unfit to give a beggar, he now donned the black robes of a Canterbury monk, attended midnight masses, and daily—with his habitual ostentation—entertained and washed the feet of the filthiest beggars in Canterbury. A shameless pluralist who had collected benefices and prebendal stalls to support his magnificent entertainments, he insisted on resigning the chancellorship regardless of the entreaties of his sovereign, who had seen in the union of the primacy and the royal chancery the solution of his problems. He gave up coursing and hunting and the hawks and hounds in which he delighted. Most surprising and, for the king, disconcerting, he embraced the extreme theories of the clerical reformers. He became an ardent, unbending champion of the papacy. When the pallium—the symbol of spiritual authority—arrived from Rome, he walked barefoot through the streets to receive it.

For, with the thoroughness with which he did everything, Becket refused to serve two masters. Having been the most loyal of royal lieutenants, he now transferred his allegiance to a more powerful master and, as it seemed to the king, most ungratefully sacrificed his interests. Instead of applying his vast legal and business experience to subject ecclesiastical encroachments to Exchequer scrutiny, he used them to extend the rights and revenues of his see. He revived long-dormant claims, demanded the restoration of estates alienated by his predecessors, and insisted on receiving homage in place of the Crown from knights holding church-lands. When a fellow tenant-in-chief usurped an advowson, he summarily excommunicated him, thus depriving the Crown of his services, for no-one could have dealings with an excommunicated man. Nor would he yield an inch to the king's demands about criminous clerks. A tax reform, to which as chancellor he would have given whole-hearted support, was fiercely resisted by him in the Council. "By the eyes of God," declared the furious king, "it is not seemly for you to gainsay me." "By the reverence of those eyes by which you have sworn, my lord king," Becket replied, "not a penny shall be given from all my land or from the jurisdiction of the Church."[1] Even when Henry sought a papal dispensation for his bastard brother to marry an heiress within the prohibited degrees, instead of facilitating matters as a normal archbishop would have done, the primate refused to consider it. He seemed to go out of his way deliberately to enrage his former friend and benefactor.

Thus the king's attempts to bring the Church under the law was frustrated by the very man who had been his chief assistant

[1] *Materials for the History of Thomas Becket*, II, 373, cit. *English Historical Documents* II, 714.

and who, as the repository of his secret plans, was ideally situated to defeat them. His love for his brilliant lieutenant turned to bitter hatred. With all his resolution and cunning he set himself to remedy his mistake. He had at all costs to get Becket out of the key position in which he had so injudiciously placed him.

. . . .

The two men—the one with the strongest throne in Europe, the other representing the international Church—seemed well matched. They had been the complement of one another and now became the antithesis. Each had the same imperious, over-bearing will, each was thorough, persistent, and electric with restless energy, each had behind him a career of unbroken triumph. And each knew, or thought he knew, his opponent by heart, for they had worked together in close companionship for seven years, and, so far as either was capable of love, had been fascinated by one another.

Yet within a year the king had completely outmanœuvred the tall, gaunt, dark archbishop. For, with all his boldness and courage, Becket lacked the virtues in which Henry, the Achilles-heel of his temper apart, was so strong. He had none of his capa-city for patient statesmanship and *finesse* in handling political opinion. He was a perfectionist rather than a man of the world. During his seven years as chancellor he had shown himself a tireless organiser and worker, with a wonderful quickness and versatility. He possessed dazzling address and charm; could be all things to all men and, so long as he was not personally con-cerned, show considerable tact, and, though revealing his heart to none, win from subordinates affection and even devotion. But while he appealed to the multitude by his dramatic genius and emotional power, his equals could not depend on him. He was far too much of an egotist to be a good colleague. He lacked constancy and stability: was a man of extremes who lived on his nerves. He seemed capable of every attitude except moderation. He constantly laid himself open to criticism and suspicion by sudden changes of mood which appeared to responsible men insincere and in bad taste. They saw him as an exhibitionist who could never stop playing a part. To Gilbert Foliot, the austere and learned bishop of London who had been the leader of the Church party before Becket's elevation to the primacy, he seemed as much an upstart ecclesiastically as to the feudal magnates socially: a careerist who had never been a monk or even a priest and whose pretences to devotion were utterly insincere.

The king, who had been so well served and delighted by his chancellor's genius, understood his weaknesses perfectly: his vanity and hypersensitiveness, his inability not to overstate and dramatise his case, his pathological desire—the result of a lonely childhood—to win applause and justify himself. And in their relations with the English bishops and the pope, both of whose support was essential to Becket's position, he played the brilliant, excitable archbishop like a fish. First he joined issue with him over what was by far the weakest point in the Church's position —the trial of criminous clerks, to which a notorious murder and an equally notorious acquittal had just drawn everyone's attention. It was an issue on which the Church was divided and about which doubts were felt even by the pope. In October 1163 at a Council at Westminster Henry outlined his proposals for dealing with this pressing scandal. He did not challenge the Church's right to try its members, but demanded only that clerics found guilty by ecclesiastical courts of major crimes should be degraded and handed over to his officers for punishment. Those who could not be restrained from such outrages by the thought of their sacred orders, he pointed out, could scarcely be much wronged by the loss of them.

To this Becket, incapable of moderation and taking up, as always, the extreme position in any cause with which he was identified, replied that it would be a monstrous injustice to punish a man twice for the same offence. In a long, passionate speech he urged the king not to introduce into the kingdom a new discipline contrary to the decrees of the ancient fathers—"a new law of Christ," he called it, "by a new and strange kind of lord."

At this Henry asked angrily whether he and his fellow bishops were prepared to swear to abide by the ancient customs of the realm. This put them in a quandary, for in the time of Henry's grandfather the Church had been subjected to many restraints which it had since shaken off. Yet in England an appeal to ancient custom was always hard to refuse. After a consultation, therefore, the archbishop replied that they would swear as their liege-lord requested, but with the customary proviso, "saving the rights of their order." At this Henry became extremely angry and stamped out in a rage, leaving the bishops to digest the fact that they were in for an uncomfortable and dangerous struggle. Next day he demanded from the primate the return of the castles and honours of Berkhamsted and Eye which he had granted him during his chancellorship.

Having set the issue before the world—one in which he appeared to be asking nothing of his bishops but what was fair and reasonable—the king proceeded to drive a wedge between them and their leader. His instrument was the pope, Alexander III, a sensible man and no extremist, who, being engaged in a life-or-death struggle with the Emperor of the Germans, Frederick Barbarossa, during which he had been forced to take refuge in France, was exceedingly anxious to stand well with the English king. He therefore responded willingly to Henry's suggestions that he should hint to his quarrelsome metropolitan that it was no service to the Church to insult the Crown by refusing to swear to the ancient customs of the realm, and that some reasonable compromise over the trial of criminous clerks would be in the Holy See's interest. Confronted by surrender in such a quarter Becket—still a parvenu in the Church—felt that he had no choice but to give way. He therefore privately, and it seems rather impulsively, informed the king that the next time he was asked to swear to the ancient customs of the realm in public, he would do as he wished. It was characteristic of him that in taking this step he consulted nobody and refrained from informing his fellow bishops who had stood behind him so firmly at Westminster.

Immediately, in the January of 1164, the king called a council at his hunting-lodge at Clarendon. In that simple, childlike age, when men's minds were swayed by outward forms and ceremonies, it seemed essential to obtain from the archbishop and his colleagues a solemn and public declaration of what had been promised. Once more the primate was asked, in the presence of the barons and bishops, whether he would agree to clerics, found guilty of felony by ecclesiastical courts, being degraded and handed over to the king's judges for punishment. And once more the archbishop, who seemed almost incapable of meeting his old master in public without falling into a furious altercation, contended that it was contrary to divine law to punish a man twice for the same offence, and that a priest was a sacred being who could no more be sentenced by laymen than a father by his own child. Thereupon the king reminded him of his promise to swear to the ancient customs and constitutions without insulting qualifications. Then he sprang a bombshell on everyone by producing these in written form and asking the prelates to acknowledge them.

These sixteen carefully-prepared clauses, known to history as the Constitutions of Clarendon, set out, not unfairly, the relationship that had existed between Church and State in the time of Henry's grandfather Henry I. Some of them, like the proviso that no peasant's son should be ordained without his lord's assent, were undisputed. Others traversed what in the past thirty years had become the accepted practice of the Church. They included provisions for trying in the king's courts disputes about advowsons as a species of landed property, and for regulating reckless and blackmailing accusations brought by archdeacons against laymen for moral offences. And they laid down a procedure for dealing with criminous clerks: preliminary investigation before a lay judge, trial in the ecclesiastical courts in the presence of a royal observer, and, where guilt was proved, degradation and delivery to the king's officers for sentence and punishment.

The most contentious provisions were that no tenants-in-chief should be excommunicated, no cleric leave the realm and no appeal be made to Rome without the king's leave. And appeals in ecclesiastical disputes were to go from the archdeacon's court to the bishop's, from the bishop's to the archbishop's, and, unless permission were given for an appeal to Rome, from the archbishop to the king, who was to direct the archbishop's court how to decide the issue. This was tantamount to making the king supreme ecclesiastical judge in the realm—a principle which, however much it might conform with ancient English practice, ran diametrically counter to existing canon law. It struck at the international sovereignty of the Church and made the crown, as in Saxon and early Norman times, the constitutional link between the pope and the English clergy.

It was one thing for Henry to try to restore the ancient un-written and peculiarly English relations between Church and State in a tacit agreement with his own bishops, some of whom at least were sympathetic to views which had been held only a century before by such a primate as Lanfranc. But it was another to reduce these to writing and demand from churchmen a public avowal of principles which violated the disciplinary canons of their Church. The episcopal bench was appalled. For three days, in a series of violent arguments, the bishops stood solidly behind the primate in defence of what they deemed the liberties of the Church. Even when "the princes and nobles of the realm, waxing hot in their wrath, burst into the chamber, muttering and clamouring," and, shaking fists in their faces, declared that those who resisted the king were in deadly peril, they remained firm.

At this point Becket—vehemently reproached by the king for promising his agreement in private and humiliating him by breaking it in public—suddenly gave way. Without consulting his colleagues he announced that, as his lord and sovereign would have him perjure himself, he must do so. By refusing to add his seal to this grudging agreement, he made his surrender seem as great an insult to Henry as it seemed a betrayal to his colleagues. Subsequently he made his position still more invidious by suspending himself from the service of the altar as a penance for perjury. He also sent an emissary to the pope to ask forgiveness for betraying the Church.

The archbishop could hardly have played his cards worse. His colleagues, hopelessly confused and divided, had lost all confidence in him. Even those who most strongly upheld the principles for which he had contended felt that, as he had abandoned them, it was a needless and dishonest continuance of a regrettable controversy to qualify and repudiate his undertaking. The view of responsible laymen was that he had made himself ridiculous and, by his vanity and ungrateful provocation of his royal master, compromised the Church's position.

Henry had put his adversary in a cleft stick; the latter's resignation now seemed inevitable. Yet, in his determination to crush him, he had blundered himself. By setting down his claims in black and white, he had put the Church's defenders on their guard. This became apparent when he sent the Constitutions to the pope for ratification. For though the Holy Father, confronted by an imperialist anti-pope in Rome, was in greater need than ever of the English king's support, he could not publicly repudiate the doctrines for which his predecessors had fought. The denial of the right of ecclesiastical appeal struck at the Church's independence and unity and at one of the papacy's principal sources of income. While agreeing to six of the clauses, Alexander, as tactfully as possible, withheld his assent from the remainder. And he released Becket from any oath he might have made to observe them. He did not approve of the archbishop's attitude, but he could not do otherwise.

The pope's refusal to underwrite his Constitutions only made Henry the more determined to get rid of the man to whom he attributed the refusal. Meanwhile the latter further prejudiced his position by trying to escape from the country in a fishing-smack. That October the king called a meeting of the Council at Northampton and summoned the archbishop to appear before it for a technical breach of feudal law—the lonely, passionate man's failure, in his alternating moods of defiance and despair, to respond to a sheriff's writ, which should never in any case have been addressed to him. Working himself into one of his famous rages, Henry browbeat the Council, whose members needed little encouragement to avenge themselves on the primate, into sentencing him for his contempt of the royal court to the loss of all his own and his see's moveable goods. Then, without notice, he called on him to account for the vast sums which had passed through his hands as chancellor. When Becket, seeing that the king was resolved on his ruin, offered a compensation of 2000 marks, it was contemptuously refused.

·　·　·　·　·　·　·　·

At that moment Henry seemed to hold all the cards. He was the most powerful ruler in Europe, and the head of a State in which respect for the Crown was more deeply rooted than in any other. He had behind him a baronage which he had taught to join with him in governing the realm, and a knighthood deeply attached to the throne. Becket, in the eyes of every king's man and of many of his fellow prelates, was a low-born clerk, a parvenu whom his royal master had raised from a merchant's counter. In opposing his benefactor he had laid himself open to charges of the basest ingratitude.

Yet, by making him desperate, Henry drove his adversary back on something greater than either himself or the Church. He forced him on to the rock of the inner spirit. Though ill and afraid, the archbishop resolved to compromise no more and to take his stand, not merely on the Church's tenets, but on the cross of suffering and sacrifice it represented. By doing so he became the champion of thousands to whom the rights and wrongs of the constitutional principles under dispute meant nothing. Becket was not by nature a religious man; he was self-centred, egotistical, an artist and an autocrat. Though pure in life, and generous to his servants and retainers, he did not instinctively love men or turn the other cheek. He was neither meek nor humble. Indeed he was more arrogant than the king, who, for all his blind rages and high-handed ways, had a vein of everyday simplicity which the primate lacked.

Yet for the lonely, spectacular role he now chose Becket was superbly equipped. His towering height, his pale, sensitive face, the aquiline nose and restless penetrating eyes, the white feminine hands and quick eager movements made him look what he aspired to be, a saint and martyr. And the very theatricality and emotionalism that so annoyed high-born men of the world appealed to the hearts of common folk who only saw him from afar and knew nothing of his weaknesses. Here was a man who even in that age of pageantry and outward symbols made his meaning ten times clearer than anyone else, speaking to them across the immense barriers of rank and wealth. Almost alone among the rulers of the time he laid himself out to please the masses—the peasants and craftsmen of England who were without the rights and privileges, laws and liberties of the feudal lords. When he rode on visitation and the children of the poor were brought to him to confirm, he did not, like other prelates, bless them from the saddle. He dismounted and went through the formalities of the sacrament like a humble priest.

Through the king's vindictiveness Becket had reached solid ground. From that moment, despite all the odds against him, he never quitted it. "If you desire success in this world," one of the monks at his side counselled him, "make peace with the king. But if you wish to serve God, act fearlessly." It was what the archbishop had resolved to do. His enemies on the episcopal bench and many of his friends, faced by Henry's unrelenting fury, urged him to resign his see rather than to bring ruin on the Church. He refused either to do so or to plead in an issue which, if lost, would place every churchman at a despot's mercy. Declaring that all temporal power derived from God and that a son could not judge his spiritual father or a sheep his shepherd, he traversed his adversary's whole position and announced, in defiance of the Constitutions, that he would appeal to Rome against any sentence passed on him.

On the 13th October 1164 Becket was summoned before the
Council to receive judgment.   Before setting out from the
monastery where he lodged he deliberately said a votive mass of
St. Stephen, the first Christian martyr.   Then, ordering the
assembled bishops to excommunicate any who dared to lay
hands on him, he entered the royal castle at Northampton,
wearing his archbishop's cope and pallium and bearing his own
cross. When the bishop of London protested, saying, "If you
brandish your cross, the king will brandish his sword," Thomas
replied, "The cross is the emblem of peace; I carry it for the
protection of the whole English Church."   All day, while the
king and his barons sat in one room and Becket in another,
and pleading bishops and threatening envoys constantly passed
between them, the archbishop sat alone, hugging his cross and
gazing on the crucifix.   To his adversaries he seemed merely an
angry, unreasonable man clinging to an untenable position—one
who, as the bishop of London said, had always been a fool and
always would be.   To himself he seemed to be wrestling with
wild beasts at Ephesus.   "This is a fearful day," murmured one
of his followers as angry baron after baron came in with summons and threat.   "Ay," replied the archbishop, "but the Day
of Judgment will be more fearful!"

As the bishops—even those most opposed to Becket—dared
not, in face of his prohibition, join in judgment against him, the
king demanded it from his earls and barons alone.   But when the
magnates made their way to the archbishop's chamber to inform
him of the sentence, he rose and refused to hear them. "You are
come to judge me," he cried, "it is not your right. . . . It is no
sentence; I have not been heard.   You cannot judge me.   I am
your spiritual father; you are lords of the household, lay powers,
secular personages. I will not hear your judgment! Under protection of the Apostolic See I depart hence."   Then, rising to his
full height and bearing his cross, he swept into the darkening hall
and towards the door, while knights and royal servants, rising
from the straw-strewn floor and benches where they had dined,
shouted, "Traitor!"   "Perjurer!"   Outside in the wet streets the

people thronged round him to beg his blessing so that he could hardly control his horse.

That night, while the triumphant king issued a proclamation that no-one was to do him physical hurt, Becket rode out of Northampton in driving wind and rain and made his way in disguise to the coast. Three weeks later he landed in France.

．　．　．　．　．　．　．　．

For six years the archbishop remained an exile. The revenues of his see were confiscated, his kinsfolk banished, and his office declared forfeit. From the position he had taken up—that ultimate appeals affecting the Church must lie to the pope and not the king, and that no lay court had the right to lay hands on an anointed priest—nothing would move him. Attempts were made to negotiate a compromise by the pious king of France, who gave him shelter out of dislike for his English rival, by the pope who, despite his disapproval of the constitutions of Claren-don, was still deeply anxious to retain Henry's goodwill, by the bishops who found themselves between the devil and the deep sea and could not obey their temporal master without disobeying their spiritual. All were in vain and broke down on the enmity of two resolute and legalistically-minded men of genius, who brought out all that was most stubborn and violent in one another. From time to time, whenever the temporising pope permitted, Becket emerged from the French monasteries into which he had retired to a life of the sternest austerity, to hurl anathemas and excommunications at his fellow prelates for com-promising with the king. Only the papal prohibition stopped him from treating the latter likewise.

Henry was equally unappeasable. But in the end the logic of events was too much for him. He could not govern Christian England without the Church. And, in an international age, himself an international ruler, he could not cut the English Church off from the universal Church and make himself, instead of the pope, its ruler. To ensure the peaceful succession of the crown and secure his successor's inheritance from the uncertainties of civil war—the fate that had befallen his own on his grandfather's death—he wished to have his eldest son crowned during his lifetime: a constitutional practice familiar in France, though hitherto unknown in England. But the consecration, which in a Christian realm was the binding part of a coronation, could only be performed—according to the custom both of Church and realm—by the archbishop of Canterbury. After waiting five years and trying vainly to get a papal dispensation to allow the ceremony to be performed by deputy, Henry took the law into his own hands and in June 1170 had the young prince crowned by Becket's enemies, the archbishop of York and the assisting bishops of London, Durham, Rochester and Salisbury.

Yet the king was well aware of his danger. He knew that the pope, who was by now on firmer ground in his duel with the emperor and anti-pope, was unlikely to condone such an invasion of the Church's control of its own hierarchy, and that opinion, both in England and on the continent, was hardening against him; unless he could soon negotiate some kind of public settlement with the archbishop, his dominions would almost certainly be laid under interdict and himself under excommunication. He knew too that Becket's host and champion, the king of France, was arming against him, and that many of his own barons, galled by his firm rule and strong measures, were awaiting an opportunity to rise.

He therefore intimated to the papal legates and French king, who were still trying to negotiate a settlement, that he was ready to make his peace with the archbishop, restore his forfeited estates and receive him back into his realm. Nothing was said about the Constitutions, but the presumption was that, as neither archbishop nor pope had accepted them, their enforcement was to be tacitly dropped. The great thing was to achieve a public reconciliation and the restoration of peace and normal religious life in England. A meeting between the two disputants took place in the French king's presence and they were apparently reconciled. But, though the restoration of the archbishop's lands and dignities was agreed, the customary kiss of peace, which he had demanded at a previous abortive meeting and which had been refused by the king, was neither given nor requested. The quarrel —and at heart both men knew it—had been patched up but not appeased.

.   .   .   .

In agreeing to return to England the primate knew the risk he was running from a passionate and injured autocrat of unpredictable moods. But his own safety was by now the last thing with which he was concerned. His only thought was of spiritual victory. Nor did he return unarmed. Before setting out he secured from the pope letters of suspension and excommunication against his fellow metropolitan of York and two of his own suffragan bishops for their part in crowning the young prince. Just as he was about to embark, he learnt that they were on their way to join the king in Normandy to consecrate royal nominees to five vacant English bishoprics. Faced with the prospect of a packed and hostile episcopal bench, Becket at once used the discretionary powers with which Alexander had armed him and launched the sentences of excommunication and suspension, hastily dispatching them to England before him.

Then on December 1st, 1170, having shown that he was prepared to abate not one tittle of the Church's authority, and avoiding the royal officials who, infuriated by his latest act of war, were · waiting at Dover to seize him, he landed at his own cathedral's port of Sandwich. All the way to Canterbury the roads were lined with praying and rejoicing multitudes; it was like a triumphal procession. In the city he was welcomed with trumpets, psalms and organs. As he took his throne in the cathedral his face was transfigured with happiness. "My lord," one of his monks whispered to him, "it matters not now when you depart from the world. Christ has conquered! Christ is now king!"

When Henry in Normandy learnt what had happened and

that Becket had announced that, though ready to absolve his suffragans on their doing penance, he had no power to withdraw the papal sentence on his fellow metropolitan, he flew into an ungovernable rage. "What idle and coward knaves have I nourished as vassals," he shouted, "that, faithless to their oaths, they suffer their lord to be mocked by a low-born priest!" Four knights—Reginald FitzUrse of Williton in Somerset, William de Tracey, Richard le Breton, and Hugh de Morville of Knaresborough—took the king at his word, and, without informing anyone of their intention, set out for England. There they made their way to Saltwood castle in Kent, the home of Becket's bitterest enemy, Sir Ranulf de Broc, the man who during his absence had farmed his see's revenues and who, with his retainers, was already waging open war against him.

On December 29th the four knights, with a rabble of de Broc's followers, arrived at Canterbury where the archbishop was sitting after dinner in his chamber. Ostentatiously refusing his servants' offer of food, they strode up to his chamber and sat down on the rushes before him, watching him in grim silence. When after a time he addressed them they broke into curses, telling him that they had something to say to him by the king's command and asking if he would have it said in public. Then they told him that, unless he absolved the excommunicated bishops, he must immediately leave the realm. To which the archbishop replied that they should cease from brawling and that, as his trust was in Heaven, no sea should ever again come between him and his church. "I have not come back to flee again," he said; "here shall he who wants find me."

At that the knights sprang to their feet and began shouting. But the archbishop answered them in kind: "I am not moved by threats, nor are your swords more ready to strike than my soul is for martyrdom. Go, seek him who would fly from you. Me you will find foot to foot in the battle of the Lord." And as, amid tumult and insults, they withdrew to their waiting men, there was a flash of the same fiery spirit that had caused the archbishop six years before in the castle hall at Northampton to round on the king's mocking brother and call him bastard. He followed the intruders to the door and cried out after them defiantly, "Here, here, will you find me!"

Becket was now expecting immediate death. Indeed, it had become clear during the past few days that he was deliberately seeking it. In his Nativity sermon on Christmas Day he had told his hearers in the packed cathedral that they had already one Canterbury martyr—St. Alphege who had been pelted to death by drunken Danes—and that they might soon have another. And on the day before the knights arrived he had secretly sent two of his monks to the pope and, in bidding them farewell, shown that he never expected to see them again. That night at supper he remarked to those about him that he who must lose much blood must drink much wine.

By now it was nearly dark, and the monks had repaired to the cathedral for vespers. A few minutes later the four knights, having donned their armour in the courtyard, returned to the hall. But they found the door barred. While they were seeking another and battering in a shutter with an axe seized from a carpenter, Becket's clerks repeatedly urged him to take refuge in the cathedral. Fearing that they would all be massacred together, they dragged and pushed him as far as the church door. But when the monks, leaving their vespers, ran to meet him and tried to bolt the door behind him, he sternly refused, saying, "It is not meet to make a fortress of the house of prayer." Then, "driving all before him as a good shepherd doth his sheep," he made his way into the dark, silent cathedral. Almost immediately its peace was broken by the knights and their retainers pouring through the open cloister door, led by FitzUrse, in hauberk and with drawn sword, shouting, "Hither to me, king's men!" Then they all began shouting together, "Where is Thomas Becket, traitor to the king and realm?" The knights were completely covered in armour save for their eyes, and their swords were naked. At the sight the monks fled into the shadows and the dark crypt below.

Only three of his household now remained with the arch-

35

bishop—William FitzStephen, his future biographer, Robert of Merton, his confessor, and an English monk named Grim who was holding the cross. As the clamour behind increased, Becket suddenly stopped and, descending the steps from the choir, called out in a clear voice, "Lo! here am I, no traitor to the king but a priest. What do you seek from me? I am ready to suffer in His Name who redeemed me by His blood." Whereupon the armed men came shouting and clattering through the darkness to where he stood beside a pillar in the transept. As they closed in to seize him, apparently intending to carry him off, they again called on him to absolve the excommunicated bishops. Rising above them in his great height, he answered: "There has been no satisfaction made, and I will *not* absolve them!" "Then you shall die this instant," cried one of the knights, "and receive your deserts." "I am ready to die for my Lord; may the Church through my blood obtain peace and liberty!" As he resisted their efforts to drag him away, the knights, fearing a rescue, began to strike furiously at him with their swords. A blow cut off his scalp, while another severed his cross-bearer's arm. Two more blows brought him to his knees, and a fourth scattered his brains on the pavement. Then the murderers burst out of the cathedral to plunder his lodgings and make their escape before the city could be roused.

. . . .

When that night in the desecrated cathedral the monks bent over the body of the proud, fastidious archbishop and stripped off his bloodstained Cistercian's habit to replace it by his pontifical vestments, they found to their amazement a covering of filthy sackcloth and a horsehair shirt, long worn and alive with lice. Beneath it they saw the festering weals of repeated self-scourging. Then, through their grief and fears, they rejoiced exceedingly. For they knew that he had been a true monk and a saint of God.

By death the archbishop had triumphed. As the news became known a thrill of horror ran through Christendom. The king against whom Becket had contended, collapsed in an agony of lamentation. Exchanging his robes for sackcloth he shut himself in his chamber, where for three days he refused all food and consolation, groaning and crying exceedingly and from time to time falling into a stupor. When he at last calmed down, he threw himself and his realm on the pope's mercy. If it was not to disintegrate, it was the only thing he could do.

But it was not the great alone who were shaken. The common people left their rulers in no doubts as to their attitude. Within a few hours of the murder rumours of miracles began to spread outwards from Canterbury. Four times, it was said, the candles round the bloodstained pall had been lit by invisible hands. A monk in the abbey had seen the archbishop in a vision going towards the high altar in episcopal robes; his deep, beautiful voice had joined in the singing of the introit. A blind woman who touched her eyes with a handkerchief dipped in his blood had regained her sight; others similarly afflicted who had prayed to him had been restored. "The blind see, the deaf hear, the dumb speak" wrote John of Salisbury, "the lame walk, the devils are cast out!" Meanwhile the de Brocs, who had threatened to move the body, were besieged in their castle by a furious crowd. The murderers, who began by boasting of their deed, are said to have fled to Scotland, where the people tried to hang them.

It was easy for twelfth century kings and lords to ignore the rights of the individual poor. But they could not ignore popular beliefs. In matters of faith neither monarch nor prelate had the last word. The Church represented and embodied the beliefs of the people. Because they were convinced that Becket was a saint, the pope, who had so often tried to restrain him during his life, was forced within two years of his death to canonise him. His shrine at Canterbury, blazing with jewels and surrounded by the discarded crutches of those he had cured, became the most famous place of pilgrimage in England. For a time the cult of St. Thomas almost rivalled that of the Virgin Mary. Churches were dedicated to him and memorials erected in lands as remote as Scandinavia and Iceland.

In his own land, whose fame he had blazoned through Christendom, Becket's name became better known and more honoured than any other of his age. Before the Reformation there can have been few English churches that did not have a retable, wall-painting, window or other treasure depicting some scene in his troubled life. Even today, despite the wholesale destruction by sixteenth and seventeenth century iconoclasts, many survive, like the boss in the roof of the Norwich cloisters with its demons standing over the Canterbury murderers or the panel at Elham in Kent in which the saint defies the royal anger at Northampton. By a strange paradox—for it had been to strengthen the realm that Henry had fought against him—Becket lived on, not merely as a martyr, but as a national hero to a submerged and conquered people. A Norman born in England who had stood up to her foreign rulers and died at their hands, he became, in a modern writer's words, "one of the people of England as well as one of the saints of God."

In a constitutional historian's sense the martyrdom achieved comparatively little. It saved for English clerics the right of appeal to Rome in purely clerical matters. It established the immunity of criminous clerks from lay justice. And it brought the English Church, beyond doubt or cavil, into line with the universal practice of the Roman Catholic Church and the canon law, even though that practice conferred on churchmen a greater independence than had been customary in the Anglo-Saxon and early Anglo-Norman State. As a result power in England, as elsewhere in western Europe, continued to be regarded, not as force to be operated by a single untrammelled will, but as a balance in which rulers were subjected to the check of the organised Christian conscience expressed through the Church. When four centuries later the rulers of England repudiated the authority of Rome, the habit of thought remained—a potent check to tyranny.

In everyday administrative practice, after the first shock of the murder had passed, it was the commonsense views of Henry that prevailed rather than the extreme and unrealistic claims of the archbishop. Of the sixteen Constitutions of Clarendon only those governing the freedom of appeals to Rome and the trial of criminous clerks were abandoned. The royal courts extended their control over advowsons and kept their jurisdiction over pleas for debt, except when the latter arose from wills and marriages —matters which had always been dealt with by ecclesiastical courts. The Crown continued to control, subject to certain formalities, the election of bishops and abbots, and to deny to English prelates the right to excommunicate their fellow tenants-in-chief without permission.

Yet Becket's martyrdom created an emotional content which for centuries remained of immense significance in English life and helped to form the enduring values of England. The Canterbury martyr created *The Canterbury Tales* and all the generations of pilgrims riding or tramping through the Kentish countryside "the holy blissful martyr for to seek." It was not the worldly ends for which Becket had fought that mattered after his death. It was the spiritual means with which he had fought for them. The immunity of clerics from lay jurisdiction meant as often as not the protection from justice of rogues and scoundrels; the right of appeal to Rome meant the submission of disputes, which might have been more expeditiously and justly settled at home, to the costly processes of bureaucratic procrastination and corruption in a foreign land. But that a man in high place who had notoriously loved, and to excess, the wealth and fine things of the world and enjoyed them in dazzling splendour, should voluntarily renounce them and live in exile and poverty, should mortify his body and at the end return to his native land to brave and suffer a violent death for the sake of an ideal, was to reveal the power of Christ and enhance the spiritual dignity of man. It is not easy for one who has lived fine to subdue the flesh, to face unarmed the naked swords of brutal warriors, to place himself in the power of insulting foes. Whoever voluntarily chooses these things is, whatever his failings, a great man. In this sense Becket was great—"great," as one of his followers put it, "in truth always and in all places, great in the palace, great at the altar;

great both at court and in the church; great, when going forth on his pilgrimage, great when returning, and singularly great at his journey's end."[1] Historians, who condemn him for contending against administrative measures which were in themselves reasonable, sometimes forget this. But his contemporaries who witnessed his martyrdom or those who heard of it from their fathers and went on pilgrimage to kneel on the steps where he died or touch with trembling fingers the bloodstained hem of his garments, saw it very clearly. For all the world's coarse obsessions and stupidity and blindness, the saints and martyrs have the last word. It is their triumph over the frailty of the body that causes man to believe in God.

[1] Herbert of Bosham, *Materials for the History of Thomas Becket*, III, 471, cit. M. D. Knowles, *Archbishop Thomas Becket*. Proceedings of British Academy XXXV (1949), 23.

CHAPTER 2

The Grey Goose Feather

" No warring guns were then in use,
 They dreamt of no such thing;
Our Englishmen in fight did use
 The gallant grey-goose wing.

And with the gallant grey-goose wing
 They shew'd to them such play
That made their horses kick and fling,
 And down their riders lay."

Old Ballad

THE LONG-BOW FIRST appeared in England at the end of the thirteenth century, among the yeomen of the Cheshire and Midland forests who had learnt its use from the Welsh hillmen during the wars of Edward I. Under that king's statute of Winchester, and by the old Anglo-Saxon rule under which every free man between the ages of fifteen and sixty was expected to turn out with his personal arms in the shire levy to defend the realm and maintain the peace, the English countryman was trained to arms, unlike his counterpart on the continent where fighting was the preserve of heavily armoured mounted nobles and knights.

His chief arms were a long-bow and a sheaf of arrows. By the time of Edward III, after half a century of almost continuous campaigning against the Welsh and Scots, skill at archery in the woodland areas of England had become widespread. Practice at the village butts after service on Sundays was enjoined by law, and archery competitions were a favourite recreation on feast-days and holidays, when rustic bowmen

> " showéd such brave archery
> By cleaving sticks and wands."

According to the Robin Hood ballads, which became current about this time, there were occasions when they did so in the presence of their warlike lords and princes. "Bend all your bows," Robin bade his men,

> " and with the grey-goose wing
> Such sport now show as you would do
> In the presence of the king."

The hero of these ballads—the North Country outlaw who lived with his merry men in the greenwood and robbed the rich to right the poor—was himself a wonderful marksman. Thrice, we are told, at the sheriff's archery competitions at Nottingham,

> " Robin shot about
> And always sliced the wand."

And when he and his followers switched their aim from the butts to the sheriff's men, the latter had to run for their lives under a hail of arrows.

Originally in its native Wales made of rough, unpolished wild elm, in England the long-bow was usually of yew. It was drawn not by strength of arm but of the whole frame. Bishop Latimer in a later century was taught as a boy to lay his body to the bow and was given weapons of increasing size as he grew bigger, "for men shall never shoot well unless they be brought up in it." The arrows, a cloth-yard long, were plumed with the feathers of the geese that had fed on the village greens and commons:

> " Their arrows finely pared, for timber and for feather,
> With birch and brazil pierc'd to fly in any weather,
> And shot they with the round, the square or forkèd pile,
> The loose gave such a twang as might be heard a mile."

Even before the outbreak of the Hundred Years War with France the long-bow had become the English weapon *par excellence*—one which no other people could use and which seemed designed for the Englishman's physique. A century later a foreign visitor noted that the bows employed by the island commonalty were "thicker and longer than those used by other nations, just as their bodies are stronger than other people's." In the hands of such masters as the Sherwood and Cheshire foresters the long-bow was a more deadly and accurate instrument of destruction than any hitherto known.

The first to feel its power were the Scots. Nineteen years after Robert Bruce's great victory over England's chivalry at Bannockburn, a Scottish army was attempting to relieve Berwick, then besieged by the young English king, Edward III. When on July 19th, 1333, it came within sight of the town, it found the English barring its path on the northern slopes of Halidon Hill. They were drawn up in a long thin line from which projected four triangular salients formed by archers, one on either flank and two in the centre. The three gradually narrowing funnels formed by these salients were closed at the top of the hill by three brigades of dismounted but armour-clad knights and men-at-arms with banners and pennons fluttering above the sheen of their swords and lances. Behind was a reserve brigade to deal with any attempt to drive in the archers on the wings, while in the rear, encircled by baggage-wagons, were laagers packed with horses awaiting a summons from their riders in the battle-line and guarded by the pages who looked after their master's steeds and armour.

The trap set by the English king for the Scots was even more deadly than the Bannockburn bogs and the pits which Bruce had dug on the road to Stirling. For in the hands of English archers the long-bow of Gwent had come of age, and Edward and his lords had found a way to turn it into a military arm of startling mobility and killing-power. One of them, the crusader Henry of Grosmont—son of the king's cousin, the earl of Lancaster—had fought at Bannockburn, and it may have been this brilliant, imaginative commander who first saw how the long-bow could be used to revolutionise the art of war. What seems certain is that during those waiting weeks while the English army was blockading Berwick the archers, whom Edward's commissioners of array had gathered from the northern and midland counties, were trained to manœuvre and exercise their art under orders, just as Bruce's pikesmen before Bannockburn had been trained to fight the battle he had foreseen. Brigaded with men-at-arms from their native shires and disciplined by veterans who had learnt war the hard way on the Welsh and Scottish hills, they were taught to operate, not only as individual marksmen, but in massed phalanxes from which, at the word of command, rhythmic volleys of arrows, travelling at incredible speed, could be directed first at one part of an attacking force, then at another, until every living thing in the target area had been killed or maimed. In their metal helmets and padded deerskin jackets these light, active men could manœuvre in extended order, enfilade a column from flank or even rear and, combining fire and movement, at a bugle call or other signal reform, under cover of their comrades' volleys, in massed ranks in which, so long as their ammunition lasted, they were virtually unassailable.

As the Scottish pikesmen moved forward in dense schiltrons across the marshy ground at the foot of the hill, they suddenly came into range of the archers. Though hundreds fell as the showers of steel-tipped arrows struck home, they pressed stubbornly on. Lowering their heads against the blinding hail and closing their ranks, they instinctively edged away from the salients of archers on either side of them and started to climb. Packed together till they were almost suffocated, riven and tormented by the shooting of the marksmen and the massed volleys from the formations into which the archers withdrew at every attempt to attack them, they stumbled up the slope towards the waiting line of English armour and the one place on the battlefield where no arrows were falling. When, breathless from the ascent, the survivors reached that hedge of levelled lances, the knights and men-at-arms started to hack at them with great swords and battle axes, forcing them down the slope where they came once more into that enfilading hail. The regent of Scotland was mortally wounded, and six earls were left dead on the field.

Altogether seventy Scots lords and five hundred knights and squires fell, and almost the entire infantry. The defenders lost one knight, one man-at-arms and twelve archers.

. . . .

Four years after this battle—which attracted little notice outside the British Isles—England became involved in a long, inconclusive war with France, originally caused by French attempts to whittle away the hereditary rights and domains of the English king in Gascony. During its course, in order to forestall charges of treason against his allies, the Flemish weavers—vassals of the French king and the chief buyers of English wool—Edward III advanced a dubious dynastic claim to the throne of France. In its pursuit, in the summer of 1346 he crossed the Channel with a small, well-equipped army, raised, unlike the feudal hosts of the continent, by indenture—a system under which fighting lords recruited, at agreed rates of pay, the numbers and types of fighting men required by the Crown. Such retinues comprised both armoured and mounted knights and men-at-arms and large numbers of bowmen. The latter, who were paid at the then high rate of sixpence a day, carried, in addition to their bows and sheaves of arrows, short swords, knives and steel-tipped stakes for building protective hedges against cavalry.

The English landed on July 12th at St. Vaast in Normandy almost without opposition. Once ashore, the king wasted no time. On the 18th, after knighting the sixteen-year-old Prince of Wales, he began his march on Rouen with the intention of joining hands with the Flemings in the north. Crossing the marshes at the south-eastern foot of the Cotentin peninsula, where his pioneers and carpenters repaired the demolished bridges over the Vire, he reached St. Lo on the 22nd. By keeping abreast with the army's left flank the fleet provided a moveable base, while the troops lived on the countryside, avenging the raids of Norman seamen on the English south-coast towns by burning their harbours and ships. After a few days of this atrocious business—the usual accompaniment of fourteenth-century

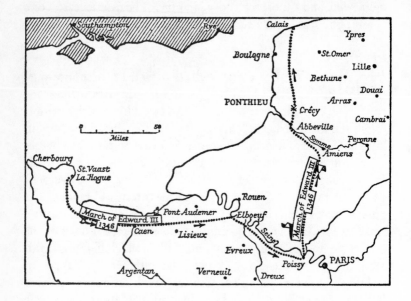

The Campaign of 1346

warfare—the king, as claimant to the French throne, issued an order threatening death to any soldier who should "set on fire towns or manors, . . . rob churches or holy places, do harm to the aged, the children or women of his realm."

Edward's French subjects showed no enthusiasm for their would-be sovereign. The peasants fled in terror from his march and, when on July 25th he summonsed Caen, the bishop of Bayeux tore up the summons and imprisoned his messenger. Yet, though a formidable town—larger, a chronicler wrote, than any English city save London—the invaders carried it in a day after the archers had out-shot the cross-bowmen defending the Orne crossings, and the fleet, sailing up the river from Ouistreham, had joined in the fight. They took a rich haul of prisoners and a copy of a treaty made eight years before by King Philip

46

of France with the Norman authorities for an invasion of
England. This Edward sent home to be read in parliament.

On the last day of July the march to the Seine was resumed.
On August 2nd the army reached Lisieux. But on the same day
the French king entered Rouen forty miles ahead, interposing
his force between the English and their Flemish allies who, two
hundred miles to the north, were just setting out from Ypres.
As soon as news had reached him of Edward's landing he had
raised the oriflamme at St. Denis and, recalling his son, who was
attacking the English in Gascony, hurried to the Norman capital,
gathering troops as he marched. The Seine here was three
hundred yards wide and, with the city held in force, the English
could not hope to cross.

Instead, on reaching the river at Elboeuf, twelve miles above
Rouen, they turned upstream to seek a narrower crossing. By
doing so they abandoned their communications with England but
threatened Paris. For the next six days the rival armies marched
south-eastwards along opposite sides of the Seine. Everywhere
the English found the bridges demolished or strongly held. But
on the 13th, when they were only a dozen miles from the capital,
Edward allowed the French to outmarch him and, by a sudden
feint, turned back to Poissy where the bridge, only partially
destroyed, was lightly guarded. Crossing by a single sixty-foot
beam only a foot wide, Northampton, the constable, got a detachment to the far side. For the next two days, while skirmishing parties set fire to St. Cloud and other villages under the
western walls of Paris to deceive the enemy, the carpenters
worked feverishly to repair the bridge. Meanwhile, though by
now in far superior strength, King Philip remained in a frenzy of
indecision, marching first to one side of his capital and then the
other, uncertain whether the English were about to assault it or
move south to Gascony.

On August 15th the carpenters finished their work, and
during that night and next morning the army and its baggage
train crossed the Seine. In the next five days it marched seventy
miles due north, hoping to cross the Somme between Amiens

and Abbeville and join hands with the Flemings who were besieging Bethune, fifty miles beyond that river. But though he
had been temporarily outwitted, when he found that his foe had
crossed the Seine King Philip acted with equal speed. Realising
at last Edward's weakness, he covered the seventy-three miles
from Paris to Amiens in three days, ordering the feudal levies of
the north to join him there. With him were the flower of
France's chivalry, together with King John of Bohemia and his
son, Charles of Moravia—titular King of the Romans.

The position of the English was grave in the extreme. Between
them and their Flemish allies in Artois lay the marshy valley of
the Somme, with the French king at Amiens only a day's march
away and every bridge over the river in his hands. All contact
had been lost with the fleet, whose seamen had returned to
England in the wake of the ships that had taken home the sick
and the spoils of Caen. The army's food supplies were almost
exhausted and in the closing stages of their march the troops had
been living on unripe fruit. After covering nearly three hundred
miles their boots were worn out and the horses dying for lack of
forage.

Edward had been far too bold. But he showed no sign of his
anxiety; "he was so great hearted," a contemporary wrote
"that he never blanched or changed countenance at any ill-
hap or trouble soever." On August 23rd he started westwards in
the hope of finding a crossing above Abbeville, but, as the estuary
here widened to two miles, the prospect was unpromising.
Scarcely had he set out when news arrived that Philip had left
Amiens and, moving up the south bank of the river to attack, was
already within a mile of Airaines where the English had spent the
previous night.

Cut off in a strange land and without maps—a military commodity then unknown—the king ordered the prisoners to be
brought before him and offered a huge reward for anyone who
would reveal a crossing place. A native of the district told him
of a concealed causeway across the estuary at Blanchetaque, mid-
way between Abbeville and the sea, where at low tide a man

could cross waist-deep. Without hesitation Edward decided to take the risk.

It was a hundred and thirty years since his great-great-grand-father, John, had lost his baggage and treasure in the Wash in a similar crossing. Before dawn on the 24th, marching the six miles to the ford in single column his advance-guard reached the river. The far bank was held by a French force of between three and four thousand men. As soon as the tide was low enough for a man to stand without being swept away, the troops started to cross, led by Hugh Despenser, whose father had been hanged on a fifty-foot gallows by Edward's mother. Carrying their bows above their heads to keep them dry, the archers struggled through a mile and a half of water, while the knights followed on horse-back. A few hundred yards from the northern bank they came within range of the enemy's cross-bowmen but continued to advance until they were in killing distance. Then, standing ten abreast on the causeway and shooting over one another's heads, they loosed their usual devastating hail. When their arrows were exhausted they stepped into the deeper water on either side and let the mounted armour splash past them into the shallows where, after a brisk skirmish, it put the French cavalry to flight.

Meanwhile on the south bank Edward's rear-guard had been holding off the advance echelons of Philip's host until the baggage wagons, with their precious load of arrows and cannon, had passed through the water, now starting rapidly to rise. Save for a few stragglers who were caught by the tide the whole army passed over in safety. The enemy, barred by the rising flood, could only watch in amazement.[1]

After crossing the Somme the English fanned out. The con-stable pursued the enemy towards Abbeville, while Hugh Despenser pushed down the estuary as far as the little port of Crotoy where he seized some wine-ships. By nightfall the whole

[1] The man who led the archers and who died three years later during the Black Death, lies in his armour of alabaster, his hands crossed in prayer and a lion at his feet, in the Despenser tomb in Tewkesbury abbey whose glorious vaulting posterity owes to his and his wife's munificence.

army was encamped in the forest of Crécy, a few miles north of the ford. Though the troops were still short of rations, their morale was high, for in a deeply religious age the passage of the river seemed a miracle. The king therefore decided to stand and give battle. The odds against him were immense, but with so cautious an adversary such an opportunity might never recur.

All day on Friday the 25th, while the French were recrossing the Somme he searched for a defensive position. He found it on a low ridge facing south-west, between the villages of Crécy and Wadicourt. Behind lay a wood—the Bois de Crécy-Grange —into which and the forest of Crécy on his right his woodland-trained archers could withdraw in case of need.

. . . .

On the morning of August 26th, 1346, having attended Mass and "committed his cause to God and the Blessed Virgin," Edward marched his army to its position. Allowing for losses he had now about 13,000 men, of whom more than half were archers, and, at the outride, some three thousand knights and men-at-arms. Under his directions the marshals deployed the latter in three divisions or "battles," two of them a little way down the forward slope of the ridge, which was about a mile long, and the third under his personal command in reserve. He himself took up his station in a windmill in the centre, with an extensive view of the valley which the French would have to cross. The right-hand division was under the earls of Warwick and Oxford with the Prince of Wales in titular command, and the other commanded by the constable. As usual, the knights and men-at-arms were dismounted in single line, their horses being taken by the pages to the wagon-laager in the rear.

Forming four projecting salients on the flanks of each of the forward divisions were the archers, with Welsh spearmen in support. Before retiring to their laager, the baggage-wagons un-loaded a supply of arrows along their lines. In front, to protect themselves from the cavalry, they hammered in iron-pointed

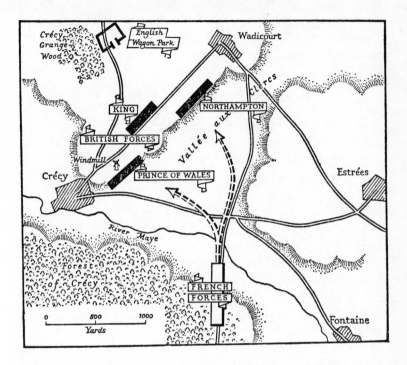

Crécy

stakes and dug pot-holes as the Scots had taught their predecessors to do. Such a formation, like that at Halidon Hill, was
calculated to force the attackers into two narrowing gulleys where
they would have to contend with the English armour while raked
by arrows from the flanks.

When the troops were all posted, the king rode along the
ranks on a small palfrey, carrying a white wand and wearing a
crimson surcoat of golden leopards. To each contingent he spoke
a few words. Beside him was Sir Guy de Brian,[1] bearing the

[1] His effigy, still coloured in faded Garter blue, can be seen in Tewkesbury
abbey. He married the widow of Hugh Despenser, hero of the Blanchetaque
crossing.

dragon banner of Wessex—the standard under which the English had fought at Hastings. It was a symbol of the national character Edward had given his army—so different to that of the feudal hosts of the past. "Next to God," it was said of him, "he reposed his confidence in the valour of his subjects."

After the king's inspection the army dispersed for the midday meal, which the cooks had been preparing in the baggage-laager, the men-at-arms leaving their helmets to mark their stations and the archers their bows and arrows. It had been arranged that the trumpets should recall them at the first sign of the enemy, who were now believed to be moving up from Abbeville. During the afternoon there was a heavy shower, which brought the archers scurrying back to their lines to guard their bowstrings, each man unstringing his and placing it in a coil under his helmet. Afterwards the sun came out and the men sat down in their lines with their weapons in front of them. There was still no sign of the French, and it was felt that there would be no battle that day.

But a little before four o'clock the trumpets sounded and everyone stood to arms. Coming out of the woods three miles to the south-east along the track still known as *le chemin d'armée* was the French vanguard. For a whole hour the English watched as Philip's immense host moved into view, "the fresh shining armour, the banners waving in the wind, the companies in good order, riding a soft pace." According to the lowest estimate that has come down from the fourteenth century, they were 40,000 strong, of whom more than 12,000 were mounted knights and men-at-arms. They rode forward in eight successive divisions, so that there seemed no end. The advance-guard was commanded by the blind King John of Bohemia—a romantic figure and world-famous warrior—who was accompanied by the French king's brother, the Count of Alençon, and the Count of Flanders whom Edward's allies, the burghers of Ghent, had driven from his country. The centre was under the Duke of Lorraine with Philip's nephew, the Count of Blois, as lieutenant.

The king—"Philip Valois tyrant of the French," as the English

chroniclers called him—followed with the reargua
with the German King of the Romans, Charles of M
the exiled King of Majorca. There were nearly a score
counts, French, German, Luxemburger and Spanish. It
so much a national army as the embodiment of the intern
chivalry which for three centuries had dominated the battlefields
of the continent, commanded by the greatest monarch in
Christendom. Above him waved the oriflamme—the sacred
banner flown when no quarter was to be given to France's
enemies. For there had been disputes on the previous night about
the allocation and ransom of the prisoners, and to prevent
quarrelling the king had given orders to slay them all.

In addition to this array of chivalry there marched among the
vanguard six or seven thousand Genoese cross-bowmen, the best
trained troops on the continent and the only professionals in the
host. The rest of the army was composed of peasant levies—the
"communes" as they were called—low-spirited serfs considered
incapable of standing up to gentlemen, but useful to follow in the
wake of their mounted superiors and help crush the foe by sheer
weight of numbers. In the French army infantry were despised;
it was knights—"the crested helmets"—who counted.

Goliath was pitted against David, but David had a sling.
David, too, had discipline which Goliath lacked. When the
French vanguard reached the valley in front of the English
position the sun was already starting to sink, and Philip's advisers
urged him to halt for the night and deploy for battle in the
morning. To this, the only sane course, the king, who had not
expected to find the English barring his path, agreed. But his
vassals had other views. Seeing the English with their banners
on the ridge, the young knights—arrogant and inexperienced—
pressed forward, impatiently confident that they were at their
mercy. Before even a blow had been struck the French army was
out of control and committed to an attack undeployed.

The vanguard, therefore, came straight on, halting only to let
the Genoese bowmen open the attack. With trumpets and
clarions sounding they started to climb the ridge. The setting sun

was in their eyes and it was hard to focus their target, waiting motionless and ready.

At this point, wrote Froissart, "when the Genoese began to approach, they made a great leap and cry to abash the Englishmen. But they stood still and stirred not for all that. Then the Genoese again the second time made another leap and a fell cry and stept forward a little, and the English removed not one foot. Thirdly again they leapt and cried and went forward till they came within shot; then they shot fiercely with their cross-bows. Then the English archers stept forth one pace and let fly their arrows so wholly together and so thick that it seemed snow." Firing four or five times faster than the cross-bowmen, they shot them out of the field. To add to the Italians' confusion and terror, two or three English cannons—a novelty from the Tower armoury which had been dragged round France and concealed among the archers—opened fire, sending their balls of iron and stone rolling through the densely packed ranks amid flames and smoke.

As the Genoese broke, the French knights, with a cry of, "Ride down the rascals," charged through their ranks, trampling down the wounded and dying. They rode in a dense, glittering line of solid armour, waving plumes and levelled lances. Everyone expected them to crush the thin, defending line of the Prince of Wales's division before them. But they never reached it. For once again the English archers stepped forward.

As their arrows, aimed at the chargers, struck home, the stately advance dissolved into disorderly heaps and clusters of dead and wounded horses and of dismounted knights weighed down by their armour. Those who went forward on foot or succeeded in driving their terrified beasts through the hail of arrows came up against a solid line of English men-at-arms, as steady as the archers who continued shooting down each new batch of attackers as they struggled up the hill through the fading light.

The fight had now become general, with the second French wave assailing the constable's division. But everywhere the result was the same; the mounted knights struggling to reach and break the line of the English armour above them and the archers continuing to massacre their horses. There was no-one to give the former orders and no-one to co-ordinate the attack. For five hours, though darkness had fallen, the mêlée continued, wave after wave of knights entering the fight only to meet the same fate. At one moment it seemed as if the Prince of Wales's slender force would be overwhelmed, and Godfrey de Harcourt hurried across to the nearest unit of the constable's division to beg its commander, Lord Arundel, to make a flanking attack to relieve the pressure. But when a similar appeal reached the king, he only remarked, "Let the boy win his spurs." For he knew that the moment to throw in his reserves had not yet come. When the messenger returned he found the prince and his companions leaning quietly on their swords, taking breath as, amid mounds of French corpses, they waited for the next attack.

Soon after midnight, after fifteen or sixteen assaults had failed, the French army began to dissolve. The dead were now piled in walls before the English lines. Among them was the blind King of Bohemia, the reins of his bridle tied to those of the knights with whom he had charged. Two archbishops, the royal Count of Alençon, the Duke of Lorraine and the counts of Blois and Flanders had all fallen. King Philip himself, his horse shot under him, was led from the field as Edward II had been from Bannockburn. There was no pursuit, for the English king, who had never once lost his grip on the battle, had forbidden his men to break rank.

As the French melted away into the darkness and no more attacks came, the exhausted victors lay down, supperless and waterless, to sleep where they had fought. When, on the misty morrow they counted the dead they found the bodies of more than 1,500 knights and 10,000 common soldiers. The French army had ceased to exist. Edward himself with his son attended the burial of John of Bohemia—a paladin after his own heart, who had long predicted that he would die in battle against the bravest knights in the world.

A new phenomenon had appeared in the western world: the military power of England. "The might of the realm," wrote the astonished Froissart, "most standeth upon archers which are not rich men." The English had shown that on their own ground they could conquer against any odds and almost without cost. Their losses at Crécy were forty dead, only three of them men-at-arms.

CHAPTER 3

The Hurling Time

" Englishmen suffer indeed for a season, but in the end they repay so cruelly
that it may stand as a great warning. . . . There is no people under the sun so
perilous in the matter of its common folk as they are in England."

Froissart

TWO YEARS AFTER Crécy, England suffered the greatest social
disaster in her history. The Black Death or bubonic plague
carried off a third of her people, and in three further outbreaks
during the next quarter of a century, the population fell to about
half its pre-1348 figure. One result was a grave labour shortage
and a spectacular rise in wages, which the Council and successive
parliaments of landowners tried to prevent by punitive ordin-
ances and legislation. These statutes of Labourers aroused bitter
class-feeling.

Yet for a century before the Black Death the position of the
English peasant had been slowly improving, whether he was a
well-to-do yardlander farming two or three hundred acres or a
landless cottar earning his daily bread by wages. Compared
with the wretched peasantry of the continent, he was not too
badly off except when the harvest failed; the bowmen of Crécy
had not been drawn from an oppressed populace. It was a
commonplace to contrast the lot of the stalwart English husband-
man with that of the French serf, wrapped in sacking and living
on apples and bitter rye-bread.

Yet probably somewhere near half the English people were not
legally free but tied by inheritance to the soil they cultivated.
Described as villeins and subject to the discipline of the lord's

manorial court—on whose juries and inquests they served—
they could not claim a free man's rights under the Common Law,
let alone representation in parliament. Like the feudalism of
which it was part, the servile manorial system of the open field
villages of central and southern England had long been in decline
and was gradually giving way to an economy based on paid
labour and rented farms. But it was still the basis of life for nearly
a million men and women who, though not technically slaves,
were bound by birth to the soil and compelled to perform un-
paid menial services for its lord. They could only gain release by a
formal grant of manumission or by flight from their homes and
fields to some chartered borough where servile status had been
abolished and residence for a year and a day gave a man his
freedom.

The extent of the services the villein had to perform for his
lord varied with the size of his holding and the custom of the
manor. But wherever the open-field system operated, as it did
in most parts of England except the pastoral north and west and
in Kent, the peasant was confronted by uncertain demands on
his time and galling restrictions on his freedom of action. Among
these were the obligations to grind his corn, bake his bread and
brew his ale at the lord's mill, oven and brewery—"suit of mill"
and "suit of oven," as they were called—which not only en-
riched the lord, but offered opportunities for every kind of
chicanery and oppression by those to whom the latter leased his
rights. An equally resented monopoly was the lord's dovecot
and "free warren" from which hordes of pigeons and rabbits
descended on the peasant's crops, while if he retaliated by
trapping such pests he faced a heavy fine in the manorial court.
If he wished to sell a beast, if he wished to reside outside the
manor, if he wished to marry his son or daughter, even if the
latter became pregnant—for this depreciated her value—he was
fined. And on his death his widow or heir was forced to pay a
heriot—the value of the best beast and chattel—and an entry-fine
equivalent to a year's rent as the price of taking over the family
holding.

All this had come to be intensely resented. Villeinage was seen by the bondsman as an economic imposition and a degrading distinction. It was no longer taken for granted, and every opportunity was taken to escape or evade its burdens. Those who resented them most were the richer villagers who occupied the traditional yardlands—holdings of thirty acres or more in the arable fields, with corresponding rights in the manorial meadowland, waste and woodland. A yardlander had to perform for his holding, in person or by proxy, not only a full half-day's labour on the lord's land for three or four days a week throughout the year but additional services called "love-boons" —given, in theory, out of love for his feudal protector—at the very seasons, haymaking and harvest, harrowing and sowing times, when he needed all the labour he could command to wrest a living from his own soil.

Those who could afford it, therefore, seized every opportunity to commute as many of such services as possible for money payments. In the expanding agricultural economy of the thirteenth and early fourteenth century many peasants were able to free themselves from the more onerous burdens, for progressive land-owners often found it paid them to hire labour rather than depend on the unwilling services of disgruntled serfs. The halving of the national labour-force by the Black Death halted this gradual emancipation. Labour suddenly became the most precious commodity in the kingdom. A landowner who had made no concessions to his serfs found himself able to cultivate his depopulated estates far more cheaply than one who had commuted his villeins' services for a cash payment. Bound by agreements to let their serfs enjoy their holdings at rents which now bore no relation to what they themselves had to pay for hired labour, and desperate for lack of workers, many lords tried to enforce rights that had lapsed or to stretch those that remained.

If the Black Death made lords more conscious of the value of compulsory services, it made every serf more eager to evade them. Shaking off their ancestral shackles, bondsmen fled from their homes and took service for wages with distant employers who asked no questions. It was the poorer members of the village community who had no land to lose who were able to seize such opportunities—the young and those with no possessions but their tools and skill as husbandmen or craftsmen. The attempts of the Commons and local justices to keep down wages by branding, imprisonment and the stocks drove them to make common cause with their richer neighbours, who were confronted by demands from their lords for services which they regarded as unjust and oppressive.

It was against the lord's officers and agents that the peasant's indignation was, in particular, directed. From the receivers and bailiffs who wrung from him the services and rents on which the landowner lived, from the steward who presided at his manorial court and the lawyers who made extreme claims on his behalf, he received little mercy. Times were bad, money hard to come by for a luxurious ruling-class in need of the income it could no longer obtain from victories abroad. The business of its agents was to exact the uttermost service and payment obtainable. In the process they often took—and even more often were suspected of taking—more than was due or than the lord himself received.

Some of the hardest task-masters were the monasteries who, hit by the economic recession and the plague, had never enjoyed, like the secular lords, the opportunity of making good their losses by the plunder and ransoms of war. Intensely conservative and, like all corporations, impersonal in business relationships, they had the justification that their exactions were for the service of God. More easily than most they were able to prove rights to long-lapsed services by the charters which every religious house preserved, added to by cultivating the friendship of the great and sometimes, if their critics are to be believed, improved by a little pious and skilled forgery. Nor, conscious of the sanctity of their claims, were they always very tactful with those whose labour they exploited; the abbot of Burton told his tenants that they owned nothing but their bellies.

Of all who enforced the lord's rights the lawyer was the most hated. To the peasant the purpose of the law seemed to be to keep him down and enforce the servile status that deprived him of liberty and opportunity. In the thirty years after the first post-Black Death statute against what Council and parliament called "the malice of labourers," nearly nine thousand cases of wage enforcement were tried by the courts and in nearly all judgment was given in the employer's favour. The peasant's indignation at those who put such restraints on him was increased by the spectacle of expanding freedom in the chartered towns which had sprung up in every part of England and to which so many of the younger men of his village had fled to better their conditions. Some of these, who had survived the harsh conditions and competition of the medieval town, had grown rich and famous.

Because of this, and for other reasons, there was a captious, bitter, disillusioned spirit abroad. The strain and cost of the long war with France, which after its resumption in 1369 turned against England, tended like the successive visitations of the Black Death to shake men's faith in society. The pestilence which had driven weak natures to a hectic pursuit of pleasure, elevating the self-indulgence of the moment above duty and morality, had left only half the labour formerly available to do the nation's work and supply the luxuries of the rich. For a generation the burden of war debts and taxes had borne with what seemed insupportable severity on the survivors. The result was a widespread sense of frustration, of loss of familiar standards, of resentment between employer and employed, landowner and husbandman, government and taxpayer. Everyone tended to blame someone else for his sufferings.

Deep down the malaise of England after the Black Death was spiritual. It was the sickness of soul of a people who felt that justice was being outraged. The old static feudalism, in which every man knew and accepted his place, was disintegrating; the more fluid society that was replacing it was on the make and given to lavish and ostentatious luxury. The reign of Edward III had witnessed a steady rise in the standards of comfort, not only of the aristocracy but of new classes—financiers, merchants, wool-

61

masters, franklins, master-craftsmen. Hearths with chimneys had taken the place in rich men's houses of sooty open fires; Flemish glass had appeared in traceried windows; dovecots, fishponds and nut-alleys were laid out in parks and gardens; manor-houses and fine merchants' dwellings, with private bedrooms and plastered walls, were rising in place of the old gloomy fortresses where men and beasts had slept together on filthy, rush-strewn floors in draughty halls, full of smoke and stink. Yet such signs of progress struck moralists like the poet, William Langland, as symptoms of a diseased society:

" Ailing is the hall   each day in the week
  Where the lord nor the lady   liketh not to sit.
  Now hath each rich man a rule   to eaten by himself
  In a privy parlour,   for poor men's sake,
  Or in a chamber with a chimney,   and leave the chief hall
  That was made for meals   and men to eaten in."

With the advance in civilization, arts and sciences, exchange of goods and merchandise had thrown the career open to the talents. In every city a race of men had arisen who pursued money-making as an end in itself, who bought and sold not primarily to supply the consumer with goods but to increase their stock of money and use it for making more. Usury, fore-stalling, regrating, making a corner in commodities and arti-ficially lowering market-prices in order to buy and raising them in order to sell—all the practices which the Church had taught were unchristian and unneighbourly—were pursued as a pro-fession by men who made fortunes by doing so and put ordinary folk out of countenance by extravagant living and the grandeur of their ways. Merchants whose grandfathers or even fathers had been simple craftsmen or serfs were addressed by their fellow townsmen as worshipful or sire, wore scarlet robes and costly furs as masters and liverymen of monopolistic merchant com-panies founded originally to protect and foster honest craftsman-ship. By their own standards most of them were worthy, if self-important, men whose bond could be trusted by their fellows;

they could hardly have continued to succeed otherwise. Yet there was a widespread feeling that vintners diluted wine, that wool-mongers cheated wool-growers, that grocers and corn-merchants sold false measure, that those who lent money to the Crown cheated the tax-payer, and that if a man had grown rich by trade he must be a rogue. And some of those who had made money out of the French war were vulgar upstarts with extravagant standards of display and notorious for jobbery and corruption. "Soapmongers and their sons for silver," wrote the indignant Langland, "are made knights." "Covetise hath dominion over all things," complained his fellow poet, Gower; "there is no city or good town where Trick does not rob to enrich himself. Trick at Bordeaux, Trick at Sevile, Trick at Paris buys and sells; Trick has his ships and servants, and of the noblest riches, Trick has ten times more than other folk."

Running through society, including the Church, was this sense of division, strife and covetousness. "Avarice," a preacher said, "makes men fight one another like dogs over a bone." By its side went "the foul sin of pride." Both the old ruling class and the new vied in the extravagance of their clothes, feasts and enter-tainments; "in such manner they spent and wasted their riches with abuses and ludicrous wantonness that the common voice of the people exclaimed." Contrasted with "the gay robes, the soft sheets, the small shirts" of the rich was the peasant, with his garment of hodden grey, living on cold cabbage, bacon and penny ale; his wattle-and-log hut full of holes; the poor Norfolk deer-stalker whose feet were so putrefied by the dungeons of Norwich castle that he could not walk at his trial, and his eight fellow-prisoners who died in Northampton gaol from hunger, thirst and want. "I have no penny," declared Langland's Piers Plowman,
" pullets for to buy

Neither geese nor gris   but two green cheeses,
A few curds and cream   and a cake of oats,
And two loaves of beans and bran   to bake for my bairns."

To him it seemed a denial of Christianity that the honest poor should be defrauded. His heart was stirred and his indignation

roused for "prisoners in pits" and poor folk in cottages "charged
with children and chief lord's rent," and country women "rising
with rue in winter nights to rock the cradle,"

> " To card and to comb   to clout and to wash; . . .
> Many the children   and nought but a man's hands
> To clothe and feed them   and few pennies taken."

Out of the air of fourteenth-century England, with all its
glaring inequalities, arose the conviction—so strangely contrasted
with the assumptions of the warrior and prelate class—that "the
peasant maintained the state of the world" and was receiving less
than justice. It was put in its highest form by Langland, who in
his *Vision of Piers Plowman* voiced the recurring English reaction
to the contrast between ill-used wealth and undeserved destitu-
tion, with its characteristic resolve, not to destroy society, but to
redress the balance. Though it never seems to have attained the
dignity of an illuminated manuscript—the *imprimatur* of fashionable esteem in that intensely aristocratic age—his poem had an
astonishing success; some sixty copies have survived and, since
it circulated among the poor and lowly, far more must have
perished. Overlooked by the rich like the *Pilgrim's Progress* of a
later age, its readers and copyists were probably parish priests and
it may have been through them and their sermons that the name
of its humble peasant hero and his identification with the crucified
Christ became so widely known. At the end of the fourteenth
and the beginning of the fifteenth century there appeared on
the nave walls of parish churches in southern England a number
of paintings, crude and almost certainly executed by local hands,
of Christ naked, lacerated and bleeding, with a carpenter's tools—
mallet, hammer, knife, axe, pincers, horn and wheel—haloed
round his head. This figure of "Christ of the Trades," is to be
found in churches as far apart as Pembrokeshire and Suffolk.
Many more probably disappeared during the Reformation;
among the best preserved are those at Ampney St. Mary in the
Cotswolds—not far from the hillside on which Langland saw
silhouetted the tower of Truth—at Hessett in Suffolk and at
Stedham in Sussex. In the first, the labouring Christ faces a

painting of the hero of knightly chivalry, St. George slaying the dragon; in the last, of the Virgin sheltering the congregation under her cloak.

.   .   .   .

There was a wide gap between the patient, Christ-like crafts-man and peasant of the wall-paintings and Langland's dream, and the angry labourer refusing service for his lord, cursing land-lords, monks and lawyers and fingering his bow. It was not hard to inflame uneducated men with a sense of injury, and it was not the selfless side of human nature that was inflamed. The poet himself was well aware of it. "Then," he wrote,

"would Wastour not work   but wandren about. . . .
Labourers that have no land   to live on but their hands,
Deigned not to dine today   on yesterday's cabbage,
No penny ale may please them   nor no piece of bacon,
But if it be fresh flesh or fish   fried or baked."

He depicted the runagate villein, demanding ever higher wages, who, when refused,

"would wail the time   that ever he was workman born;
Then curseth he the king   and all his Council with him
That lay down such laws   the labourers to grieve."

Parliament was being flouted and the Statute of Labourers made a dead letter by surly villeins standing idle in the fields or tramp-ing in angry companies to the nearest town to sell their labour to those who would pay highest for it. Phrases like "stand to-gether!" "make a good end of what hath been begun!" passed from shire to shire, and wandering agitators preached incendiary sermons on village greens. "Things will never go well in England," proclaimed the defrocked hedge-priest and dema-gogue, John Ball, "so long as goods be not in common and so long as there be villeins and gentlemen. By what right are they whom we call lords greater than we?" "We are formed," he declared, "in Christ's likeness and they treat us like beasts."

It was an age of war and violence; war always breeds violence.

Resentment amongst the labouring classes against their oppressors was not confined to England. In the middle of the century
the Roman mob had risen under the demagogue Cola di Rienzo;
a decade later occurred the terrifying Jacquerie or peasants'
revolt in northern France. Wherever men were brought together in large numbers to serve masters who catered for the
luxuries of the rich, the spirit of rebellion was present. In 1378
the oppressed wool-carders of Florence revolted against the
merchant oligarchs of the city, stormed the palazzo of the Com-
mune and installed one of their members as Gonfalonier of Justice.
A year later the weavers of Ghent and Bruges and the Flemish
cloth towns had risen and were still defying their count and the
French king.

In England unrest so far had mainly taken the form of mass
withdrawals of labour-services, particularly in places where the
lord was an impersonal ecclesiastical corporation. When the
jurymen of Harmsworth, Middlesex—the property of a Norman
abbey—defied the lord's steward by returning a false verdict in
favour of their fellow villeins who had absented themselves from
the previous year's haymaking, the villagers deliberately opened
the river sluices to flood the hay. There were mob rescues of
fugitive bondsmen as they were being haled back to their
"villein nests," and armed assemblies by night to poach the lord's
woods and slay his game. The labour laws, too, help to explain
the passion and vehemence of some of these sudden explosions of
rustic wrath, often on seemingly trivial pretexts. Englishmen
were not prepared to suffer the indignity of being branded on the
forehead with an "F" for "falsehood" because they took day-
hire or demanded more than the inadequate statutory wage
allowed by parliament. A year or two after the first Statute of
Labourers, when feeling against this form of class legislation was
running particularly strong, the peasants from the villages round
Oxford joined the townsmen in a murderous attack on the
university—later known as St. Scholastica's Day—distinguishing
themselves by their savagery and furious cries of "Havak, havoc,
smygt faste, gyf good knok."

During the opening years of Richard II's reign such riots had grown ominously in number. They were fomented by the egalitarian sermons of friars and wandering priests like John Ball, who for the past twenty years had been tramping the country preaching, in defiance of the ecclesiastical authorities, against the rich "possessioners" of Church and State. In the words of the monastic chronicler Walsingham, he preached "those things which he knew would be pleasing to the common people, speaking evil both of ecclesiastical and temporal lords, and won the goodwill of the common people rather than merit in the sight of God. For he taught that tithes ought not to be paid unless he who gave them was richer than the person who received them. He also taught that tithes and oblations should be withheld if the parishioner was known to be a better man than the priest." Forbidden to preach in church, he continued to do so in streets, villages and fields until he got himself excommunicated. Nothing, however, stopped him, and, though he several times suffered imprisonment, as soon as he got out he started again. He also took to circulating inflammatory letters full of dark riddles and rhymes calling on the virtuous poor to prepare for the day when they could fall on their oppressors. "John Ball, St. Mary's priest," ran one, "greeteth well all manner of men and biddeth them in the name of the Trinity, Father, Son and Holy Ghost, stand manlike together in truth, and help truth, and truth shall help you.

> Now reigneth price in price,
> Covetise is holden wise,
> Lechery without shame,
> Gluttony without blame,
> Envy reigneth with reason
> And sloth is taken in season
> God amend, for now is time."

. . . .

On top of this strained situation came the demand for a new and crushing tax. Like all medieval peoples the English tended to regard taxes as a form of robbery and injustice. The evolution of their government had turned largely on their rulers' recognition that the consent of the taxed to new imposts could only be won by allowing them a share in their imposition. When, Magna Carta having placed limitations on the feudal taxation of land, imposts had been levied on personal wealth and merchandise —moveables, as they were called—the same rule had been adopted. Superseding the feudal lord's right to tallage at will, the principle that the subject should be party to the fiscal burdens imposed on him had been applied at every stage of the tax-structure. Whenever parliament agreed that a fifth, tenth or fifteenth should be levied on moveables, justices had been sent into every county to assess the local proportion payable with representative knights from every hundred, who, in turn, met the representatives of every vill, where a jury of inquest swore to the number, quantity and value of taxable goods in the township. Shortly before Crécy, as a result of an agreement between Exchequer officials and representatives of the localities, a fixed proportion of the subsidy rate voted by parliament had been allocated to every county, hundred and township. During Edward III's reign, which lasted fifty years, vast sums were raised by this method for the war with France, which, after the victorious 'forties and 'fifties, ceased to finance itself and forced Government and parliament to seek ever new ways of raising money.

In 1371 the latter adopted the novel device of a tax on every parish in England at a standard rate. Six years later a still more revolutionary innovation was adopted by the aged king's last parliament. This was a poll-tax of fourpence a head on the entire lay adult population except beggars. This "tallage of groats," as it was called, mulcting the poorest at the same rate as the richest, proved intensely unpopular and very hard to collect. But it appealed to a parliament of landowners and employers, since for the first time it imposed a direct fiscal burden on the peasant and unpropertied wage-earner.

Three years after Richard II's accession, faced by the Government's now desperate need, a new parliament, meeting at Northampton, in the autumn of 1380, imposed the tax for a third time, trebling the rate per head. For a poor rustic householder with a large family who might have to defray the tax of several aged or female relatives, this was a crushing burden. Reflecting the belief of the rich that the labour-shortage caused by the Black Death had placed "the wealth of the kingdom in the hands of artisans and labourers," it not only showed astonishing ignorance of the circumstances of "common folk whose occupations standeth in grobbying about the earth"; it ignored the principle for which parliament had long contended: that there should be no taxation without representation and consent. The peasantry and town-artisans on whom the tax bore so hardly were completely unrepresented in a parliament of magnates, prelates, landowners, merchants and lawyers.

The consequence of the shilling poll-tax was a wholesale falsification by the villages of southern England of their tax-returns. When these reached the commissioners appointed to collect the money, it seemed as though the population had shrunk by a third since the last poll-tax of two years before. The amount brought in fell far below what was expected, and the Government was furious. On March 16th 1381 the Council found that the local collectors had been guilty of gross negligence and favouritism and appointed a new commission to scrutinize the lists and enforce payment from evaders.

The decision was received with universal execration. It was spoken of as a corrupt job engineered for the private profit of the head of the commission of revision, John Legge, a serjeant-at-law, and of the treasurer, Sir Robert Hales—"Hob the robber," as he was called. When news of a further descent of tax assessors reached the villages, the ignorant supposed that a new tax was to be levied on top of that already paid. Everywhere in the populous counties of the south-east, rustic opinion was at boiling point against tax-collectors, escheators, jurymen, lawyers and royal officials in general and against the chancellor and treasurer in particular and, illogically enough, for he was no longer actively engaged in government but absent on a mission in Scotland, the young king's uncle, John of Gaunt, Duke of Lancaster.

No-one in authority treated the dissatisfaction of the peasantry very seriously. But when at the end of May the new poll-tax commissioner of Essex, Thomas Brampton, appeared at Brentwood with two serjeants-at-arms to open enquiries into the returns for the hundred of Barstaple, he was met by the representatives of the defaulting townships with a sullen refusal to pay. They possessed, they said, their receipt for the subsidy and would not pay a penny more. But it was the fishermen and fowlers of the Thames estuary—the men of the sea and salt-water creeks—who provided the spark that fired the revolution of working-class England. Summoning to their aid their neighbours from Corringham and Standford-le-Hope, the men of Fobbing-by-Tilbury met Brampton's threats of arrest with open violence, and with sticks and stones drove him and his men out of the town.

This was more than the Government could ignore. On Sunday, June 2nd, the chief justice of the Common Pleas, Sir Robert Belknap, descended on Brentwood with a commission of trailbaston and an escort of pikesmen. His business was to punish the rioters and hang the ringleaders. He found the place in a ferment. For by now the rebellious fishermen had prevailed on the entire neighbourhood to rise. Armed with staves, pitchforks and bows, a mob surrounded the judge, seized and burnt his papers and made him swear on his knees never to hold another commission. They then murdered his three clerks and three local tax-assessors or jurymen whose names they had made him reveal. Sticking their heads on poles they bore them in triumph round the villages of south-east Essex, while the terrified Belknap fled back to London.

On the same day trouble began on the other side of the Thames. At Erith in Kent a band of rioters broke into the monastery of Lesnes and made the abbot swear to support them. The ringleaders then crossed the river tó take counsel of the men of Essex. During the next few days rebellion spread northwards across the county as rioters carried their messages from parish to parish. Everywhere government agents were attacked, their houses plundered and their records and papers thrown into courtyard or street and burnt. The admiral of the Essex coast, Edmund de la Mare of Peldon, and the sheriff, John Sewall of Coggeshall, had their homes sacked, the former's papers being carried on a pitchfork at the head of the triumphant fishermen. At every manor visited, a bonfire was made of all charters and manorial rolls.

It was as though the whole system of law and government, built up over centuries, was being repudiated by the common people. Yet though damage to property was widespread, there was comparatively little loss of life, most of the local lords managing to escape. The chief escheator of the county was murdered as well as a number of Flemish merchants in Colchester where the mob rose at the approach of the peasantry. Had the treasurer been at his home at Temple Cressing instead of in London, he would certainly have been torn to pieces; as it was, his "very beautiful and delectable manor," as a chronicler described it, was burnt to the ground after the populace had eaten the fine fare and broached "the three tuns of good wine" which he had laid in for an impending meeting of the chapter-general of the Order of St. John of Jerusalem of which he was master.

Meanwhile trouble was growing in Kent. On the day after the assault on the chief justice at Brentwood two serjeants-at-arms acting for Sir Simon Burley, the boy-king's tutor, arrested a respected burgess of Gravesend on the ground that he was a runaway serf. When the townsfolk declined to pay £300 for his manumission—at least £15,000 in today's purchasing-power—the poor man was sent to the dungeons of Rochester castle. Two days later, on Wednesday June 5th, heartened by the arrival of a hundred insurgents from Essex, the people of all the towns and villages on the south bank of the river between Erith and Gravesend rose in rebellion. They were careful, however, to stress in a proclamation listing the crimes of their young sovereign's ministers that, though there were "more kings than one in the land," they wished for none but Richard. Patriotically they added, that "none dwelling within twelve miles of the sea should go with them but should keep the coast of the sea from enemies."

Next day, June 6th, decided the fate of Kent. At one end of the county the men of Gravesend and Dartford marched on Rochester. At the other end a commission of trailbaston, directed against tax-evaders and accompanied by the hated John Legge, was prevented from entering Canterbury. Rochester Castle, though strong enough to withstand a siege for weeks, was surrendered by its constable that afternoon after several ineffective attempts to storm it. Probably it was under-garrisoned, but, like almost everyone else, the defenders were bemused by the fury and turbulence of the mob. For the rustic population of England to behave in such a way seemed something outside nature: it was as though the animals had rebelled.

Certainly the Government seemed unable to grasp the situation. Like the local authorities it remained inert throughout that critical first week of June, helplessly watching the course of events. The chancellor, its head, was the gentle primate, Simon Thebaud of Sudbury—the son of a Suffolk trader whose family had grown rich supplying the local gentry with luxury goods and developing the new rural cloth industry. He was utterly without martial instinct or experience. The king's uncles were far away; John of Gaunt was in Edinburgh negotiating a truce with the Scots, Thomas of Woodstock was in the Welsh marches and Edmund of Cambridge had just sailed for Portugal. On news of the outbreak a messenger had been sent to Plymouth to countermand the expedition but arrived too late. Owing to the needs of the English garrisons in France and Brittany the country was almost denuded of troops except on the remote Scottish and Welsh borders. In the capital and the crucial south-east there were only a few hundred men-at-arms and archers guarding the king, and a small force which the old condottiere, Sir Robert Knollys, had started to collect in his London house to reinforce

Brittany. Nothing was done to call out the country gentry and their retainers who in the insurgent counties to the east and north of London were paralysed with fear.

But if the Government was without an active head, the insurgents had found one. On Friday June 7th the men of Kent marched up the Medway valley from Rochester to Maidstone, where they were welcomed by the populace who rose and plundered the richer inhabitants, murdering one of them. Here they chose as their captain one Wat Tyler. Little is known of his past, but according to Froissart he had seen service in the French wars and, it subsequently transpired, like many old soldiers, had since been earning a livelihood by highway robbery. He was clearly a mob orator of genius, for he immediately reduced to discipline the motley throng of excited peasants and artisans. And he quickly showed himself a man of action and exceptional military talent.

On the day he assumed command Tyler issued a proclamation setting out the insurgents' aims. They would admit, he said, no allegiance except to "King Richard and the true commons"— in other words, themselves—and have no king named John, a reference to the Duke of Lancaster. No tax should be levied "save the fifteenths which their fathers and forebears knew and accepted," and everyone should hold himself in readiness to march, when called upon, to remove the traitors around the king and root out and destroy the lawyers and officials who had corrupted the realm.

The rebels not only found a military leader. They acquired a spiritual one. Among the prisoners released from Maidstone gaol was John Ball. Only a few weeks before, the long-suffering archbishop had clapped him in again, describing how he had "slunk back to our diocese like the fox that evaded the hunter, and feared not to preach and argue both in the churches and churchyards and in markets and other profane places, there beguiling the ears of the laity by his invective and putting about such scandals concerning our person and those of other prelates

73

and clergy and—what is worse—using concerning the holy
father himself language such as shamed the ears of good Chris-
tians." The irrepressible preacher now found himself free again
and with a ready-made congregation of twenty thousand ragged
enthusiasts after his own heart. According to Froissart, who,
though often an unreliable witness, visited England soon after the
rising and was clearly fascinated by the whole affair, he addressed
them in these terms:

" My good friends, matters cannot go well in England until
all things be held in common; when there shall be neither
vassals nor lords; when the lords shall be no more masters
than ourselves. How ill they behave to us! For what
reason do they thus hold us in bondage? Are we not all
descended from the same parents, Adam and Eve? And
what can they show, or what reason can they give, why
they should be more masters than ourselves? They are
clothed in velvet and rich stuffs, ornamented with ermine
and other furs, while we are forced to wear poor clothing.
They have wines, spices and fine bread, while we have
only rye and the refuse of the straw; and when we drink,
it must be water. They have handsome seats and manors,
while we must brave the wind and rain in our labours in
the field; and it is by our labours that they have where-
with to support their pomp. We are called slaves and, if
we do not perform our service we are beaten, and we have
no sovereign to whom we can complain or would be willing
to hear us. Let us go to the king and remonstrate with him.
He is young and from him we may obtain a favourable
answer, and, if not, we must ourselves seek to amend our
conditions."

At the same time the preacher sent out to the villages of Kent
and Essex more of his inflammatory missives:

> " John Ball
> Greeteth you all,
> And doth you to understand
> He hath rung your bell.

Now with right and might,
Will and skill,
God speed every dell!"

Another, written under a pseudonym and addressed to the men of Essex, was subsequently found in the pocket of a rioter condemned to be hanged.

"John Schep, sometime Saint Mary's priest of York, and now of Colchester, greets well John Nameless and John the Miller and John Carter and bids them that they beware of guile in the town, and stand together in God's name, and bids Piers Plowman go to his work and chastise well Hob the Robber. And take with you John Trueman and all his fellows and more, and look sharp you to your own head and no more.

John the Miller hath ground small, small, small.
The King's Son of Heaven shall pay for all.
Beware or you will be in woe
Know your true friend from your foe,
Have enough and say "Hello!"
And do well and better and flee from sin,
And seek true peace and hold therein.
And so bids John Trueman and all his fellows."

Tyler and Ball—brigand and hedgerow preacher—were the leaders "the true commons" needed. While Ball addressed himself to his sympathizers, Tyler acted. Sending emissaries to urge the surrounding villages to rise and join him at Maidstone, he set out with several thousand followers for Canterbury. By midday on the 10th he had reached the city, where he was greeted with enthusiasm by the inhabitants, all those, that is who had nothing to lose. On enquiring whether there were any traitors in the town, he was directed to the houses of the local notables, three of whom he had executed on the spot. Then, having burnt the judicial and financial records of the shire, beaten up the sheriff and sacked the castle, letting out the prisoners from the gaols, he and his followers poured, a vast tumultuous multitude, into the cathedral during Mass. Here with one voice

75

they cried out to the monks to elect a new archbishop of Canterbury in place of Sudbury whom they declared to be a traitor and "about to be beheaded for his iniquity." They also extracted an oath of fealty to the king and true commons from the mayor and corporation and—for the summer pilgrimage season was at its height—recruited their ranks by a number of pilgrims. At the same time they dispatched agitators to the towns and villages of East Kent.

Early on Tuesday June 11th, having spent less than twenty-four hours in Canterbury and set the eastern weald and coast from Sandwich to Appledore aflame, Tyler set off again. Reinforcements poured in as he marched. By nightfall he was back in Maidstone, having covered eighty miles in two days. Then, pausing only for the night, he marched with his entire host before dawn on the 12th for the capital, sending messengers into Sussex and the western counties to summon the commons to join him and "close London round about." Simultaneously on the other side of the Thames the Essex insurgents, who by now had won complete control of the county, began a parallel march under the captaincy of Thomas Farringdon, an aggrieved Londoner.

While the two hosts converged on the capital, terror reigned on either side of their march as village mobs smoked out royal and manorial officials, lawyers and unpopular landlords, breaking into their houses, and burning every record they could find. They would have, they declared, "no bondsmen in England." Many of the gentry took to the woods, among them the poet John Gower, who afterwards recalled in his long Latin epic, *Vox Clamantis,* the pangs of hunger he suffered while living on acorns and trembling for his life in wet coppices. Others, less fearful or unpopular, made timely contributions to the "cause" and took the oath of fidelity to the "king and true commons." A few, but only a few, were murdered, while others, being persons of distinction who had not done anything to make themselves unpopular, were carried off as hostages to grace Wat Tyler's entourage, including Sir Thomas Cobham and Sir Thomas Tryvet, a hero of the wars.

Meanwhile the authorities had at last resolved to act. On either the Tuesday or Wednesday Tyler's men, pouring towards the capital, were met by messengers from the king at Windsor to ask why they were raising rebellion and what they sought. Their answer was that they were coming to deliver him from traitors. They also presented a petition asking for the heads of the Duke of Lancaster and fourteen other notables, including the chancellor, treasurer and every leading member of the Government. On receipt of this the fourteen-year-old king and his advisers left hastily for London and the Tower to form a focus of resistance round which the forces of order could rally. The king's mother and her ladies, who had been on a summer pilgrimage to the Kentish shrines, also set out for the same place of refuge. On the way they encountered the rebel vanguard. Yet, though greatly frightened, they were subjected to nothing worse than a little ribald jesting and were allowed to continue their journey to the capital. Here the mayor, William Walworth, after escorting his sovereign to the Tower, was busy putting the city into a state of defence.

That evening the Kentish host encamped on the Blackheath heights, looking down across the Thames to the distant city. On the opposite bank the Essex men took up their station in the Mile End fields outside the suburb of Whitechapel and about a mile to the east of the walls and the Aldgate. Some of the less exhausted Kentish rebels continued as far as Southwark, where, welcomed by the local mob, they burnt a bawdy house rented by some Flemish women from Mayor Walworth and let out the prisoners from the Marshalsea and King's Bench. Finding the drawbridge in the centre of London Bridge raised against them, they went on to Lambeth where they sacked the archbishop's palace and the house of John Imworth, the warden of the Marshalsea.

It was not only the proletariat of Southwark who sympathized with the insurgents. There were thousands of journeymen, apprentices and labourers inside the city walls who did so too. On the mayor's orders the gates had been closed and entrusted to the aldermen and watch of the adjacent wards. But there were bitter rivalries among the city's rulers. The victualling interests were at daggers drawn with the older merchants, drapers and mercers, who, employing labour on a large scale, favoured a policy of free trade and low-priced food in order to keep down wages and feed their journeymen and apprentices cheaply—a matter of vital importance to them since the labour shortage caused by the Black Death. Both were monopolists, but, to overthrow their rivals, the victuallers had formed an alliance with the discontented city proletariat—wage-earners and small craftsmen —who regarded their employers and the capitalists who controlled the market for their handiwork in much the same light as the villeins regarded their lords. Among three aldermen whom the mayor dispatched to urge the insurgents to keep the peace was a certain John Horne, a fishmonger, who, separating himself from his companions, sought a private interview with Tyler and secretly promised his support. When he returned to London he not only assured the mayor that the marchers were honest patriots who would do the city no harm but, under cover of darkness, smuggled three agitators across the river to stir up the mob.

Earlier that evening an emissary from the rebel camp had travelled by boat from Greenwich to London to seek an interview with the king and council. This was the constable of Rochester castle, Sir John Newton, who for the past week had been a prisoner of the insurgents. Brought into the presence and given leave to speak, he explained that, though his captors would do the king no harm, they were determined to meet him face to face to communicate certain matters of which he had no charge to speak. Since they held his children as hostages and would slay them if he failed to return, he begged for an answer that would appease them and show that he had delivered his message.

To this after some hesitation the Council agreed. Next morning at prime the king and his lords embarked in five barges for Greenwich. Here, on the shore below Blackheath the Kentish men, after a hungry and sleepless night, were assembled in battle array under two great banners of St. George. While they waited,

Mass was celebrated, it being Corpus Christi day, and afterwards John Ball preached, taking as his text the old popular rhyme:

" When Adam delved and Eve span
Who was then the gentleman?"

According to the St. Albans chronicler, "he strove to prove that from the beginning all men were created equal by nature, and that servitude had been introduced by the unjust oppression of wicked men against God's will, for if it had pleased Him to create serfs, surely in the beginning of the world He would have decreed who was to be a serf and who a lord. ... Wherefore they should be prudent men, and, with the love of a good husband-man tilling his fields and uprooting and destroying the tares which choke the grain, they should hasten to do the following things. First, they should kill the great lords of the kingdom; second, they should slay lawyers, judges and jurors; finally they should root out all those whom they knew to be likely to be harmful to the commonwealth in future. Thus they would obtain peace and security, for, when the great ones had been removed, there would be equal liberty and nobility and dignity and power for all." "When he had preached this and much other madness," wrote the disgusted chronicler, "the commons held him in such high favour that they acclaimed him the future archbishop and chancellor of the realm."[1]

Whether it was this sermon or the presence of the archbishop in the royal barge or the fact that the Kentishmen had not breakfasted, they greeted the king's arrival with such a tumult of shouting that he was unable to make himself heard. "Sirs," he kept calling across the water as the rowers rested on their oars just out of reach of the frantic multitude, "what do you want? Tell me now that I have come to talk to you." But as the crowd steadily grew more threatening, fearing lest some of the bowmen might start to shoot, the Earl of Salisbury—by far the most experienced soldier present—ordered the boats to put out into midstream and return to the Tower.

At that both the Kentish host and the Essex men who had

[1] T. Walsingham, *Historia Anglicana* II, 32.

been watching from the other shore set up a great shout of
"Treason" and, with their banners and pennants, moved off
towards London. Access to the city's markets and provision
shops had by now become essential if they were not to have to
disperse through hunger—a fact on which the authorities were
counting. Within the city, processions of clergy were marching
through the streets praying for peace, while crowds of sympathizers with the insurgents were gathering in the poorer lanes
and alleys. For, though the city gates were still barred against
them, the agitators whom Horne had slipped into the town had
not been idle. As Wat Tyler's men neared the southern approaches to the bridge they were again met by this liberal-minded
fishmonger waving a royal standard which he had procured by a
trick from the town clerk. And as, headed by this emblem of
loyalty and respectability, they surged on to the bridge, the
drawbridge in the midst of its shops and houses was lowered to
them by the alderman of the Billingsgate ward. About the same
time another alderman of the opposition faction let in the Essex
men through the Aldgate.

Once the head of the rebel columns was in possession of the
southern and eastern entrances the whole multitude poured in to
the city, while the apprentices and journeymen and the labouring
poor of the slums flocked into the streets to greet them. For a
time the newcomers were too busy eating, drinking and gaping
at the city sights to do much harm. But presently, refreshed by
several huge barrels of ale which some rash philanthropists had
broached in the streets and incited by the apprentices who had
old scores to pay off against John of Gaunt, they set up a cry of
"To the Savoy! To the Savoy!" The duke might be in Edinburgh, but the superb palace he had furnished from the plunder
of France—and, as many supposed, of England—stood a mile outside the western walls where the fields and gardens sloped down
to the riverside from the Strand that linked London to Westminster. Thither the men of Kent, with thousands of excited
apprentices—a great company with torches—made their way in
an angry tumult, breaking into the Fleet prison on the way and

letting out the criminals, while the duke's servants fled as the shouting came nearer.

No time was wasted. In the general desire for justice or revenge even plundering was forbidden. Everything in the great house was hurled out of the windows—tapestry, sheets, coverlets, beds—and hacked or torn to pieces. Then the building was set on fire and burnt to the ground. At the height of the fire there was an explosion caused by three barrels of gunpowder, which were thrown into the flames in the belief that they contained specie. Some of the rioters afterwards continued towards Westminster where they destroyed the house of the under-sheriff of Middlesex and let the prisoners out of the gaol. Others, on their way back to the city, broke into the lawyers' home in the Temple, tore the tiles off the roof and took all the books, rolls and remembrances from the students' cupboards to make a bonfire. They also fired some shops and houses which had recently been built in Fleet street, declaring that never again should any house deface the beauty of that favourite country walk of the Londoners. Those who had gone on to Westminster returned by way of Holborn, setting light to the houses of several "traitors" pointed out to them by their London comrades and breaking open Newgate still further to enlarge their company. Meanwhile the men of Essex descended on the priory of St. John's, Clerkenwell, the headquarters of the Knights Hospitallers just outside the city's northern wall. Here they burnt the priory and hospital—"a great and horrible piece of damage for all time to come"—and murdered seven Flemings who had taken sanctuary in the church.

That night, while the insurgents camped round the royal fortress in the open spaces of Tower Hill and St. Catherine's wharf and while their leaders drew up lists of persons to be liquidated, the king and Council debated long and anxiously what was to be done. Since the morning their position had changed dramatically for the worse; instead of waiting behind London's walls while the rebels starved outside, they themselves were hemmed in the Tower, and the city it was supposed to dominate was in possession of a fanatic, uncontrollable mob.

From a garret in one of the turrets into which he climbed the boy king could see twenty or thirty fires burning in different parts of the town. Beyond, the whole of the home counties to south and east were in revolt, while, unknown as yet to the beleaguered Council, the revolutionary ferment had spread that afternoon into Hertfordshire and Suffolk, where burgesses and bondsmen had risen together against the monks of England's two most famous abbeys, St. Albans and Bury.

The key to the situation lay, however, in the capital. If the mob who had taken possession of it could be defeated, the flames of revolt might be put out elsewhere. But, with London lost and the court imprisoned inside it, there was nothing round which the forces of order could rally. Mayor Walworth, a bluff and vigorous man, urged an immediate sally against the insurgents while they were sleeping off the effects of their evening's debauch. There were six hundred armed men-at-arms and archers in the Tower and a hundred or so more in Sir Robert Knollys's house and garden; with a bold front they would probably be joined by all the law-abiding in London. Only a small minority of the insurgents wore armour; if the loyal forces struck at once, thousands might be slain as they slept. But the Earl of Salisbury, who had fought with the king's grandfather and father at Crécy and Poitiers, thought otherwise. Once fighting began in the narrow streets and lanes, the rebels' immense superiority in numbers would tell and total disaster might ensue. "If we should begin a thing which we cannot achieve," he said, "we should never recover and we and our heirs would be disinherited and England would become a desert." Instead, he offered the Ulysses-like counsel that an attempt should be made to induce the rebels to disperse by fair words and promises, which could afterwards be repudiated as obtained under duress.

An earlier attempt that evening to persuade them to do so by putting up the king to address them from the ramparts and offer a free pardon to all who should go home had been shouted down in derision. Some more signal mark of royal trust was needed if the populace was to be appeased. It was, therefore, proposed that the king should offer to confer with the rebels in the Mile End fields and to ride out there next morning through their midst with such of his lords as were not expressly marked down for execution. While under cover of this bold move the crowds were drawn away from the Tower, the archbishop and treasurer and John of Gaunt's son and heir, young Henry Bolingbroke, earl of Derby, could be smuggled out to safety by water.

The plan depended on the king's readiness to take the risk. But, though he appeared a little pensive, the boy was ready and even eager. He was now fourteen, and it was something to find that at last all the great lords and counsellors around him looked to him for leadership. As soon as it was light a proclamation was made from the walls and soon afterwards, surrounded by an immense multitude of excited country folk, the royal cortège set out along the Brentwood road for Mile End. But many of the Londoners stayed behind to watch the Tower, for the rebels' leaders were not so easily fooled. When the boat by which their intended victims attempted to escape appeared, it was forced to put back as soon as it emerged from the water-gate.

Nor did the royal ride to Mile End prove easy or pleasant. At one moment the Essex leader, Thomas Farringdon, a highly excitable man, seized the king's bridle, demanding to be avenged on that false traitor Prior Hales, the treasurer, who he said had deprived him of his property by fraud. So threatening was the crowd that the king's half-brothers, the Earl of Kent and Sir John Holland, finding themselves at the edge of the throng, seized the opportunity to gallop away and escape to open country to the north. When, however, the royal party arrived in the Mile End fields the simple country folk who were waiting there knelt before the king crying, "Welcome, our lord King Richard, if it pleases you we will have no other king but you." It was like the scene in the ballads when the sovereign whom Robin Hood and his men had captured revealed his identity and promised to restore every honest man to his own.

It must have seemed to many present that such a golden time had come when their young king—the son of England's hero, the

Black Prince—announced that he would grant all their demands. He promised the abolition of serfdom, of villein services and seigneurial market monopolies, and that all holders of land in villeinage should henceforth become free tenants at the modest rent of 4d. an acre a year. Nor did he only promise them all free pardons and an amnesty if they would return quietly to their villages, but offered to give a royal banner to the men of every county and place them under his special protection and patronage. His words, as Froissart put it, "appeased well the common people, such as were simple and good plain men." They rather took the wind, however, out of their leaders' sails. The latter, therefore, returned to the charge. "The commons," Tyler told the king, "will that you suffer them to take and deal with all the traitors who have sinned against you and the law." To which the king replied that all should have due punishment as could be proved by process of law to be traitors.

This, however, was scarcely what Tyler and his fellow-leaders wanted. While the king, surrounded by the better disposed of his humbler subjects, was helping to set them on their way to their distant villages, the two captains of the commons of Kent and Essex hurried back with a band of picked followers to the Tower where a large crowd was still waiting outside the gates, clamouring for the archbishop's and treasurer's blood. Pushing through them they succeeded in bluffing their way into the fortress itself either through the treachery of the guards or, more probably, because, with the king and his lords expected back at any moment, the portcullis was up and no one knew what to do. Fraternizing with the soldiers, shaking their hands and stroking their beards, the crowd pressed after their leaders into the royal apartments, shouting for the traitors' blood. In their search the king's bed was hacked to pieces and his mother, the Princess of Wales, subjected to such rude treatment that she was borne off in a dead faint by her pages and put into a boat on the river. John Legge, the serjeant-at-law who had drawn up the poll-tax commission, and three of his clerks, the Duke of Lancaster's physician, a Franciscan friar named Appleton, and several others were found. The duke's son, Henry Bolingbroke—who eighteen years later was to become king—was more fortunate, being saved by the resource of one of his father's retainers. The archbishop and treasurer were taken in the chapel, where, expecting death, the former had just received the confession of the latter and administered the last rites. Dragged by the mob into the courtyard and across the cobbles to Tower hill, they were summarily beheaded across a log of wood. It was the third time in the country's history that an archbishop of Canterbury had been assaulted at the altar and brutally done to death.

After that, all pretence of moderation and order vanished. While the primate's head, stuck on a pike and crowned with his mitre, was being borne round the city before being set over the gateway to London Bridge—the traditional place for traitors—and the king, shunning the desecrated Tower, made his way with his escort to the royal wardrobe at Baynard's Castle near St. Paul's where his mother had taken refuge, the riff-raff of the capital and the peasants' army ran riot in the streets, forcing passers-by to cry, "With King Richard and the true commons" and putting everyone to death who refused. By nightfall "there was hardly a street in the city in which there were not bodies lying of those who had been slain." The chief victims were the Flemish merchants who were hunted through the streets and killed wherever found; more than a hundred and fifty are said to have perished, including thirty-five who had taken shelter in St. Martin-in-the-Vintry and who were dragged from the altar and beheaded outside on a single block. Every disorderly person who had old grudges to pay off or property he coveted seized his opportunity; Alderman Horne, with a mob at his heels, paraded the streets bidding anyone who wanted justice against a neighbour to apply to him. Tyler himself hunted down and cut off the head of the great monopolist, Richard Lyons, whose servant he was at one time said to have been, while his lieutenant, Jack Straw, led a gang to burn the home of the murdered Sir Robert Hales, the treasurer, at Highbury. Far away in Suffolk at about the same hour the head of Sir John Cavendish, chief justice of the

King's Bench, was being carried on a pike through the rejoicing streets of Bury St. Edmunds,[1] while his friend and neighbour, the prior of the great abbey, who had been hunted all day on the Mildenhall heaths, cowered before his captors, awaiting the trial that was to lead to his death next morning. Later, on the Saturday, when his head, too, was borne back on a pike to Bury, the crowd carried the heads of the two friends round the town together, making them converse and kiss one another.

Dawn on Saturday June 15th saw the nadir of the once proud kingdom whose princes a quarter of a century before had led the French king captive after Poitiers through the streets of London. From Lincolnshire, Leicester and Northampton to the coasts of Kent and Sussex its richest and most populous counties were aflame, while, as the news spread of London's capture and the king and Council's humiliation, other shires as far as Cornwall and Yorkshire crackled with rumours of impending rebellion. The greatest officers of state—the primate and chancellor, treasurer, and chief justice—had all been brutally done to death, and everywhere magnates and gentry were flying to the woods or, isolated and helpless in their homes, awaiting the sound of mobs and the light of torches. In London riot, plunder, arson and murder had continued all night and, though thousands of law-abiding peasants had returned to their homes on receiving the king's promise, thousands more, including their leaders and all the more violent and criminal elements, were in control both of the capital and what remained of the government.

The king spent the night at the wardrobe in Baynard's Castle comforting his mother. His surrender at Mile End seemed to have achieved nothing, and, though thirty royal clerks had been employed all the previous afternoon copying out pardons and charters, the hard core of the insurgents remained both un-satisfied and seemingly unsatiable. Yet, since there was no other way of loosening their stranglehold, Richard resolved, regardless

[1] He had been caught at Lakenheath as he was trying to cross the Brandon, a country woman having recognised him and pushed the ferry boat into mid-stream so that he should not escape his pursuers, who executed him on the spot.

of the risks involved, to try again. Accordingly on the morning of Saturday the 15th he proposed a further meeting with the commons and their leaders. This time the rendezvous was to be the cattle market at Smithfield, just outside the city's north-western walls close to the church of St. Bartholomew the Great and the smoking ruins of the priory of St. John's, Clerkenwell.

Before proceeding there the king rode to Westminster Abbey to pray at the shrine of his ancestor, St. Edward the Confessor. Murder and sacrilege had been there that morning before him, a mob having broken into the sanctuary, tearing from the pillars of the shrine to which he had clung in terror the warden of the Marshalsea—a man hated by the populace as being "without pity as a torturer." The monks of Westminster and the canons of St. Stephen's met the king at the abbey gates, barefooted and carrying their cross. For a while all knelt before the desecrated shrine while the young king confessed to the abbey's anchorite and received absolution, afterwards repairing to the little oratory in the royal closet of St. Stephen's chapel to pray before a golden image of the Virgin which had been a treasured possession of his family since the days of Henry III and was believed to have special protective powers. It is possible that it is this deeply moving incident in the king's life rather than his coronation four years earlier that is depicted in the Wilton Diptych—the young Plantagenet, robed and crowned, kneeling before the figures of St. Edward, King Edmund the Martyr and St. John the Baptist whose hand rests on the boy's shoulder and all three of whom seem to be gazing fixedly and sternly as at some threatening force, while a winged galaxy of guardian angels, wearing Richard's badge of the hart, gather round the Virgin and her child beneath the banner of St. George.

The king and his retainers, about two hundred strong, now mounted and rode on to Smithfield. Because of their peril they wore armour under their robes. They were joined at St. Bartholomew's church by Mayor Walworth and a small party, while on the opposite side of the market-place the entire insurgent army awaited in battle order. It must by now have been about five o'clock of the afternoon and the weather very hot.

Tyler now felt himself to be master of the kingdom. He was at the head of a host which outnumbered by many times the little royal band, and all day news had been coming in from every quarter of new risings. On the previous evening he had boasted that he would shave the beards—by which he meant slice off the heads—of all who opposed him and that in a few days there would be no laws in England save those which proceeded from his mouth. "He came to the king," wrote the Anonimalle chronicler, "in a haughty fashion, mounted on a little horse so that he could be seen by the commons and carrying in his hand a dagger which he had taken from another man. When he had dismounted he half bent his knee and took the king by the hand and shook his arm forcibly and roughly, saying to him, 'Brother, be of good comfort and joyful, for you shall have within the next fortnight 40,000 more of the commons than you have now and we shall be good companions.'

"When the king asked Tyler, 'Why will you not go back to your own country?' the insurgent chief replied with a great oath that neither he nor his fellows would depart until they had their charter such as they wished to have, and such points rehearsed in their charter as they chose to demand, threatening that the lords of the realm would rue it badly if the points were not settled to their satisfaction. The king asked him what were the points that he wanted, and he should have them freely without contradiction written down and sealed. He then rehearsed points which were to be demanded. He asked that there should be no law except the law of Winchester, and that there should be henceforth no outlawry on any process of law, and that no lord should have any lordship ... and that the only lordship should be that of the king; that the goods of Holy Church should not remain in the hands of the religious nor of the parsons and vicars and other churchmen; but those who were in possession should have their sustenance from the endowments, and the remainder of their goods should be divided amongst their parishioners; and no bishop should remain in England save one, and that all the lands and tenements now held by them should be confiscated and shared amongst the commons, saving to them a reasonable substance. And he demanded that there should be no more bondsmen in England, no serfdom nor villeinage, but that all should be free and of one condition. And to this the king gave an easy answer, and said that he should have all that could fairly be granted, saving to himself the regality of the Crown. And then he commanded him to go back to his home without further delay. And all this time that the king was speaking no lord nor any other of his council dared nor wished to give any answer to the commons in any place except the king himself.

"After that Tyler, in the king's presence, called for a flagon of water to rinse his mouth because he was in such a heat, and when it was brought he rinsed his mouth in a very rude and disgusting fashion before the king; and then he made them bring him a flagon of ale of which he drank a great deal, and in the king's presence mounted his horse. At this time a yeoman of Kent, who was among the king's retinue, asked to see the said Wat, the leader of the commons; and when Wat was pointed out to him, he said openly that he was the greatest thief and robber in all Kent. Wat heard these words and commanded him to come out to him, shaking his head at him in sign of malice; but the yeoman refused to go to him for fear of the mob. At last the lords made him go out to Wat to see what he would do in the king's presence; and, when Wat saw him, he ordered one of his followers, who was riding on a horse carrying his banner displayed, to dismount and cut off the yeoman's head. But the yeoman answered that he had done nothing worthy of death, for what he had said was true and he would not deny it, but in the presence of his liege lord he could not lawfully make debate without leave, except in his own defence. . . . For these words Wat would have run him through with his dagger and killed him in the king's presence, and because of this, the mayor of London, William Walworth by name, reasoned with the said Wat for his violent behaviour and contempt done in the king's presence and arrested him. And because he arrested him, the said Wat struck the mayor with his dagger in the stomach with great anger; but, as God would have it, the mayor was wearing armour and took no harm. But like a hardy and vigorous man the mayor drew his cutlass and struck back at Wat and gave him a deep cut on the neck and then a great cut on the head. And in this scuffle a yeoman of the king's household drew his sword and ran Wat two or three times through the body, mortally wounding him. And the said Wat spurred his horse, crying to the commons to avenge him, and the horse carried him some four score paces, and there he fell to the ground half dead. And when the commons saw him fall and did not know for certain how it was, they began to bend their bows to shoot."[1]

It was thirty-five years since Crécy and a quarter of a century since Poitiers, and even the youngest who had shared in these masterpieces of the bowman's art were now, by the standards of the fourteenth century, old men. Even Najera was fourteen years away, and few of the English archers who had wrought that Pyrrhic victory can ever have returned to England. Yet there must have been at least several hundreds in the insurgent host who had served in the French and Breton wars and many thousands more who had learnt to use the long-bow at the butts after church on Sundays and were armed with the terrifying weapon —the most formidable in the world—which the Plantagenet kings had given the yeomanry of England. It seemed, as hundreds of bows were drawn in the rebel ranks, that it was going to cost the last of them his life and throne.

At that moment Richard clapped spurs into his horse and rode straight across the square towards the massed insurgents. "Sirs," he cried as he reined in before them, "will you shoot your king? I am your captain. I will be your leader. Let him who loves me follow me!" The effect was electric; the expected flight of arrows never came. Instead, as the young king slowly wheeled his horse northwards towards the open country, the peasants in ordered companies followed him like the children after the piper of Hamelin.

[1] *The Anonimalle Chronicle*, (ed. V. H. Galbraith).

As they did so, the mayor galloped back into the city to rouse the loyalists and call them to rescue their sovereign. His chief adversary—Alderman Sibley who had lowered the river draw-bridge two days before—arrived just before him, spreading the rumour that the whole royal party had been killed. But Wal-worth's appearance gave him the lie and, sickened by the plunder, murder and arson of the last forty-eight hours, the shopkeepers and wealthier citizens flocked with their arms into the streets as the sole hope of saving their homes and possessions. Mustered by the aldermen and officers of their wards and led by old Sir Robert Knollys with his archers and men-at-arms, they hurried in thousands out of the Aldersgate in pursuit of the imperilled king and his rabble following. They found them in the Clerken-well cornfields with the boy, still unharmed, sitting on his horse in their midst, arguing with the insurgents, now leaderless and confused in the absence of Tyler who had been borne dying into St. Bartholomew's hospital. While they were so occupied, Knollys quietly deployed his men, outflanking and surrounding the multitude, while a band of heavily armoured knights pushed through the crowd to the king's side.

The threat to the Crown and capital was over. The insurgents made no resistance; it was the end of a long hot day and they must have been parched and exhausted. Encircled by armed men and appeased by the king's promises, even the extremists had no more fight in them and were ready to return home. He refused to listen to the proposal of some of his rescuers that, as his former captors were now at his mercy, he should order them to be massacred; "three-fourths of them," he is said to have replied, "have been brought here by force and threats; I will not let the innocent suffer with the guilty." Knollys, who was himself of yeoman birth, strongly counselled the course of mercy and helped to organize the march of the Kentish men through London to their homes.

The whole multitude now dispersed. When Richard re-turned to the Wardrobe amid the rejoicings of the Londoners whose mayor he had just knighted in the Clerkenwell fields, he said to his anxious mother. "Rejoice and praise God, for today I have recovered my heritage that was lost and the realm of England also."

. . . .

Had the king fallen at Mile End or Smithfield there would have been no authority but that of the rebellious peasantry left from Yorkshire to Kent and from Suffolk to Devon. When he and Walworth so unexpectedly, and at the eleventh hour, turned the tables on Tyler, the revolution was on the point of complete success. For on the very afternoon that Richard, preparing for death, confessed and received absolution in the desecrated abbey, the fires of rebellion, fanned by the news of the previous day's massacre in the Tower and the insurgents' triumph, spread from St. Albans to Cambridge and Ipswich and into Bedfordshire, the Fens and Norfolk. At St. Albans, led by a local tradesman called William Grindcobbe—a brave man with a burning love of freedom—the townsfolk invaded the abbey, seized its charters and burnt them in the market place, ripping up the confiscated millstones—symbols of the abbey's monopolistic privileges—with which the abbot had paved his chamber, while the country-folk drained the fishponds and trampled down the fences enclosing the monastic woods and pastures. At Cambridge, as during that Saturday village after village rose in the fenland, the bell of Great St. Mary's brought out the mob in a riotous crusade against the university and the adjacent priory of Barnwell. Corpus Christi College, the chief owner of house-property in the town, was gutted, and the university charters, archives and library were burnt next day in the Market Square while an old woman shouted, as she flung parchment after parchment into the flames, "Away with the learning of the clerks! away with it!" During the weekend other risings occurred in hundreds of villages in East Anglia, the Fenland and east Midlands. In all of them justices of the peace, tax commissioners, lawyers and unpopular landlords, particularly monastic ones, were attacked, their houses sacked or burnt and their charters and court-rolls destroyed.

The most formidable of all the risings outside the capital occurred in Norfolk, the richest and most populous as well as most independent-minded county in England. In West Norfolk, where it broke out during the weekend of the king's triumph and lasted for ten days, it was without a leader and apparently quite purposeless, the one common denominator being robbery under threats of violence. In the eastern half of the county, where a leader of Tyler's calibre appeared, rebellion took a political course, though a different one to that of the home counties. Its aim, natural in so remote an area, was not the reform and control of the Government, but the setting up of an independent East Anglia. But though for a week its leader, a dyer named Geoffrey Litster, kept regal state in Norwich, with the king and Council in possession of the capital the revolution collapsed as suddenly as it had begun. It disintegrated piecemeal. By the end of June all resistance was over.

Except for the summary execution of a few ring-leaders like Tyler's lieutenant, Jack Straw, and John Starling—the Essex rioter who had decapitated Archbishop Sudbury and who was taken still carrying the sword that had done the deed—the insurgents were tried and punished by the normal processes of law. Though a large number of persons were charged with treason or crimes of violence, only about a hundred and fifty[1] suffered the death penalty, nearly all of them after being found guilty by a local jury. Most of the ring-leaders perished including John Ball, who was found in hiding at Coventry, and John Wraw, another priest who had led the Suffolk insurgents and who tried to save his life by turning king's evidence. The noblest of all—the leader of the St. Albans townsmen against the tyranny of the great abbey that held them in bondage—died with sublime courage, protesting the righteousness of his cause. "If I die for the liberty

[1] Froissart's estimate of 1500 hanged or beheaded, like most of his figures, seems wildly inaccurate. In his detailed but unfinished study of the rising, André Réville made a list—admittedly incomplete—of a hundred and ten persons who suffered the supreme penalty. André Réville, *Le Soulèvement des Travailleurs d'Angleterre en 1381.*

we have won," he said, "I shall think myself happy to end my life as a martyr for such a cause."

Before the end of the summer the king put a stop to further arrests and executions, and in December a general amnesty was declared. The peasants' revolt and its repression were over. Only the smouldering ashes of anger and resentment remained; that and fear of its recurrence. But for two circumstances the king would have perished with his ministers. One was his courage, the other the deep-seated loyalty to the throne which transcended the sense of injustice and desire for revenge of the peasant multitude. Fierce as were the passions aroused during the "hurling time," and cruel and atrocious some of the deeds done during it, the majority of those who had marched under the banner of "King Richard and the true commons" sincerely believed that they were restoring the realm to justice and honest government and rescuing their young sovereign from traitors and extortioners. They did not seek to destroy either him or his kingdom, and, even at the height of the rebellion, provided for the defence of the country. And, though they released the criminals from the jails and allowed the more savage of their companions to wreak their will on those whom they regarded as oppressors, they made no attempt to massacre their social superiors like the French Jacquerie of a generation before. When in their wretchedness after their ruler's defeat in war the French peasants had risen, they had loosed their vengeance on the entire ruling class, murdering, raping, torturing and mutilating every man, woman and child within their reach. In the contemporary accounts of the English peasants' revolt no instance is recorded of violence to a woman, though for three days the capital and for several weeks the richest parts of England lay at their mercy.

Yet they and their leaders came very near to overthrowing the government of their country, far nearer than the rebellious peasants of France, Flanders and Italy had ever come. They had done so because their cause was based, not on mere desperation or unthinking anger, but on certain principles of justice on which, when they could free their minds from class prejudice, all Enklishmen were agreed. And though they seemed to have been defeated and to have been reduced once more to bondage, they had, in fact, as time was to show, achieved their object. When, a week after the Smithfield meeting, a delegation of peasants waited on the king at Waltham to ask for a ratification of the charters, he replied that his pledges, having been extorted by force, counted for nothing. "Villeins you are still," he told them, "and villeins ye shall remain!" He was wrong. For the present the lords might enforce their rights; they could not do so permanently. The magic of their old invincibility was gone. Given arms by the Statute of Winchester and taught to use them on the battlefields of France, the peasants had tested them on the manor itself and knew their strength. They would no longer brook servitude.

As an economic means of cultivating the soil for profit, villeinage was doomed. With such surly and mutinous labour and no police to enforce it, it proved impossible to make it pay. Faced by the growing competition of the towns the lord had to make concessions to keep his villeins on the land. And as the population began to rise again after the first waves of Black Death, the process of commuting services for money payments was resumed and paid labour increasingly took the place of servile. In other places, lords found their demesnes so hard to work that to maintain their incomes they were forced to let them to the wealthier and more industrious peasants. Within half a century of the revolt, even in the open-field villages of the Midlands, tenant-farming with hired labour had become the norm, and hereditary servile status had ceased to have any practical significance. It was only a question of time, before the common law, with its bias in favour of freedom, had transformed villein tenure into copyhold. The propertyless bondsman became the copyholder enjoying, by virtue of his copy from the manorial rolls, the same protection from the king's courts and the same right to enjoy or dispose of his hereditary holding as a free-holder.

Interlude

CHAPTER 4

The Miraculous Providence

"It being so rare, so excellent, that aged Time out of all the archives of antiquity can hardly produce a parallel."

AS THE LAST STREAKS of daylight, September 3rd, 1651, fell on the Worcestershire landscape, a tall dark fugitive drew in his horse on a lonely heath. About him clustered some sixty lords and officers, whose looks told a tale of peril and defeat.

At that moment the young king of England had touched a lower point than any to which his twenty-one chequered and poverty-stricken years had yet brought him. A few weeks before he had ridden at the head of a Scottish army along the moorland road by Shap Fell, watching, across the unclouded atmosphere of summer, the distant Derbyshire heights beckoning him on to London and a golden crown. Now his gallant gamble had ended in dust. All day he had fought at the head of outnumbered and despairing men as Cromwell's net closed in on Worcester. Only at evening, as the shattered Scots poured out through St. Martin's Gate, had King Charles the Second, protesting that he would rather die than see the consequences of so fatal a day, been swept by the rout from the doomed city.

At Barbourne Bridge, where the grass highway to the north was crowded with flying men, there had been a hasty consultation. The king himself had wished to ride alone to London, trusting to arrive before news of the battle and so take ship to France. But the day was already waning, and his companions had dissuaded him from this desperate course. Leaving the main line of fugitives to the west, they rode with him across a land of wooded valleys and little hills, until at nightfall they reached Kinver Heath. Here the scout, who was leading, admitted that he was lost.

In the confusion that followed, the Earl of Derby brought forward a Catholic gentleman, Charles Giffard, owner of a remote house in Shropshire, near which he had found shelter a few days before. To Giffard and his servant, Yates, a poor rustic skilful in the ways of that country, the fugitives entrusted themselves. So guided they came down into the hidden lands below. As complete darkness fell, romance spread her cloak over the king and hid him from the thousand eyes that sought him.

Nobody suspected the little party of Cavaliers who walked their horses through the streets of sleeping Stourbridge. At an inn near Wordsley the king stopped for a hasty tankard of ale: then rode on through the night, a crust of bread in one hand and meat in the other. Giffard rode at his side, telling him of the secret hiding-places of Whiteladies and Boscobel, while the broken lords and officers trotted behind. For some hours they followed a maze of winding lanes till they came to the edge of Brewood Forest. Here, fifty miles from the battlefield, and a little before dawn, the tired king saw the dark outlines of the ruined monastery of Whiteladies.

The clatter of hooves and the whispered calls of Giffard brought down the Penderels, the poor Catholic woodcutters who tenanted the house. To these humble folk the great personages, crowding into the hall, turned for help and advice. While a hasty message was sent to bring William, the eldest of the five Penderel brothers, from Boscobel, the king, in an inner chamber, broke his fast on sack and biscuits. A few minutes later Lord Derby brought in William and Richard Penderel to him, telling them that they must have a care of him and preserve him. To this they proudly and gladly assented. Richard went out to fetch some country clothes, while the king stripped and put on a rough noggen shirt. The first lines of dawn were appearing when Richard returned with an old sweaty doublet, a green, threadbare coat and a greasy steeple hat without band or lining. Lord Wilmot, the stoutest and merriest of the fugitives, began to cut the royal locks with a knife, but did the job so badly that Richard was commanded to finish it, which he did in great pride with a basin and a pair of shears. Placing his hands up the chimney, Charles, who, despite peril and weariness, could not refrain from laughing, completed his make-up by blacking his face. Then, while his companions rode off to join the flying Scots, he went out into the dawn with Richard Penderel and a bill-hook.

It was raining. All day the king crouched in the damp under-growth of a little wood, called Spring Coppice. About midday Penderel's sister-in-law, Elizabeth Yates, brought him a blanket to sit on and a mess of milk, butter and eggs. She told him news of the world outside the woods—of long streams of Scottish fugi-tives and pursuing Roundheads and of search-parties already at Whiteladies. Afterwards he fell into a broken slumber.

Charles had changed much since Vandyke had painted him amid the silken dresses, the flowing hair, the lace, the pearls, the roses of his father's court. Before his twelfth year he had seen the lights of Whitehall darken into tragedy, while a blind mob, which cared for none of these things, bawled out for reform and liberty. While still a child, he had become a wanderer on the face of the earth. For three years he had followed his ill-fated father; seen the royal standard raised and blown down one tempestuous autumn evening at Nottingham, seen Rupert's men charge across the Warwickshire plain, and played where gown and sword mingled in Christ Church meadow. Sent at fifteen to preside over the king's ruined fortunes in the west, he had spent a last year of boyhood on English soil, amid the squabbles and debaucheries of a broken army, driven back week by week towards the sunset until the royal banner floated in solitary loyalty above Pendennis castle. Thence, on a March night in 1646, he had passed out of England.

He had become king at eighteen—of an estate of broken men and women, dangers, debts and beggary. Nor had he had any-where to lay his head, for the rulers of Europe, overawed by the "powerful devils at Westminster," had little wish to shelter him.

Then the tempter had appeared in the homely guise of an elder of the Presbyterian Kirk and offered him the Scottish Crown in return for the renunciation of the Anglican cause for which his father had died. After many pitiful evasions, to find bread for himself and his followers he had taken the Covenant and sailed for Scotland. In the year that followed, he had learnt many things. He had been humiliated and catechised; subjected to an infinity of dull, tedious sermons, made to do penance for the sins of his father and the idolatry of his mother, and threatened with betrayal to his iron foes. Yet by patience and a certain gentle persuasiveness he had at last overthrown the supremacy of Argyll and the Kirk, and at the eleventh hour rallied a united Scotland behind him. But his triumph had come too late; half the country was in Cromwell's hands, and the sequel had been that bold, desperate march into England. Now an adventure, which had begun in shame, degradation and the sorrow of honest men, was ending in a little wet wood in a corner of the land he had come to conquer. But it was pleasanter to sleep under a hedge in England than in a palace in Scotland: even the rain and the weariness were better than that.

In the intervals of sleep the king talked to Penderel. He had still hopes of reaching London and there taking ship for France, but his companion knew of no one on that road who could assist him. It was therefore decided that he should make for Wales, where he had many friends, and that Penderel should escort him that night to Madeley, ten miles to the west, where a Catholic gentleman of his acquaintance might secure them a passage across the Severn.

A little before dusk the two left the wood and made their way across a heath to Hobbal Grange, the cottage where Richard lived with his widowed mother. The old peasant came out to welcome her king, blessing God that she had raised up children to succour him in his time of need. She gave him bread, cheese and a fricassee of bacon and eggs, and wondered to see his appetite, half regal and wholly boyish. While she waited at the table, her son-in-law, Francis Yates—who not long after was hanged at Oxford for his share in the affair—came in with thirty pieces of silver, his all, which he offered to the king. The latter, who—though he perhaps did not realise the full grandeur of the sacrifice —was not unacquainted with poverty, accepted ten of them in his necessity.

The night was pitch black, and Charles, after two days of continuous action and exposure, was tired out. He and Penderel made their way across country, avoiding the haunts of men and clambering the wet fences and pales of remote enclosures. After a few miles the trackway they were following dipped down to bridge a stream, beside which stood a mill. The miller, hearing footsteps, appeared at the door and called on them to stop. Instead of obeying, they ran blindly past him. The lane beyond the river was muddy and steep, and the darkness was such that Charles had nothing to guide him but the rustling of Penderel's breeches ahead and the miller's footsteps behind. When his breath and courage could carry him no longer he flung himself into the hedge and waited for the end. Here Penderel joined him, and the two lay listening for their pursuer. But all was quiet, and after a time they resumed their journey through the briary, dripping night. Poor Charles was now in despair. His ill-made country shoes so racked his feet that he threw them away and walked in his slashed stockings. His nose began to bleed, his head throbbed and his limbs trembled with cold and weariness. "Many times he cast himself upon the ground with a desperate and obstinate resolution to rest there till the morning, that he might shift with less torment, what hazard so ever he ran. But his stout guide still prevailed with him to make a new attempt, sometimes promising him that the way should be better, sometimes assuring him that he had but a little farther to go." Shortly after midnight they came to Madeley.

At the edge of the village Penderel left the king in hiding and made his way to Francis Wolfe's house. The old gentleman—he was sixty-nine and lived to see the Restoration—came to the door. Penderel asked him if he would help a royalist fugitive of rank to cross the Severn. Wolfe replied that the town was full of

troops, and all the passages across the river guarded, and that he
would not undertake so perilous a task for anyone but the king
himself. But when Penderel blurted out the truth he expressed
his readiness to venture his life and all that he had.

As the priest-holes in the house were known, the Wolfes and
their daughter, Anne, sheltered the king all that day in a hayloft.
In the evening they brought him food and money and new shoes
and stockings. Then, as the passage of the Severn was judged
impossible, the two travellers started on the return journey for
Boscobel. At Evelith Mill, fearing their challenger of the previous
night, they left the roadway, intending to ford the river above the
bridge. Here Penderel's courage, for the first and last time, failed
him. The heavy rain had swollen the little stream, and, child of
the Midlands that he was, he confided that he could not swim
and that it was a scurvy river. Thirty years afterwards Charles
dictated the story of that passage to Pepys. "So I told him that the
river, being but a little one, I would undertake to help him over.
Upon which we went over some closes to the river side, and I,
entering the river first to see whether I could myself go over, who
knew how to swim, found it was but a little above my middle,
and, thereupon, taking Richard Penderel by the hand, I helped
him over." At about three o'clock that morning they passed the
gateway of Whiteladies and came into the woods between that
place and Boscobel.

Leaving the king in the wood, Penderel went on to Boscobel
to consult his brother as to the next step in their desperate enter-
prise. Here news awaited him. Lord Wilmot had found a refuge
at the house of a neighbouring Catholic gentleman, Mr. Whitgreave of Moseley Hall, through the offices of Father Huddleston,
a priest, who lived there. The other piece of news was that
Colonel Careless, who two days before had led the last charge
over the cobblestones of Worcester, was in hiding at Boscobel.

Careless accompanied Penderel back to the wood. He found
the king, at the first stroke of dawn, sitting forlorn on a tree-
stump, and could not refrain from weeping at the sight. The
three then walked together across the high ground towards

Boscobel, looking back, as the sun touched the Wrekin, on the far Welsh mountains beyond the Severn.

At Boscobel, a black and white hunting-lodge amid a jumble of barns and hayricks, the king breakfasted off bread, cheese and small beer. Joan Penderel, William's wife, washed and dressed his feet, cutting the blisters and inserting pads of paper between his toes. Then, as it was probable that the house would be searched by one of the numerous companies of soldiers in the neighbourhood, Charles and Careless went out again into the wood.

At the edge of the copse, overlooking the highway, was an old hollow oak. Into this, at Careless's suggestion, they climbed. The road below was soon busy with passers-by, and through the veil of leaves that concealed them they could see a party of soldiers searching the woods, where the Penderels, to allay suspicion, were "peaking up and down" with their nut-hooks. After a time Charles, worn out, fell asleep with his head in Careless's lap. As the hours passed and the king's fitful slumber continued, Careless's supporting arm became completely numbed. With infinite difficulty he awoke him, motioning him to silence lest the troopers below should hear.

At nightfall, when the seekers had gone home to prepare for the Sabbath, the Penderels brought a ladder to the tree, and Charles and Careless, tired, cramped and hungry, returned to Boscobel. They passed through the big parlour of the house—it still stands—and up the stairs to a long attic gallery, used for storing cheeses. Here Mrs. Penderel, whom Charles christened Dame Joan, brought them a supper of chickens. Afterwards, as the night was fine, Charles sat for a while drinking wine in the garden, where Humphrey Penderel, the miller, came with news. While in the town that day he had been questioned by a republican officer, who suspected that he knew of the king's whereabouts. Humphrey had stoutly denied all knowledge, whereupon the officer showed him a proclamation, threatening death to all who should aid "Charles Stuart, a long dark man above two yards high," and offering a reward of £1,000 to anyone who should betray him. On hearing this Charles could not help reflecting on the temptation to which the poor men who sheltered him were exposed, but Careless, divining his thoughts, assured him that had the reward been a thousand times as great it could not have shaken their fidelity.

Before the king retired to rest, Careless asked him what he would like for breakfast. Charles suggested mutton—a reply which caused the Penderels to exchange glances, for suspicion might be aroused should they attempt to obtain so unusual a luxury from their neighbours. He then made his way upstairs to a hiding-hole beneath the attic floor, where he spent the night on a straw pallet in a space little bigger than his own body.

He awoke early on Sunday morning, and the first sounds he heard were the church bells of Tong. Careless had been up before him and brought home his breakfast from Farmer Staunton's sheepcote. Together they fried the mutton collops before the fire.

Charles spent the greater part of the day reading in a "pretty arbour" in the garden, where there was a stone seat and table. "He commended the place for its retiredness," and so rested. Here, as in other places, there is a touch of the *Pilgrim's Progress* in the narrative: one is reminded of the shepherd's boy in the Valley of Humiliation. The king's state was indeed very low. He was surrounded by his enemies, a price was set on his head, and his poor protectors were hard put to it to know where to turn for food for another day.

While the king spent that Sabbath in the garden John Penderel made his way to Moseley to consult Lord Wilmot and ask his help. He found Whitgreave and Father Huddleston, who informed him that Wilmot had left Moseley for Colonel Lane's house, Bentley, beyond Wolverhampton, intending thence to travel to the coast. As every hope of Charles's escape now depended on Wilmot, Penderel persuaded the others to take him to Bentley. Here Wilmot was found. In consultation with this cheerful, self-confident fugitive, who himself scorned any disguise but a hawk on his sleeve, it was decided that Charles should be brought that night from Boscobel to Moseley and that Wilmot should meet him there. On the way back Penderel revealed the identity of their intending guest to Whitgreave and Huddleston. Having fixed a rendezvous at the foot of the garden, he returned with the news to Boscobel.

From Boscobel to Moseley was eight miles: the night was dark and stormy. Charles was still too lame to walk, and Humphrey Penderel's aged mill-horse, with a "pitiful old saddle and rough bridle," was requisitioned for him. He bade farewell to Careless and set out, surrounded by the five Penderel brothers and Yates who marched beside him armed with bill-hooks and pistols, ready to sell their lives in his defence. With this curious and devoted army the king crossed Chillington Park and the dark Staffordshire woods. At Pendeford old mill, two miles from his destination, he dismounted, leaving the horse with William, Humphrey and George Penderel. He had gone a few paces on his way when he turned back and, begging their pardon that his troubles had made him forgetful of his friends, gave them his hand to kiss. The peasant brothers kneeling before the king in the storm are the epitome of this night. It was the supreme moment of their simple and pious lives.

In a little grove of trees in the corner of a field called the Moor, Father Huddleston was waiting for the king. He led him down a long walk of trees, through a gateway and across a garden. At the darkened door of the house Whitgreave did not know before which of the eight shadowy figures, all habited alike, he should kneel, until the light of the hall fell on the pale, kingly boy with his cropped hair and shabby clothes, and Wilmot said: "This is my master, your master, and the master of us all."

While Whitgreave fed the Penderels, Wilmot led the king through the hall and up the broad staircase to a panelled chamber. Here Charles, sitting on the bed, asked questions about the fate of his companions. Presently Whitgreave and Huddleston joined them with sack and biscuits and a change of shirt. Refreshed, Charles expressed himself fit for a new march and ready, should God bless him with an army of resolute men, to drive all the rogues out of his kingdom.

Next morning, Monday September 8th, the king awoke after the first night of comfort he had enjoyed since the battle. At breakfast he saluted old Mrs. Whitgreave, his host's mother, and made her sit with him at table while Huddleston and Whitgreave waited. The latter had sent all his servants to work in the fields, except a Catholic cook, who could be trusted with the half truth that the house sheltered a fugitive from Worcester. Charles spent most of this day sitting in a room over the porch, watching the high road that ran past the house. Three boys, who were living at Moseley as pupils of Huddleston's, were released from their lessons and told to keep guard, a task which they thoroughly enjoyed. That night at supper the eldest of them called to his companions, "Eat hard, boys, for we have been on the life-guard this day," an observation, as Whitgreave remarked, "more truly spoken than he was aware."

On Tuesday a message arrived that Colonel Lane would ride over that night to escort the king to Bentley, where he had arranged for him to start next day for the coast, disguised as a servant of his sister Jane, who had obtained a pass to visit a pregnant friend near Bristol. That morning Charles was in good spirits. He joined Huddleston and Whitgreave in the latter's study and amused them by stories of his usage by the Scots. Seeing a volume of Catholic devotions on the table, he picked it up and read for a time, commending several passages to Huddleston's great joy and edification. In the afternoon there was an adventure. A servant arrived with news that a company of militia was on its way to search the house and arrest Whitgreave on a charge of having been present at Worcester. The latter at once hid Charles in the priest-hole, and, leaving all doors open to avert suspicion, went downstairs to meet the soldiers. A long and angry altercation took place in the doorway; in the end Whitgreave's neighbours were able to persuade the search-party that he had never left Moseley during the battle. When at last he was free to let Charles out of his narrow hiding-place, he found him in some fear that he had been abandoned for ever.

That evening the king asked Huddleston to show him his

master's oratory, saying "he knew he was a priest, and he needed not fear to own it, for if it pleased God to restore him to his kingdom, they should never more need privacies." The priest led him to the little secret oratory. Charles looked with respect on this plain, decent room with its crucifix and candles, and with regard at the man, who, without fear or cant, faced poverty and death in order to minister to his flock. Brought face to face with the same poverty and peril, Charles was perhaps nearer the inner truth of religion at that moment than at any other in his life. He stood there before the altar, no longer boy or king, but man in his simple dignity, humble in the presence of God.

At midnight Lane arrived from Bentley with two horses and waited in an orchard at the foot of the garden. At the top of the stairs old Mrs. Whitgreave was waiting to bid farewell to her king. Pressing sweetmeats into his hands, the old lady knelt down before him, and in this posture she, her son and Huddleston prayed God to preserve him. Charles, deeply touched, gave them his hand to kiss, thanking them for their love and care and telling them that, if ever it pleased God to restore him, he would not be unmindful. After that he went into the garden. In the orchard the horses were waiting. The night was cold, and Huddleston lent the king his cloak; once more squire and priest knelt: then Charles and Lane rode off into the darkness.

They made their way eastwards across a wilderness of heaths and wide fields. On the high land between Willenhall and Walsall, where now the night sky is lit by blast furnaces, they came to Bentley Park. Wilmot was waiting for them in the hall, and the three sat down to supper. It was arranged that Charles was to start for Bristol at dawn, riding pillion with Jane Lane and disguised as William Jackson, a tenant's son in attendance, while the pair were to be escorted by Henry Lassels, a young cousin of the house. Wilmot, who still refused to compromise his nobility by a disguise, was to travel with Colonel Lane at a short distance from the main party. Charles retired to bed for the remainder of the night in the servants' quarters.

A little before dawn Lane called the king and gave him £20,

a suit and cloak of country grey and a high black hat. When Charles had dressed himself like a sober farmer's son on holiday and received the final instructions as to his part, he fetched the horses from the stables and waited, with his hat under his arm, before the house for his mistress.

Jane mounted and took her seat behind the king. Her mother stood at the door to see her go, ignorant of the honour done her daughter. But the girl knew her prince and trembled as she touched his shoulder. For the next week she carried the crown of England in her hands, and never was trust more bravely or delicately performed.

For the greater part of the first day's journey the travellers were accompanied by a self-opinionated brother-in-law of the Lanes, John Petre, who was taking his wife to Buckinghamshire and knew nothing of the identity of Jane's servant. All morning they rode through the broad, undulating country which now marks the western fringe of Birmingham, but which was then rural enough. At Bromsgrove, "a poor scattering village," Charles's mare cast a shoe. While he worked, the smith discoursed of current politics. No, he replied to the king's inquiry, he had heard no news since that of the victory of Worcester, nor had he heard that the chief rogue, Charles Stuart, had yet been captured. The king remarked that if that rascal were taken he deserved to be hanged for bringing in the Scots, on which the smith replied with an oath that he spoke like an honest man.

In the afternoon they skirted the Forest of Arden. A little beyond Wooton-Waven an old woman, gleaning by the wayside, called out to them to have a care of the soldiers on the main Stratford road. Charles was for riding on, but Petre, who had once been beaten by a band of drunken troopers, insisted on turning out of the way. Passing through Snitterfield, Shakespeare's paternal home, they came to Stratford by another route, only to meet the soldiers entering the town. Their foes, however, merely opened their ranks to let them pass, duly returning Charles's respectful salute. Here the Petres turned towards Banbury, while Charles, Jane and Lassels pursued their way southwards towards the Cotswolds. At Long Marston, having ridden fifty miles that day, they halted for the night at the house of John Tomes, a cousin of the Lanes. Charles supped in the kitchen, and, when the maid asked him to wind the jack, the well-nourished Cotswold servants gathered round, wondering what kind of a countryman he might be who could not perform so simple a task. But Charles knew his Staffordshire. "We seldom," he replied, "have meat, and when we do we rarely use a jack."

Next day, September 11th, the travellers were abroad early, and the view from the Cotswold edge across western England was their recompense. As they crossed the hills by Chipping Campden, Charles could see a dark patch in the north, Worcester of fatal memory, westwards wooded Bredon and the Malverns, and far off the hills of Wales. For the next few hours, in all that busy, seeking kingdom, the pure winds and the tinkling sheep-bells were their only companions. They rode through Stow-in-the-Wold and Northleach, coming at dusk to Cirencester. Here Charles and Lassels slept together in the low upper room of an inn. After the chamberlain had taken away the candles, they changed beds, Lassels taking the little truckle mattress on the floor and resigning his bed to his king.

On Friday they reached Bristol. They entered the city at Lawford's Gate and crossed the Avon at Rownham Ferry. Charles remembered Bristol well; he insisted on riding about the town, inspecting the site of the former Royalist fortifications and noting with surprise the many changes and improvements. Then, skirting the left bank of the Avon, they climbed the upland to Abbots Leigh, the home of Jane's friend, Mrs. Norton, and her husband. As they reached the summit, the sun was sinking over the Bristol Channel. Below them in the dusk was a gabled Elizabethan house, and from its trees and lawns arose the sound of rooks and of men playing bowls.

As they rode past the little group of players, Charles saw to his dismay a former chaplain of his, Dr. George—a most loquacious man—leaning against the railings watching the game. He took

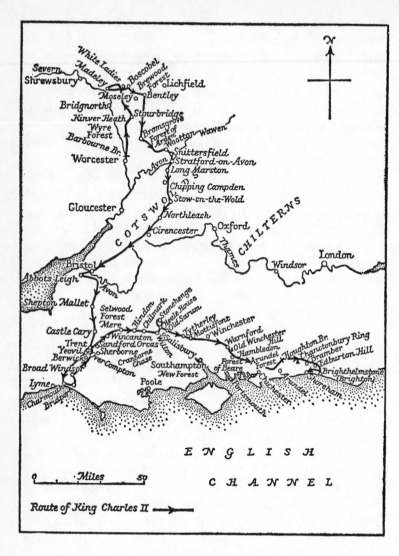

The Escape from Worcester

the horses to the stable, and Jane Lane, on entering the house, told Pope, the butler—an old Royalist soldier—that her servant was sick of an ague and not fit to be below stairs. Accordingly Charles, who must have been feeling lonely on his separation from his charming fellow-traveller, found himself accorded a private room and a fire away from the other servants. At supper Miss Lane filled a little dish of broth and asked Pope to carry it to her retainer, telling him that he should have some more presently. Pope took it with a napkin, spoon and bread, and spoke kindly to the young man, who he found very willing to eat. Meanwhile in the dining-hall, Dr. George, "being a man of a cheerful conversation, asked Mistress Lane many questions concerning William of whom he saw she was so careful by sending up meat to him, how long his ague had been gone and whether he had purged since it left him and the like." To these embarrassing questions poor Jane gave what answers she could. After supper Dr. George, who much fancied himself as a physician, paid a call on the invalid. He felt his pulse, asked many questions, and wondered why he shrank from him. His patient was not a little relieved when he heard that he was leaving Abbots Leigh next day.

In the morning the king rose early and, having an excellent appetite, went downstairs to get his breakfast at the buttery-hatch. Here he found Pope and two or three other men. While they ate bread and butter, washed down by the butler's ale, one of the men started to give a detailed account of the battle of Worcester. Charles, asking him how he came to know so much of the engagement, was not a little alarmed to learn that he had actually been a trooper in his own guards. Hoping to allay suspicion, he asked him to describe the king's clothes and appearance, which the other did most accurately, looking hard at him and explaining that the king was at least three inches taller than he. "Upon which," Charles afterwards related, "I made what haste I could out of the buttery, for fear he should indeed know me."

The surprises of that morning were not yet over. As Charles

stood by Pope's side, bare-headed at the hall door, to let Mrs. Norton pass, he noticed that his companion was staring at him very earnestly. Worried by this attention, he went out into the fields for half an hour. On his return to his chambers Lassels came to him and told him that he thought Pope had recognised him. Charles asked what kind of a man he was, and, on being assured of his proven loyalty, decided to place his safety in his hands. He accordingly sent for Pope, who, looking upon him, fell upon his knees with tears in his eyes.

The good butler, hearing that Wilmot, who was lodging at a neighbouring house, was proposing to pay a visit to Abbots Leigh that afternoon, warned Charles that the servants were not to be trusted and that Wilmot would certainly be recognised. He contrived, therefore, to delay the latter and to bring him that night secretly to the royal chamber. Here a consultation was held, and it was agreed that Pope should try to find a ship at Bristol to carry the king to France.

Charles spent that week-end resting quietly at Abbots Leigh, mostly sitting alone in the chimney corner and feigning illness. Miss Lane continued to express her anxiety for her servant in public, saying, "the boy will never recover—he'll ne'er be good again," while Margaret Rider, a maid of Mrs. Norton's, conceiving a romantic passion for the lonely young man, made him a carduus-posset and waited on him tenderly.

Pope's efforts to charter a vessel were fruitless. On Monday it was decided to remove Charles to Trent, near Sherborne, the home of an enthusiastic royalist, Colonel Frank Wyndham, a brother-in-law of Charles's old nurse. Wilmot went on at once to warn Wyndham, while the others prepared to set out next morning. Just before announcing their intentions to the household, a disaster occurred. Their hostess miscarried, and poor Jane was at her wits' end to know what excuse to make to enable her to leave her friend at such a moment. The butler's resource saved them. He concocted a letter from Bentley, announcing the sudden illness of Jane's father, and handed it to her at supper: the girl's skilful acting did the rest.

Early on Tuesday Charles, Jane and Lassels set out for Trent. They travelled eastwards for a few miles, as though heading for Bentley, and then turned south. Following the old Roman track-way past Shepton Mallet, they reached Castle Cary, where they were met by Lord Hertford's steward, who found them accommodation for the night. Next morning, a fortnight after the battle, they came at about ten o'clock to the retired and beautiful village of Trent, where Wyndham and his young wife were awaiting them. Charles, who was in good spirits, called out, "Frank, Frank, how dost thou?" He was escorted to the house, where a suite of black panelled rooms had been set apart for him. Here he was to make his longest stay during the period of his flight, and here, in a household of twenty persons, his presence remained unknown to all but his host and hostess, their little cousin, Juliana Coningsby, and two loyal maids. Their names, Eleanor Withers and Joan Halsenoth, are worthy of remembrance; they waited upon him, passing the food, cooked in the kitchen below, to his room by means of a rope in the chimney.

On the king's arrival a conference was held. Wyndham related a strange tale of his father, who, on his death-bed fifteen years before, had called his sons about him, telling them that they had seen serene and quiet times, but must now prepare themselves for cloudy and troublesome ones. "I command you," he had said with his last breath, "to honour and obey your sovereign, and, though the crown should hang upon a bush, I charge you forsake it not." In these dying words Wyndham perceived a prophecy, now nearing fulfilment.

The next day Jane and Lassels set out for Staffordshire, and Wyndham paid a visit to his neighbour, Giles Strangways, about finding a boat. The latter sent him on to Lyme Regis, where, after some delay, a royalist merchant, called Ellesdon, succeeded in chartering a coasting vessel, the master agreeing for a substantial sum to convey two royalist gentlemen to France. It was arranged that on the night of the following Monday, September 22nd, Limbry, the master, should bring his ship to the little coastal village of Charmouth, where Charles and Wilmot were to be in waiting. A room was booked at the inn at Charmouth, and, to avert suspicion, the landlady was informed "that there was a young man to come thither the next Monday that had stolen a gentlewoman to marry her." Having completed these romantic arrangements, Wyndham returned to Trent.

On the Monday morning Charles set out on his travels once more, riding pillion, this time in front of pretty Juliana Coningsby, with Wyndham as guide and chaperon. The undisguised Wilmot and Wyndham's servant, Peters, followed them at a safe distance. They went by Over Compton and Berwick, crossing the high Dorset downlands at Pilsdon Pen. At a house among the hills, a few miles above Charmouth, they met Ellesdon, who was able to assure them that all was ready. An hour later, as dusk fell, they rode down the steep hill into Charmouth and put up at the Queen's Arms. The wind was blowing for France and the auspices were kindly.

It had been fair day at Lyme, and the little inn was packed with horse-dealers. After supper Wyndham and Peters went to the beach to await Limbry's long boat, leaving Wilmot and Juliana, with Charles to wait on them, to masquerade, before an extremely interested household, as lovers. Hour followed hour, the disappointed company retired to bed, and still the three waited. At dawn, after what seemed an eternal night, Wyndham returned with news that the tide had gone out and no boat come.

As the people of Charmouth were obviously intrigued by their visitors, it was decided that Charles, Miss Coningsby and Wyndham should set out for Bridport, where Wilmot and Peters, after ascertaining the cause of Limbry's failure, should join them later in the day. Peters accordingly went to Lyme, while Wilmot sent his horse, which had cast a shoe, to be shod. The blacksmith noticed that the remaining shoes were of Midland make, which tallied ill with the couple's tale that they came from Exeter, and confided his suspicions to the ostler, who confirmed them by recounting the strange behaviour of these supposed lovers.

Having finished his task, the smith therefore made his way to the house of the local minister to seek advice. Finding the latter engaged in his morning devotions—a somewhat lengthy affair[1]— the honest craftsman, fearing to lose the hire of his labour, returned to the inn. But when he had been paid and had seen the fat and jovial Wilmot ride away, his suspicions revived. There was something, he reflected, very peculiar about that man. Was not Charles Stuart at large in England, seeking to escape, and was there not a reward of £1,000 upon his head? Once more he sought the house of the minister. He told his tale, confided his fears and hopes, and was rewarded when he saw the good man's eyes light with zeal. Together they hastened to the inn, where they wasted five minutes in upbraiding the indignant landlady. Then they sought a Justice of the Peace. But the latter was a true Englishman, with all an Englishman's love of deliberation and fear of rendering himself foolish in the eyes of his neighbours, and flatly refused to issue a warrant for a king's arrest upon such slender evidence. In despair the two sleuth-hounds left him and made their way to Captain Massey, who commanded a troop of Roundhead militia. He proved to be the man they were seeking, called out his soldiers and at once set out in hot pursuit along the Bridport road.

While these events were happening at Charmouth the king's party had reached Bridport. Here the town was full of red-coats on the point of embarking for the conquest of Jersey. While Wyndham and Juliana ordered a meal at "The George," Charles, with the horses, pushed boldly through the troopers in the yard. At that moment an ostler approached him and said he was sure he knew his face. Charles, after discovering that this would-be friend had been in service at a house in Exeter at which he had formerly lodged, claimed to have been a fellow-servant with him there. This satisfied the ostler, who asked him to drink, but the king begged to be excused, explaining that he had to wait on his master and mistress. He found them in an upper room, with a

[1] The minister, Mr. Benjamin Wesley, was a great-grandfather of John Wesley.

meal set before them, of which they made him eat before he returned to the horses. At this moment Juliana's sharp eyes caught sight of Peters in the street below. From him she learned that Wilmot was in Bridport and was urging an immediate departure; the imperturbable nobleman had at last sensed peril. Accordingly they set out at once along the London road, joining Wilmot and Peters just outside the town. About a mile out of Bridport they decided to turn up a lane northwards and work back across country in the hope of tidings of the lost vessel. It was well that they did so. A minute later Massey's pursuing troopers galloped past the turning towards Dorchester. Meanwhile the travellers continued their rambling journey, unconscious that a whole countryside was seeking them. They lost their way and rode all afternoon in a wilderness of downs and lonely valleys. "Providence directed these strangers," leading them at nightfall to the little village of Broadwindsor, a few miles north of Bridport.

Here, in the heart of the bleak Dorset uplands, they put up at a poor little inn, the best harbourage the place could afford. Happily the landlord was an old servant of Wyndham's family, and he and his wife were both staunch Royalists, having "according to their condition undergone their share of troubles." Though they did not know the full extent of the greatness they were entertaining, they bustled about to make their guests comfortable. But the latter's perils were not yet over. At midnight a company of soldiers arrived, on march for the coast, and demanded quarters. They swarmed all over the lower part of the house, completely cutting off the attic in which the king was trying to sleep. One of their doxies who accompanied them was unexpectedly brought to bed of a child on the kitchen table; the clamour of this event and the furious dispute as to the babe's future upkeep, which it occasioned between the military and the parish overseers, made sleep impossible. Fortunately the soldiers resumed their march at daybreak, and the fugitives were able to breathe again. During the morning Peters, who had been sent to Lyme to interview Ellesdon, returned with the explanation of Monday night's fiasco. Apparently Limbry had confided to his wife that he was about to carry a dangerous cargo to France, and the latter, much alarmed, had locked him up in his room and kept him there till he gave his word that he would not sail. Further attempts to embark from Lyme were plainly out of the question, and the little party returned to Trent.

Here the king remained for nearly another week. The two maids and his pretty hostess waited on him, and he passed his days cooking his own food and boring holes in coins as keepsakes for them. On one occasion, hearing the church bells pealing, he looked out of the window to see a crowd of villagers dancing round a bonfire in celebration of his own supposed capture and death. On another Mrs. Wyndham was put to great fear for her guest—she had none for herself—by the arrival of a mysterious troop of horse at Sherborne, but Charles, who was growing used to dangers, only laughed.

Meanwhile further attempts were being made to secure a ship. Through the suggestion of a neighbour, Wyndham had got into touch with a little group of royalists at Salisbury. One of these, Colonel Robin Phelipps, a younger son of the house of Montacute, undertook to find and charter a vessel from a Hampshire or Sussex port. His first attempt at Southampton was unsuccessful, but he transferred his efforts to Chichester. To be nearer the scene of action, it was decided to move the king from Trent to Heale, near Salisbury the residence of Mrs. Hyde, a widow.

On the evening of Sunday, October 5th, Phelipps arrived at Trent to act as guide. Next morning the king took leave of his kind hosts. That day Phelipps and Charles rode fifty miles, the latter once more in front of Juliana, while Peters followed them in attendance. They passed, by Sandford Orcas and Wincanton, through a little frequented and lovely corner of England. At Mere, eighteen miles on their way, they stopped for a drink at the George Inn, where Phelipps knew the host, a good royalist. They drank in the cellar, where the landlord turned to Charles with a "Thou lookest like an honest fellow. Here's a health to the king!" The subject of this loyal toast naturally hesitated, and mine host turned to Phelipps in disgust and asked him what kind of a Roundhead fellow he had brought.

In the afternoon the travellers, passing through Hindon, Chilmark and Teffont, skirted Salisbury Plain and came to Wilton. Here Juliana and Peters said good-bye, and Charles and Phelipps, leaving the main road, made their way across the plain towards the Avon valley. At nightfall they found the welcoming lights of Heale House.

Mrs. Hyde was waiting for them, and a cheerful little party of loyalists from Salisbury sat down together to supper, though the identity of the newcomer was not known to all. Mrs. Hyde recognised him at once and, though she tried to hide her feelings, could not refrain from showing her loyalty by helping him to two larks instead of one. Among the guests was Dr. Henchman, a canon of Salisbury Cathedral, one of the chief agents in the search for a boat. After supper this wise and brave old churchman had a long talk with his king.[1]

It was not thought safe that Charles, who had been seen by all the servants at supper, should remain publicly at Heale, and it was decided that on the next day he should pretend to depart, returning secretly in the evening. Accordingly in the morning he rode off with Robin Phelipps. The pair spent the day pleasantly enough on Salisbury Plain, where there was no one to observe or disturb them. They galloped on the soft down turf, started hares and paid a visit to Stonehenge. Here Charles stood looking upon the stones for some time and proved to his companion the fallacy of the popular belief that they could not be counted twice alike. At dusk Henchman met them in a meadow near Heale, where Phelipps took his leave. The king then re-entered the house by a back way and was escorted to a secret hiding-hole. Here he spent the next five days, waited upon by Mrs. Hyde and her sister, who alone knew of his presence. His

[1] Fourteen years later, as Bishop of London, he was to prove that his courage was as great in the day of worldly success as in that of adversity, by remaining at his post during the plague, and at the end of his long and useful life his last blessings were to rest on the rising stones of Wren's St. Paul's.

quarters were cramped, but he was probably safer at this period of his wandering than at any other. The Government had lost all trace of him.

Meanwhile his faithful friends were seeking a boat. Wilmot and Phelipps, stopping at Hinton-Daubnay, near Hambledon, had recruited George Gounter of Racton, a Sussex royalist. A much persecuted man, he had just returned from London, where he had been borrowing the wherewithal to pay the heavy fines laid on his estates. Without hesitation he undertook a new burden in the cause for which he had already given so much. His poor wife, struggling to make both ends meet, wept when she heard of the new danger he had accepted, but encouraged him in his resolve. On Saturday, October 11th, this gallant gentleman found what he was seeking at Chichester, where, with the help of Francis Mansel, a loyal merchant, he negotiated a treaty with Nicholas Tattersall, the master of a Brighthelmstone coal-brig, who, for sixty pounds down, agreed to carry two fugitives from Shoreham to France.

On Sunday, October 12th, Charles made ready for his departure from Heale. At three o'clock that night, Phelipps, with a led horse for the king, arrived at the appointed rendezvous. The led horse broke its bridle and ran up the river; with great difficulty Phelipps recaptured it. The two horsemen then rode through the night, past Clarendon Park corner and Old Sarum. Dawn found them crossing the high and lonely hills to the east of Salisbury. All that morning they rode through Hampshire, by Tytherley and through the woods of the Test Valley, and so, by Mottisfont and Hursley, to Twyford. Here, leaving Winchester and the gleaming Itchen behind them, they trotted across the sweet, wind-swept open downs.

On a hill called Old Winchester, the highest in those parts, above the little village of Warnford, Wilmot and his servant, Swan, Gounter and his brother-in-law were waiting for the king. They had left home early, calling at the house of Gounter's sister, Mrs. Symonds, at Hambledon, to borrow a brace of greyhounds on the pretence of coursing: they warned her that they might seek her hospitality that night. When the hour fixed for the rendezvous passed without any sign, Gounter rode down to Warnford. There, at the town's end, he encountered Charles and Phelipps. Pretending not to have recognised them, he continued his way into the village, drank a glass of ale and purchased some tobacco, and then rode back, catching up the travellers as they reached the summit of the hill.

On that high October afternoon, with half England—rolling down and far woodland—spread around them, they held a council of war, deciding to spend the night in some quiet neighbouring house. "I know," said Gounter, "divers yeomanry men, where for a night we may be very welcome, and there is one who married my sister and whose house stands privately and out of the way." "Let us go thither," replied the king.

As evening fell on the Hampshire landscape they rode over Broadhalfpenny Down, where men already played a quaint game with stump and ball, towards the valley. Below them lay Hambledon, on the edge of the forest. At about candle lighting they came to Mrs. Symonds's house; though all unconscious of her honour, she welcomed them and led them into a little fire-lit parlour, setting biscuits and wine before them.

That night was the pleasantest in all the king's travels. They sat down to supper at a round table, and, when the meal was almost over, the master of the house joined them. He, like an honest Cavalier, had been drinking in a tavern, and was filled with an hospitable desire to see all about him as merry as he. He settled down among his wife's guests, taking a stool by Charles, whose cropped hair and solemn aspect marked him out as a suitable object for conversion. Then, shaking his hand and mixing a bottle of strong waters in a tankard of beer, he called him Brother Roundhead and bade him drink deep. The scene is a delicious one—the wainscotted room, the firelight and the candles on the table, the faces of the hunted fugitives lit by the glow and the wine, and the hiccoughing host, half scared by the king's puritanical appearance and wholly jovial. Whenever a bibulous oath escaped him, Charles was ready with the appropriate rebuke:

"Oh, dear brother, this is a scape: swear not, I beseech you." But the other was incorrigible. At ten o'clock, in order to let Charles escape to bed, Gounter suggested to his host that the Round-head would be better away. Symonds gladly assented.

It is not improbable that Charles awoke with a headache. That day, the 14th of October, was the last of his pilgrimage. Before he left Hambledon a message arrived from Lord Southampton, who had somehow learnt of his presence in the neighbourhood, offer-ing his services and hospitality. Charles, having the promise of a ship, would not allow him to run the risk, but ever afterwards gratefully acknowledged his obligation to a nobleman, who, having great possessions, was ready to sacrifice them all for his sake.

Phelipps went to London to make arrangements for a supply of money to await the fugitives in France, and the king, Gounter, Wilmot and Swan set out alone. For thirty miles they rode east-wards through the forest. On the fringe of Arundel Park they saw the Governor of the castle and his men riding out to hunt; they did not like the look of his "starched moustaches," so turned aside and led their horses up the slope of the high woods. Beyond the downs they crossed the Arun at Houghton Bridge. In the quiet village street they halted before the ale-house door and, while they drank, Gounter pulled out a couple of Mrs. Symonds' neats' tongues from his pocket.

East of the Arun they climbed, and for eleven miles rode along the downs. The thrill of the upland air caught their hearts and, as the king gazed northwards from Chanctonbury over the Weald, England seemed to him a country worth fighting for. In Bramber, where they came down to cross the Adur, the street was full of soldiers, and in the narrow lanes beyond they heard horse-hooves close behind them. Boldly they slackened pace, and the troopers, on some military errand, pushed by unregarding.

Near Beeding they parted company, preferring to approach Brighthelmstone by different routes. Charles and Wilmot climbed Edburton Hill and cantered over the nine miles of down which divided them from the sea. At Brighthelmstone, then only a cluster of fishermen's cottages, they pulled up at the George. When Gounter and Swan arrived they could hear the king's voice in the parlour, toasting Wilmot: "Here, Mr. Barlow, I drink to you!"

At the inn Mansel and Tattersall, who as yet only knew of Charles as a royalist fugitive, met them. They all sat down together to supper. Though there was some anxiety about the wind, the king was in excellent spirits.

That evening witnessed two last touching pieces of loyalty. After supper Tattersall, who had looked much at Charles during the meal, drew Mansel aside and told him that he had not dealt fairly with him, "for, though he had given him a very good price for the carrying over of that gentleman, yet he had not been clear with him; for he was the king, and he very well knew him to be so. But, said he, be not troubled at it, for I think I do God and my country good service in preserving the king, and, by the grace of God, I will venture my life and all for him and set him safely on shore if I can in France." To such simple men it was given to see further than the politicians in their wisdom.

There was a further incident. As the king was standing alone by the fireside after supper, with his hand leaning on his chair, the innkeeper, an old guardsman, came in and started to talk. Suddenly he raised the king's hand and kissed it, saying, "God bless you wheresoever you go; I do not doubt before I die to be a lord and my wife a lady." Charles laughed and hastily left the room, but he had no cause to fear the old soldier's loyalty.

For a long time they sat up drinking and smoking, Charles desiring to keep Tattersall with him, lest he should decline the venture at the last moment, as Limbry had done. When it became known that the wind had changed and set fair for France, Charles and Wilmot lay down for a brief rest. At two o'clock Gounter called them, showing them the time on his watch. They rose and made their way on horseback through the night to a creek at the mouth of the Adur, where Tattersall's brig, *The Surprise*, was lying. They climbed aboard and lay down in the little cabin, waiting for the tide. Here Gounter bade them farewell.

At about seven o'clock of the morning, being high water, they went out of the port, steering a westward course as though for Poole, the boat's normal destination. At that very hour another fugitive from Worcester, less fortunate than Charles, was waiting for the axe to fall in Bolton market square. A few days before his death Lord Derby had written to his wife: "Though I be never so close, my heart is my own—free as the best." It was such a spirit that made the Restoration a certainty.

All that day Gounter followed on the beach with the horses, watching those vanishing sails. On board *The Surprise*, the king, who had learnt to love ships during his first exile in Jersey many years before, suffered a sea change; he walked the deck, happy and at home, talking to Tattersall and winning that loyal sailor's admiration by directing the course. The crew, four men and a boy, stood watching and smoking.

One further subterfuge was necessary, Tattersall had not broken the news of the vessel's unwonted destination to his men. He now approached the king and begged his help. The latter accordingly confided to the crew that he and Wilmot were merchants, who had suffered losses and were in debt, and offered them twenty-five shillings to drink if they would second his endeavours to persuade the master to set them in France. This speech made a strong appeal to the thirsty throats and romantic hearts of the English seamen. They at once agreed, and the master was quickly persuaded. About five in the afternoon, while still in sight of the Isle of Wight, the brig stood off with a northerly wind for France.

At dawn on Thursday, October 16th, Charles landed at Fécamp. When his mother's Court rode out to welcome him back to the Louvre his friends could scarcely recognise him. The gentle boy, who had left Paris two years before, was now shorn and bearded, his build was manly and powerful, his features had coarsened, his expression grown reckless. Yet to shrewd observers the long mouth and level eyes told their tale. Young though he was he had met as intimates hunger, weariness and peril; he had shared the companionship of the very poor; he had known courage and fidelity. And, if the Commonwealth's spies noted, beneath his outward cheerfulness, a certain sadness, it was because his heart was still in England with the loyal men and women who had shared his perils and from whom he was now divided.

Part Two

CHAPTER 5

The Revolt of Tom Bowling

"If there is, indeed, a rot in the wooden walls of old England, our decay cannot be very distant."

R. B. Sheridan

THE ROYAL NAVY HAD MADE its entry onto the world stage under Drake and the Elizabethans, had sunk into insignificance under the early Stuarts, recovered under Cromwell and the second Charles to wrest the sceptre of ocean commerce from Holland, and, given administrative discipline by the life-long labours of Pepys, became during the eighteenth century the chief arbiter of human affairs at sea. Yet until the age of Nelson its ascendancy was never undisputed. For over a hundred years monarchical France, with its much greater population and resources, contended with Britain for command of the sea and, on more than one occasion, all but attained it. Britain's danger was greatest when France and the Atlantic empire of Spain joined hands against her, as they did during the American War, when, with her fleets outnumbered, she had had to fight for her very existence.

Yet Britain had always triumphed in the last resort because the sea was her whole being, whereas with her Continental rivals it was only a secondary consideration. "The thing which lies nearest the heart of this nation," Charles II had written, "is trade and all that belongs to it." Being an island, her commerce was maritime and its protection an essential interest of an ever-growing number of her people. They were ready to make sacrifices for the Navy which they would never have done for the

Army or any other service of the Crown. For it was on the Navy, as the Articles of War put it, that under the Providence of God the safety, honour, and welfare of the realm depended.

Because of these things the Navy touched mystic chords in the English heart which went deeper than reason. The far sails of a frigate at sea, the sight of a sailor with tarry breeches and rolling gait in any inland town, and that chief of all the symbolic spectacles of England, the Grand Fleet lying at anchor in one of her white-fringed roadsteads, had for her people the power of a trumpet call. So little Byam Martin, seeing for the first time the triple-tiered ships of the line lying in Portsmouth harbour, re-mained "riveted to the spot, perfectly motionless, so absorbed in wonder" that he would have stayed there all day had not his hosts sent a boat's crew to fetch him away. From that hour his mind was "inflamed with the wildest desire to be afloat." Bobby Shafto going to sea with silver buckles on his knee was an eternal theme of eighteenth century England: of such stuff were admirals made.

They had a hard schooling. Flung, like Nelson, at twelve into an unfamiliar world of kicks and cuffs, crowded hammocks and icy hardships, or after a few months under "Black Pudding," the omnipresent horsewhip of the Naval Academy, Gosport, ap-prenticed as midshipmen to the cockpit of a man-of-war, they learnt while still children to be Spartans, dined off scrubbed boards on salt beef, sauerkraut and black-strap, and became com-plete masters before they were men of a wonderful technical skill in all that appertained to the sailing and fighting of ships.

They were as inured to roughness and salt water as gulls to wind. Boys in their teens would spend days afloat in the maintop, ready at any moment to clamber to the masthead when top-gallant or studding sail needed setting or taking in. They grew up like bulldogs, delighting to cuff and fight: in some ships it was the practice while the officers were dining in the wardroom for the midshipmen to engage regularly in pitched battles on the quarterdeck, Romans against Trojans, for the possession of the poop, banging away, "all in good part," with broomsticks,

handswabs, boarding pikes and even muskets.   Midshipman
Gardner of the *Edgar*, being pinked in the thigh by a comrade
with a fixed bayonet in the course of one of these friendly scraps,
retaliated by putting a small quantity of powder into a musket
and firing at his assailant, marking "his phiz" for life. So tough-
ened, they faced the world on their toes ready for anything and
everyone. Such were the high-spirited midshipmen who pelted
the British ambassador with plums at the Carnival at Pisa and, as
he looked angry, hove another volley at his lady, observing that
she seemed better tempered than his Excellency. So also the
officers of the wardroom, dining at the best inn in Leghorn and
growing somewhat merry, rolled the waiter among the dishes
in the table-cloth and pelted the passers-by with loaves and
chicken legs.

These were the permanent cadre of the Navy; the officers of
the establishment, "born in the surf of the sea," who, unlike the
lower deck, coming and going as occasion demanded, lived in the
Service and died in it. They were bound together by the closest
ties of professional honour, etiquette and experience. Socially
they were of all sorts: one high-born captain filled his frigate with
so many sprigs of aristocracy that his first lieutenant—no re-
specter of persons—was wont to call out in mockery to the young
noblemen and honourables at the ropes, "My lords and gentlemen,
shiver the mizen topsail!" The majority were of comparatively
humble origin, occasioning Sir Walter Elliot's remark that,
though the profession had its utility, he would be sorry to see any
friend of his belonging to it. Few had much of this world's goods
nor, unless exceptionally lucky over prize money, could hope for
much. Some were scholars—for it was a literary age—and read
their Shakespeare or discoursed learnedly on the classical associa-
tions of the foreign ports they visited: more often they were
simple souls, "better acquainted with rope-yarns and bilge water
than with Homer or Virgil." But one and all were masters of
their profession, proud in their obedience to king and country
and ready to give their lives and all they had whenever the
Service demanded. "A bloody war and a sickly season!" was the

closing toast of many a jovial evening in the wardroom: it was so that men rose in their calling.[1]

Such men not only officered the fleet: they gave it their own tone and spirit. They were often rough teachers, full of fearful oaths like the master's mate of the *Edgar* who ended every sentence with a "Damn your whistle," and too fond of enforcing their commands with the lash. But the men they commanded were rough too; hard-bitten merchant seamen and fishermen, brought into the Service for the duration by the pressgangs, with always a sediment in every ship of jailbirds and incorrigibles whose only chance of freedom was the hard life of the sea. The unresting, automatic discipline which the handling of wind-propelled warships in northern waters demanded could not have been enforced by gentler souls: it was that which gave Britain command of the waves and kept the Royal Navy from the slovenly, helpless degradation which befell that of revolutionary France. From the admiral, piped on board, to the boatswain's mate with his colt ready to "start" the lower deck to action, strictly ordered subordination and readiness to obey were the hallmarks of the Service.

The life of the seamen was a life apart; something that was of England and yet remote from it. A king's ship was a little wooden world of its own, with its peculiar customs and gradations unguessed at by landsmen; its proud foretopmen, the aristocrats of the sea, and far down out of sight its humble waisters: pumpers and sewermen, scavengers and pigsty keepers. In such a community, often years together away from a home port, men learnt to know each other as they seldom can on shore: to love and trust, to fear and hate one another. There were ships that became floating hells, ruled by some sadistic tyrant, with drunken,

[1] So Nelson wrote to his father: "I wish I could congratulate you upon a rectory instead of a vicarage; it is rather awkward wishing the poor man dead, but we all rise by deaths. I got my rank by a shot killing a post-captain, and I most sincerely hope I shall, when I go, go out of the world the same way; then we all go in the line of our profession—a parson praying and a captain fighting."

flogging officers "crabbed as fiends," and savage, murderous crews such as that which flung Bligh of the *Bounty* to perish in an open boat in a remote sea. There were others commanded by captains like Nelson, Pellew and Duncan, where the men looked on their officers as fathers and were eager to dare and do anything for them. Here something of the unspoken sympathy between experienced rider and horse entered into the relationship between quarter and lower deck.

The nation honoured its rough, simple seamen, as it had cause to, though it usually saw them at their worst: ashore on their brief spells of leave, with discipline relaxed and their hard-earned money riotously dissipated on brandy and the coarse Megs and Dolls of the seaports. But it saw too, as we also can glimpse from the prints of the old masters, the fine manly faces, the earnest gaze, the careless attitudes so full of strength and grace for all the gnarls and distortions of weather, accident and disease: symbols of rugged-headed courage, manly devotion and simple-hearted patriotism. They were children—generous, suspicious, forgiving, with the fortitude and patience of men: rough Britons tempered by the unresting sea into virtue of a rare and peculiar kind. The sight of a Monsieur's sails roused in them all the unconquerable pugnacity of their race: the whine of Johnny Crapaud's shot whipped their quick tempers to savagery. Though chivalrous and generous victors, they were not good losers like the courtly Spaniards and the aristocrats of the old French navy; they had to beat their adversary or die. As they waited at quarters before a fight, "their black silk handkerchiefs tied round their heads, their shirt-sleeves tucked up, the crows and hand-spikes in their hands and the boarders all ready with their cutlasses and tomahawks," they reminded an eye-witness of so many devils.

Yet from such scenes the British sailor could pass in a few hours to the buffoonery and practical jokes dear to the lower deck, the fiddler's lively air, the droll or pathetic ballads with their rhythm of the waves, while the seas broke over the forecastle and the ship pitched and rolled; and to those tenderer moments when, homeward bound, hearts panted with the anticipated happiness of meeting wives and sweethearts and the headwind's moping contrariness was lulled by the chorus of "Grieving's a folly, Boys!"

> " And now arrived that jovial night
> When every true bred tar carouses,
> When, o'er the grog, all hands delight
> To toast their sweethearts and their spouses."

History loves to linger over the good-humoured jollity between decks when port was reached: the girls on the seamen's knees with sturdy, buxom arms around their necks; the reels and gigs as Susan's bright eyes promised her Tom Tough his long-awaited reward; the grog and flip that passed about under the light of the flickering lanterns. And judging by the popularity of Dibdin's songs, the nation liked to think of such scenes too and took deep comfort in the thought of the hearts of oak and jolly tars that kept its foes at bay.

. . . .

In 1797—the fifth year of Britain's struggle against the militant power of Revolutionary France—the Royal Navy alone stood between her and defeat. One by one her continental allies had collapsed before the élan of the ragged revolutionary armies; Prussia and Holland had given up the fight and entered the enemy camp, Piedmont had sued for an armistice, and, in the autumn of 1796, the sudden defection to the French cause of Spain and its powerful navy—lying athwart Britain's trade and ocean communications—had forced her to withdraw her fleet from the Mediterranean, where that summer a young general named Napoleon Bonaparte had overrun northern Italy in a series of dazzling victories over her ally, Austria. The three chief naval powers of the continent—France, Spain and Holland—were now aligned against her, outnumbering her ships of the line by nearly two to one. Ireland was on the verge of revolution, the working-class population of the industrial north was hungry and restless, and powerful invasion-forces were waiting with transports at Brest and Texel for a chance to break the blockade and strike at

England or Ireland. During the last fortnight of 1796, the Brest
expedition got to sea and reached the Irish coast, only to be driven
back by gales; in February, after an abortive attempt to burn
Bristol, a raiding force made landings on either side of the
Bristol Channel, causing a panic in the City, during which Pitt's
Government suspended cash payments and seemed about to fall.

The last British ships to leave the Mediterranean were two
frigates under Commodore Horatio Nelson who had been sent
back just before Christmas to evacuate troops and stores from
Elba. On his return voyage through the Straits of Gibraltar on
February 12th 1797, Nelson—then unknown outside the Service
—had encountered a Spanish fleet of twenty-seven battleships
and twelve frigates sailing from Cartagena to join the French
fleet at Brest, which, with its aid, was to drive the overstretched
British blockading squadrons from the Channel and escort an
army of invasion from Holland to Ireland. Forced to pass through
them as they battled with an Atlantic gale, and hotly pursued by
two of their largest ships, Nelson lost a man overboard. To save
him and his first lieutenant, who had lowered a boat, Nelson,
checking course, risked certain destruction. But, bewildered by
their tiny prey's unaccountable conduct, the Spaniards checked
too and enabled him to escape. Next day he rejoined the Mediterranean Fleet off Cape St. Vincent, where his Commander-in-
Chief, the sixty-one year old Sir John Jervis, was waiting with
fifteen battleships to intercept the Spaniards.

While only two of Jervis's ships carried 100 guns, of the
Spaniards' twenty-seven no less than seven were three-deckers
with 112 guns or more, and one of them—the four-decker
Santissima Trinidad—was the largest fighting ship in the world.
In the early morning of February 14th—St. Valentine's Day—
they were sighted approaching Cape St. Vincent from the south-
west—"thumpers," the signal lieutenant reported, "looming like
Beachy Head in a fog!" Yet "old Jack," as the seamen called
Jervis, was determined to force a battle. For he knew that a vic-
tory at that moment was essential to his country.

The old admiral was no gambler. He knew the strength of

the Spanish fleet but he also knew its fighting capacity. As the mist lifted and his flag-lieutenant called out the odds, he remained grimly unperturbed. "There are eighteen sail of the line, Sir John." "Very well, sir,"—"There are twenty sail of the line, Sir John." "Very well, sir,"—"There are twenty-five sail of the line, Sir John." "Very well, sir,"—" There are twenty-seven sail of the line, Sir John; near double our own." "If there are fifty sail of the line, I will go through them."—"That's right, Sir John," cried the Canadian, Captain Hallowell, in his enthusiasm actually slapping his admiral on the back, "and a damned good licking we'll give them!"

In two columns imperceptibly merging into an impenetrable line with sterns and bowsprits almost touching, the British fleet bore down on the enemy, making straight for a gap—nearly three miles wide—between the main force and a straggling division to leeward. The Spanish admiral made an effort to close it, but too late. It was like the inexorable thrust of a sword into a careless giant's guard.

Down in the dark of the gun-decks and in the "slaughter houses" near the mainmasts, the men were waiting with the precision born of long practice. As each enemy drew alongside and all was ready—the ports open, matches lighted, the guns run out—they broke into three tremendous cheers more daunting to their foes even than the thunder of their broadsides. "We gave them their Valentines in style," wrote one of the *Goliath's* gunners; "not that we loved fighting, but we all wished to be free to return to our homes and follow our own pursuits. We knew there was no other way of obtaining this than by defeating the enemy. 'The hotter war, the sooner peace,' was a saying with us."

The climax of the battle came at about one o'clock. At that moment the head of the Spanish line was nearing the tail of the British. Nelson, flying his flag in the thirteenth ship in the British line, the 74-gun *Captain*, saw with the instinct of genius that only one thing could prevent the main Spanish division, which had suddenly turned to leeward, from rejoining its isolated ships and confronting Jervis with a reunited fleet before he could alter course. The Spaniards were battered but they were still intact: another few minutes and the chance of the decisive victory that England so sorely needed would have passed. Without hesitation, disregarding the letter of the orders he had received and anticipating those there was not time to transmit, Nelson bore out of the line and placed the *Captain*—the smallest two-decker in the British fleet—straight in the course of the giant *Santissima Trinidad* and four other ships. For ten minutes, her foremast shot away and her wheelpost broken by a tornado of fire, it looked as though the *Captain* would be blown out of the water. But when the smoke cleared she was still there, and the *Excellent* under Captain Collingwood was coming to her aid. The Spaniards' line was inextricable confusion, all hope of a junction between their sundered divisions at an end, and Jervis beating back into the fight with the remainder of his fleet.

Before the victory was complete, Nelson did a remarkable thing. Crippled though she was from her duel with the *Santissima Trinidad*, he placed the *Captain* alongside the 80-gun *San Nicolas* and prepared to board. Climbing through the quarter-gallery window in her stern, the little one-eyed commodore led the boarders through the officers' cabins to the quarterdeck where they hauled down the Spanish ensign. At that moment fire was opened on the boarding party from the stern-gallery of the three-decker, *San Josef*, which in the confusion of the fight had drifted against the *San Nicolas*. Placing sentries at the tops of the latter's ladders, Nelson re-directed his boarding party up her side. There, as his fellow captain, Collingwood, described it, on the quarter-deck of a Spanish first-rate he received the swords of the officers of the two ships, "while one of his sailors bundled them up with as much composure as he would have made a faggot, though twenty-two of their line were still within gunshot." The cool daring of the thing tickled the imagination of the Fleet. "Nelson's patent bridge for boarding first-rates" became a lower-deck legend.

Thus it was that on the evening of March 3rd England was raised from a trough of depression by the news of a great and providential victory. Four battleships, two of them first-rates, had been taken, and the rest of the Spanish fleet had withdrawn under cover of darkness to Cadiz, nursing wounds that would avert any danger from that quarter for many months. And, as the clouds of that terrible winter parted, men saw through them the gleam of something swift and glorious and of a new name—Nelson.

But six weeks later, on the morning of April 17th, dreadful rumours began to percolate through the capital. The Navy, which had saved the country from invasion, was about to betray it to its enemies. The Channel Fleet—the buckler on which England's very existence depended—had refused to sail and mutinied for an increase of pay. By nightfall the news was confirmed. Yet at that very moment the Austrians were on the point of asking a truce from the victorious Bonaparte, Ireland—almost denuded of troops—was defenceless, and a French army of liberation was waiting to embark at the Texel under cover of the Dutch fleet. Like the Black Death four centuries before, the Revolution had crossed the Channel and broken out in England.

. . . .

Naval pay, fixed by ancient enactment, had stood for nearly a century and a half at 10s. a month for an ordinary seaman and 24s. for an A.B. But the price of the commodities on which the sailor's family depended had not remained constant. To the normal rising trend of prices had been added war inflation, now aggravated by the bank crisis. In the merchant service the laws of supply and demand had raised the seaman's pay to four times the naval rate. Prevented by the pressgang from selling their highly skilled services in the open market and forced to let their wives and children starve while they served their country, the men were conscious of a grave injustice of which their rulers—ill-served by statistics—were blissfully unaware. Even the despised soldiers had been given a small rise since the war. But the sailors—the pride and defence of the nation—had had nothing done for them, though certain of their officers had recently had increases. So strong was their feeling that at the beginning of March before sailing for the spring cruise the men of the Channel Fleet combined to send round-robins to old Lord Howe, their nominal commander-in-chief. In these they respectfully pointed out that the cost of living had doubled and that their pay was insufficient to support their families. And since it was only paid in the port of commission, whence in war-time a ship might be absent for months and even years, it was frequently in arrears.

As Howe was an invalid at Bath and about to hand over his command finally to his deputy, Lord Bridport, he merely forwarded the petitions to the Admiralty. Here they were ignored. For in the critical state of the country's finances, application to parliament for a rise in naval pay seemed out of the question, and discussion of the matter would thus obviously be undesirable. As the petitions were anonymous no reply was made. When the fleet returned to Spithead at the end of March the men found their request met by silence. They were very angry and took steps to prepare a petition to parliament and to support it by joint action. "They had better," the *Queen Charlotte's* men wrote of the Government, "go to war with the whole globe than with their own subjects."

Of all this Lord Bridport was unaware. For through an administrative oversight the Admiralty had failed to inform him of the petitions. But on April 12th he accidentally learnt of a plot to seize the ships and hold them as pledges for redress of grievances. He was naturally profoundly shocked and, hearing at second hand of the petitions to Howe, became exceedingly indignant with the Admiralty. In his heart he sympathised with the men's demands. But when he raised the matter with Whitehall he was merely told to take the Fleet to sea. For the Admiralty was determined to sidetrack the matter.

On the morning, therefore, of April 16th—Easter Sunday—

Bridport reluctantly ordered the Fleet to weigh anchor. His signal was ignored. In the *Queen Charlotte*, Howe's former flagship, the men, seeing an attempt to forestall the mutiny, manned the shrouds and gave three cheers—the pre-arranged signal for revolt. At once the leaders put off in boats and rowed round the fleet, ordering the crew of every vessel to send two delegates that night to the *Queen Charlotte*. Like all the Hoods a shrewd and sensible man, Bridport forbade his captains to resist. Instead he ordered them to muster their men and ask them to state their grievances.

That evening the delegates of sixteen battleships assembled in the *Queen Charlotte's* state-room to draw up rules for the regulation of the fleet. They ordered watches to be kept, drunkenness to be punished by flogging and ducking, and yard-ropes to be rove at every fore-yard arm to enforce their authority. Women were to be allowed aboard as usual in harbour, but to prevent tittle-tattle were not to go ashore till the matter was settled. Respect was to be paid to the rank of officers, but, until the desires of the men were satisfied, not an anchor was to be raised. To symbolise their unanimity the shrouds were to be manned morning and night and three cheers given.

It was a strange position. The fleet was in indubitable mutiny. Yet the men did not regard themselves as mutineers and persisted in trying to behave as though ordinary discipline prevailed. The country was at war with an ideological creed which glorified revolution: it was hourly expecting invasion. Yet in the rebellious ships there was no sign of sympathy with that revolution: on the contrary the delegates declared that the fleet would sail at once if the French put to sea. They even stopped the frigates and small craft from taking part in the mutiny lest the country's trade should suffer. Nervous folk on shore, imagining "secret Jacobin springs," looked for foreign agents and agitators. But if there were any such, they were unsuccessful in impressing their principles on their old foes of the Channel Fleet. In its good order, common sense and almost pathetic legalism the start of the English revolution contrasted strangely with the French.

Meanwhile Admiral Pole, dispatched post-haste with news of the mutiny, had reached the Admiralty at midnight on the 16th. In the small hours of Tuesday morning he told his horrifying story to the First Lord. Earl Spencer was the best type of patrician—an athlete still in early middle age, a scholar with liberal leanings, red-haired and handsome. He acted with promptitude and vigour. As soon as it was light he hurried to the Prime Minister and, after a day of interviews set out for Portsmouth with two junior Lords and the Secretary of the Admiralty.

Here on the 18th the Board, formally sitting in the Fountain Inn, opened its proceedings. Refusing to compromise its dignity by meeting the seamen personally, it used the flag officers of the fleet as go-betweens. It might have been wiser for Spencer, who was over-persuaded by his Service colleagues, to have settled the matter directly with the delegates, whose real weakness was not Jacobinism but excessive suspicion. As it was, in the delays and second thoughts born of too much coming and going, the sea-men's conditions tended to rise. A new petition added demands that rations—on paper a pound of meat, a pound of biscuits and half a pint of rum a day—should no longer be subjected to the purser's customary deduction of an eighth, that fresh vegetables should be provided in port, that the sick should be properly cared for, that pay should be continued to the wounded until dis-charged, and that in harbour men should have leave to go ashore instead of remaining aboard like prisoners. The unknown hand who framed this document asked that the sailors should be looked upon as a number of men standing in the defence of their country, and that they might in some wise "have the grant of those sweets of Liberty on shore when in harbour." He ended by assuring the Admiralty that the men would suffer double the hardships they complained of sooner than allow the Crown to be imposed on by a foreign Power.

The new requests were in themselves reasonable: they were all in the end granted without doing the country the least injury. Pursers who "took care of their eighths" were far too common: the meat was often uneatable, the biscuits weevily, the butter rancid and the cheese full of long red worms.[1] Many ship's surgeons were drunken wastrels who had gone to sea as the last resort in a life of professional failure. And considering that the seamen had been torn away from their homes and callings to indescribable hardships and tedium, it seemed monstrously unjust to keep them on board in harbour.

But, however reasonable, the ultimatum was presented at a time when the country was in graver danger than any since the Spanish Armada appeared off Plymouth. To yield unconditionally at the pistol's mouth might undermine the whole fabric of naval discipline and precipitate the same tragic train of events which had brought monarchical France to massacre and ruin. To aristocrats like Spencer the very discipline of the mutineers seemed ominous: it argued, as Lady Spencer wrote to "weathercock" Windham, a steadiness which overpowered her with terror. Therefore, though the Board prudently eschewed violent counsels, it determined to make some sort of a stand: to keep the seamen at a distance and, while granting the substance of their demands, to make as many minor abatements as possible. In fact it tried to avoid paying the full price for its own former and very English failure—through complacency, inertia and reluctance to inquire too closely into uncomfortable facts—to reform abuses while it had time to do so with dignity.

The results of this obstinacy were not happy. On the 20th the Prince of Wurtemberg, who had come to Portsmouth to marry the Princess Royal, had been cheered and saluted as though nothing unusual was happening while being escorted by Spencer round the mutinous fleet. This singularly English episode encouraged the Lords of the Admiralty in their firm resolve. But next day, while Admiral Gardner was arguing with the delegates in the *Queen Charlotte's* stateroom, the men—after seeming agree-

[1] It was an old saying in the Service that Judas Iscariot was the first purser. But boatswains often ran them fine in the art of peculation. It was Johnny Bone, the boatswain of the *Edgar*, to whom the great Adam Duncan observed: "Whatever you do Mr. Bone, I hope and trust you will not take the anchors from the bows." *Recollections of J. A. Gardner* (Navy Records Society), 71.

ment had been reached—grew suspicious and declared that a
final settlement must wait till a pardon had been received under
the king's hand. At this the admiral, who thought it high time
the fleet was at sea, lost his temper and denounced the delegates
as "a damned, mutinous, blackguard set" of "skulking fellows"
who were afraid of meeting the French. In his fury he even shook
one of them and threatened to have him hanged. At this there was
a riot which ended in the apoplectic old man's being hustled out
of the flagship and the red flag being hoisted in all ships. The
officers were placed under confinement or—in the case of the
unpopular ones—sent ashore.

Once more, faced by urgent crisis, Spencer acted promptly.
That night he set out for London to obtain the royal pardon,
secured next morning an immediate Cabinet council and by
midnight had obtained the king's signature at Windsor and had
had copies printed for circulation in the fleet. But by the time
that these, galloped through the night, reached Portsmouth, the
good temper of the Navy was already re-asserting itself. The
astonishing delegates, while still insisting on the redress of grievances, had apologised gracefully to Bridport for the flag striking
incident and begged him as "father of the fleet" to resume
command. This the admiral did on the morning of the 24th,
reading the royal proclamation to the crew of the flagship and
making a speech in which he promised general satisfaction of all
demands. The mutiny thereupon ended. Next morning the
greater part of the fleet dropped down to St. Helens to await an
easterly wind to carry it to Brest.

But though the country congratulated itself that a dreadful
week had been attended by no worse consequences, suspicion and
unrest remained. The men were not sure that the Government
meant to honour its promises. The inexplicable delays attendant
on parliamentary processes increased their distrust. During the
next fortnight while the fleet waited for the wind, the ferment
continued to work. The seamen had tasted power and learnt
their strength. Moreover the recognition of their principal
grievances had reminded them of others.

On several occasions in the recent past abuses in particular ships had been so serious that they had provoked isolated mutinies. Over-rapidity of war-time expansion and the difficulty of raising men and keeping them from desertion had aggravated the severity of discipline. With the jails emptied to supply the pressgangs, it is not surprising that some officers could only enforce order at the cat's tail. Such a regimen could be accompanied by a horrible brutality. "The ill-usage we have on board this ship," the crew of the *Winchelsea* wrote to the Admiralty early in the war, "forced us to fly to your Lordships the same as a child to its father." Another ship's company referred to its treatment "from the tirant of a captain" as more than the spirits and hearts of Englishmen could bear, "for we are born free but now we are slaves." These things were against the Regulations, but, with each ship a world of its own and often far from port, the Regulations were hard to enforce. In certain ships the officers, as Collingwood said, beat the men into a state of insubordination.

Grievances apart, the Fleet was ripe for trouble. The dilution of the better elements with the worse had left a dangerous sediment at the bottom of every crew. In four years of war naval personnel had swollen from 16,000 to 120,000. Many of the latest joined were "quota men" raised under the Act of 1795 which had imposed on every parish the obligation of supplying the Service. Among these were inevitably some of superior station—broken-down tradesmen, fraudulent attorneys and the like, who were disgruntled with their lot. Ten per cent of the seamen were foreigners. Another ten per cent were Irish, some of them under sentence for political offences and illegally smuggled into the Fleet by high-handed officials. Recently an increasing number had been United Irishmen and sympathisers with the principles proclaimed by France.

The agitation and struggle of those seven breathless days at Spithead stirred all this perilous matter into a ferment. This was no ordinary mutiny, for it had succeeded. Suspicion that its fruits were going to be filched by parliamentary chicanery was now aroused by two circumstances. On the 3rd the Duke of Bedford, making party capital out of a national misfortune, contrived by an awkward question in the Lords to convey to uninitiated seamen poring over their newspapers the false idea that the Government was going to drop the bill for supplementary naval pay. Simultaneously the Admiralty circulated a foolish document forbidding captains to temporise with mutiny, and directing the marines to be kept in constant readiness for action. This was no more than a childish attempt of official pride to recover official face. But by accident or design its contents became known to the fleet. On Sunday, May 7th, when on a change of wind Bridport hoisted the signal to sail, the seamen at St. Helens once more manned the shrouds and broke into defiant cheers.

This time mutiny wore a graver aspect. The seamen of the *Royal George*, swearing their officers had deceived them, seized the arms and ammunition. A broil in Admiral Colpoys's flagship at Spithead, in which a seaman lost his life while rushing the quarterdeck, nearly ended in the admiral and the officer who had fired the shot being summarily hanged. In other ships unpopular officers were bundled ashore and left with their belongings on the quayside. Some of the marines, the traditional keypins of naval discipline, joined the rest. The people of Portsmouth, confronted with the spectacle of the fleet flying the red flag and of shaken captains and admirals dumped on the sea front like *émigrés*, hourly expected the arrival of the French and the guillotine. As a Civil Lord of the Admiralty wrote to Spencer, the situation formed "the most awful crisis" the country had ever known.

Meanwhile the conflagration had spread. At Plymouth the crews of Sir Roger Curtis's squadron had mutinied on April 26th and turned most of their captains ashore. Four days later ominous cheering signalled an outbreak of revolt in the flagship of the North Sea Fleet waiting at Yarmouth for a wind to blockade the Dutch invasion fleet in the Texel. But in this case the admiral in command was equal to the occasion. Towering with rage, the giant Scot, Adam Duncan, called his men out of the foreshrouds and rated them like a father. The affair ended—for they adored the fine old man—in their promising to go to any part of the world with him and writing a letter thanking the Lords of the Admiralty for their compliance with the request of the Channel Fleet.

For underneath the suspicion, the smouldering grievances and agitation ran the English individual sense of humanity. A worthy officer remained in the seamen's eyes a worthy man, however much he might theoretically embody the forces of despotism. All the generalisations of French ideology or Irish logic could never persuade them otherwise.

It was this deep-rooted manliness of the British sailor that saved the day. The authorities, at last abandoning false pride, behaved with equal good sense. The supplementary estimates providing for the increase in pay were hurried through their remaining stages, and the one line of approach to the disgruntled seamen which was certain of success—the simple human one—was chosen. Someone with a flash of the inspiration which always seems to come to the salvation of England in the last ditch suggested the victor of the First of June as *deus ex machina*. Armed with full powers to redress grievances on behalf of the Admiralty and to grant pardon on that of the Crown, Lord Howe, overcoming gout and infirmities, set off for Portsmouth. Without wasting a minute he had himself rowed across the Solent to St. Helens where, visiting every ship in turn, he set to work to restore the confidence of the seamen in their rulers.

By May 13th, six days after the renewed mutiny had begun, the old hero had achieved his purpose of quietening what he described as "the most suspicious but most generous minds" he had ever met. The demand of the men to dismiss the more unpopular officers was tactfully turned by getting the latter to petition the Admiralty for transfer to other ships. There only remained to celebrate the reconciliation of Fleet and nation. On May 15th, after twelve hours of rowing round the cheering fleet amid the strains of "Rule Britannia," "Black Dick"—as exhausted as after the battle of the First of June—was carried by the sailors shoulder high to the port governor's house. Here in a perfect delirium of patriotic emotion he and his lady entertained the delegates to a grand dinner and jollification. At Plymouth, where a similar happy ending occurred, Captain Boger, after being kept a prisoner in the *Cambridge* guardship, was paraded with his fellow captains in open carriages round the town on a broiling summer day, amid tumultuous cheering. Dressed in full uniform, with a face scarlet from the heat, he repeatedly asked for a glass of water, but his men, who were extremely fond of him, horrified at the request, told him that "his Honour might have any sort of grog, but that as for water they would not suffer his Honour to drink it."

Two days later the Channel Fleet put to sea to seek the enemy. But the country had no time for relief. During the second Spithead mutiny the news reached London that Austria, brought to her knees by Bonaparte's advance on Vienna, had signed an armistice at Leoben and that France was free to concentrate her entire force against England. Already a Dutch army was waiting at the Texel. Every day brought new alarms. On May 12th, while Howe was completing his work of pacification, a brilliant young Tory M.P., George Canning, penned some mock verses congratulating his friend Windham, who had made a comforting ministerial reference in a recent speech to "negative successes," on a "day of no disaster." He was too soon. For on that very day, while rumours percolated through London that the Household troops had revolted, the men of the flagship at Sheerness defied their officers and turned the forecastle guns on the quarterdeck. The rest of the battleships lying in the mouth of the river at the Great and Little Nore followed their example.

The good humour and sense which had characterised proceedings at Spithead were lacking at the Nore. The chief ringleader was an ex-schoolmaster who had recently taken the Government's quota money to get himself out of a debtor's prison. The son of an Exeter tradesman, Richard Parker, now thirty years of age, had been three times to sea, had served as a midshipman and had been courtmartialled for insubordination. He marked his return to the Navy by helping to stir up trouble in the port flag and depot ship, the *Sandwich*, already rife with discontent through her foul and overcrowded condition. Like many other famous talkers he was full of good intentions, on which later apologists have dwelt at length. But he was without moral ballast. He was ambitious, vain, untruthful, weak and so excitable as to seem at times mentally deranged. In his hands the smouldering grievances and resentment of rough and ignorant men became a terrible menace.

The mutineers at the Nore formulated no specific demands. It was mutiny without an objective. It disregarded the general settlement reached at Spithead. Like the French Revolution in miniature, it proceeded on its own momentum and degenerated into rebellion for the sake of rebellion. Parker, who styled himself President and kept up an admiral's state, never stirred without the accompaniment of musical honours and banners. He told the men that the act for the increase of their pay was only a temporary Order in Council and, when shown to be wrong, declared that it had no validity beyond the end of the year. Only after repeated requests for the men's grievances did he present Admiral Buckner—in whose presence he remained contemptuously covered—with an ultimatum of eight articles. One of these affirmed the right of seamen to dismiss their officers. But he refused to discuss matters with any one but the Lords of the Admiralty, insisting that they should wait on the delegates.

Meanwhile his followers ceaselessly paraded the streets of Sheerness or rowed in procession round the port, armed with pistols and cutlasses and accompanied by brass bands playing "Rule Britannia" and "Britons, Strike Home!" For the men, though greatly enjoying their holiday and unwonted power, Englishwise refused to admit any disloyalty in their attitude. When the Government marched two regiments of militia into the place, Parker wrote to Admiral Buckner protesting at the "insult to the peaceable behaviour of the seamen." He added that the Lords of the Admiralty were themselves remiss in their duty in failing to attend where their appearance would give satisfaction.

As the Admiralty declined to obey, the mutineers proceeded to more vigorous measures. On May 23rd they seized eight gunboats lying in Sheerness harbour and carried them off in triumph to the Nore. Next day they dispatched delegates to Yarmouth to urge the men of the North Sea Fleet to join them. Here Admiral Duncan, having received news that the Dutch fleet was embarking troops at the Texel, was about to sail for Ireland. Though the fatal infection was at work in his ships, he trusted to his personal popularity to overcome it. Only a week before he had dealt with a further outbreak in the *Adamant* by hoisting his flag in her and asking the turbulent crew whether any man dared to dispute his authority. When one of the ringleaders said he did, the giant admiral had picked him up by the collar with one hand and, bearing him to the side of the vessel, had cried out, "My lads, look at this fellow who dares to deprive me of the command of the fleet!" After which incipient mutiny in that ship at least dissolved in laughter.

But on the 29th, while standing out for the Dutch coast, one after another of Duncan's ships left him and sailed home to the Nore. Only his flagship, the *Venerable*, and the now faithful *Adamant* kept their course. "I am sorry," wrote the gallant old man, "that I have lived to see the pride of Britain disgrace the very name of it." Not since an enemy sailed up the Medway had such shame befallen the Navy.

Meanwhile on the evening of the 27th the Cabinet, faced by the gravity of the situation, resolved that the Admiralty must swallow its pride and go down to Sheerness. A new Royal Pardon was made out specifically covering the post-Spithead mutinies. That night Spencer, accompanied by two colleagues and the Secretary of the Board, again set off on his travels. But on reaching Sheerness on the 28th, he found what he had already suspected, that the Fleet's attitude was not unanimous and that many of the men were already sickening of Parker's presumption. He therefore refused to receive the delegates and, remaining in the Dockyard Commissioner's house, used old Admiral Buckner as an intermediary. And as Parker refused to abate anything from his demands, the First Lord presently returned to London with

THE FIRE AND THE ROSE

his mission unaccomplished. With Parker to deal with, it is doubtful if any other course was ever possible.

It was now war to the knife. Neither side would admit of compromise. While the mutineers were enthusiastically welcoming Duncan's absconding battleships, the Government was giving orders to cut their communications with the shore. All fraternisation between the Fleet and the Army was stopped and the sailors were to be resisted by force if they attempted to land. A bill was hurried through parliament extending the death penalty to persons having intercourse with rebellious seamen. Finally the provisions of the fleet at the Nore were stopped. These measures, which passed both Houses with only one dissentient vote, were stern in the extreme. But they reflected the mood of the nation. They were an instance of the English method of grappling with a problem only when it became unmistakably dangerous but then doing so without second thoughts or hesitation. For the rulers of England weakness was a thing of the past.

Nor did they stand on pride. The Army, whose loyalty was so vital in that hour, was treated with a new consideration. Increases in pay long asked for in vain by the military authorities were immediately granted by parliament. The soldiers responded cheerfully: having been so often sneered at by the seamen for their inefficiency and defeats, it was a pleasant change to become the heroes of the nation and be set to police the proud favourites. Under the command of Sir Charles Grey, the most popular officer in the Army, the troops kept close watch along the Kent and Essex shores and scarcely allowed a man to pass.[1]

[1] The kind of treatment to which the despised "lobsters" were subjected in the seaports is illustrated by an extract from Commander Gardner's *Recollections*, describing an incident on Gosport beach when a party of soldiers was marching some French prisoners to jail: "A *posse* of women rushed out of Rime's noted alley, and, pointing to the soldiers, sang the following beautiful ditty:

> 'Don't you see the ships a-coming?
> Don't you see them in full sail?
> Don't you see the ships a-coming
> With the prizes at their tail?

Behind them was the nation. Its patriotism and sense of danger were alike aroused: fear of the invader waiting at the Texel and the intangible bogey of revolution that had grown up during the horrors of the Terror and the unreasoning years of war propaganda. To simple Britons Fox and his gang of Whig "traitors" and defeatists lurked under the delegates' table in the stateroom of the *Queen Charlotte*. To frustrate their vile tricks and save the nation, thousands of middle-class citizens enrolled as "peace officers" or volunteered to serve in the flotilla of gunboats which Commodore Gower was organising in Long Reach to defend London from the mutineers. The East India Company placed all its ships at the Government's disposal: hundreds of private merchants followed its example.

The stoppage of the fleet's victuals placed the delegates in a quandary. Since they would not go back, they had to go forward. On May 31st they decided to "show the country that they had it in their power to stop the trade of the river." But when on June 2nd they did so, seizing every ship entering or leaving the Thames, they merely united the country more vigorously than before. The trading community, attacked at its most sensitive point, was appalled and, because it was appalled, furious. So were the good people of the Thames-side towns who found tarred and feathered officers dumped by piratical crews on their waterfronts. This was plainly the prelude to the orgy of massacre,

---

Oh! my little rolling sailor,
Oh! my little rolling he;
I do love a jolly sailor,
Blithe and merry might he be.

Sailors they get all the money,
Soldiers they get none but brass;
I do love a jolly sailor,
Soldiers they may kiss my . . .
Oh! my little rolling sailor,
Oh! my little rolling he;
I do love a jolly sailor,
Soldiers may be damned for me!' "

rape and arson which the anti-Jacobin cartoonists had taught them to fear. When the Government retaliated against the blockade by removing the buoys and beacons at the mouth of the Thames, there was not a dissentient voice from a seafaring people.

As the rest of the nation became more unanimous, the seamen became less so. The mutiny was popular so long as it remained a holiday demonstration with plenty of triumphal processions ashore, patriotic songs and brass bands and an unwonted freedom for airing grievances and slighting tyrannical officers. It became another thing altogether when it meant being cooped in idle ships, denied the liberty of the shore and its taverns and kept to short commons. But what really sapped the spirit of mutiny was the realisation that the nation, which, however sparing it might be in other things, had always lavished unstinted praise on its sailors, now regarded them as traitors and French dupes. Even their brethren of Spithead and Plymouth, now returned to their allegiance, wrote to the men of the Nore expressing horror at their proceedings. This imputation was more than the sailors could bear. The sense of community and playing for one's side, so strong in Englishmen, kept them a little while longer loyal to the mutiny, but they became moody, suspicious of one another and openly critical of their leaders. "Dam my eyes," wrote one of them in desperation to a silent, unrelenting Admiralty, "if I understand your lingo or long Proclimations, but in short give us our Due at Once and no more at it, till we go in search of the Rascals the Eneymes of our Country." In such a mood their attempts to celebrate Oakapple Day and the king's birthday on June 5th, which struck their compatriots as an impertinence, assumed a pathetic significance.

On June 6th the Government formally declared the mutineers rebels, though still extending its offer of pardon to all who should submit except the ringleaders. About the same time it became known in the fleet that Parker had been keeping back the terms of this offer from his followers. Discontent at his admiral's airs and peremptory ways had been growing for some time: it now turned to open murmuring. The more popular officers detained aboard the ships were quick to take advantage of the change of temperature, and sober seamen who had never approved of the mutiny began to come into their own.

The first sign of collapse came on the morning of the 9th when Parker, sensing the altered mood of the men and desperately resolving to take the hungry fleet over to the Texel, gave the order to put to sea. Not a vessel stirred. The mutiny had come full circle. On the same day the officers of the *Leopard* seized control of the ship from the divided and disillusioned crew and set sail for the Lower Hope. The example was at once followed by the *Repulse* and, despite a desultory fire from the rest of the fleet, both ships made good their escape.

For the next few days the fleet presented a curious spectacle to watchers from the shore as red, blue and white flags fluttered up and down the mastheads while the ships' companies contended whether they should return unconditionally to their allegiance, make new attempts to parley with a stony-hearted Admiralty or sail for America or Ireland. But all the while the sands of mutiny were running out. The Admiralty refused to consider any proposition short of unqualified submission, and the men knew they had no alternative but to submit. By the 12th only two out of the twenty-two ships still at the Nore flew the red flag of defiance. Every day more of them slipped their cables and made their way up river to surrender to the authorities.

On the 15th the crew of the *Sandwich* repudiated Parker's authority and sailed under the guns of Sheerness. The mutiny was over. A few of the ringleaders made their escape to Calais. Parker, handed over to the military by his comrades, was taken to Maidstone jail under an escort of the West Yorks Militia. Here he was tried by court-martial and spent the remaining hours of his life writing an apologia for his actions and a long tirade against the men he had helped to mislead. He was hanged on the last day of June from the yardarm of the *Sandwich*. Fifty-eight others were condemned to death, of whom twenty-eight were executed. Others were flogged or sentenced to terms of imprisonment. Of the 412 ringleaders found guilty, 300 were pardoned.

No other end to the affair was possible, for any other would have spelt the loss of naval discipline at a moment when its preservation was vital to the country. When Parker demanded the submission of the Admiralty to a seamen's council and held the nation's trade up to ransom, he threatened to smash the edge of a sharp and delicate instrument which, in Nelson's hand, was to establish the Pax Britannica and keep free the sea routes of the world for a century. Only undeviating firmness on the part of Admiralty and parliament and an undivided endorsement by the nation could have saved the Navy from the fate of that of Republican France. Mutiny at the Nore had arisen from the same causes as at Spithead and Plymouth. But, with Howe's redress of wellnigh insupportable grievances, naval rebellion in the Thames lost its justification. Its continuance exposed the country to dangers greater than any in her history. In acting as they did, the Government and country showed the soundness of their instincts. So did the seamen in repudiating their leaders.

Yet the mutinies, terrible as they had seemed at the time, had served a purpose. They had brought home to the Government and country the abuses which were impairing the discipline and spirit of the Fleet and which, persisted in, must have proved fatal. Though at first they shook, they helped in the end to restore confidence between ruler and ruled: to re-establish the conditions in which alone officers like Nelson could operate. They began a slow but steady improvement in seagoing conditions: a kind of practical English revolution based not on abstract theories but on concrete needs. Before the Spithead mutiny the men of the Royal Navy, though praised and fêted, were not treated as human beings but as automata: after it their right to decent living and feeding conditions and proper care in sickness, disablement and retirement became gradually recognised. It was something for Englishmen to have initiated such a revolution in time of war and national crisis, and to have done so without disaster.

CHAPTER 6

Touch and Take

"I will try to have a motto, or at least it shall be my watchword—Touch and take!"   *Nelson*

I

AFTER THE NAVAL MUTINIES and the withdrawal of Austria from the war, everyone expected that the hero of the hour, General Bonaparte, would attempt to invade a now isolated England or her restless subject island, Ireland. But, deterred by the destruction of the Dutch fleet that autumn at Camperdown by Admiral Duncan, the young conqueror of Italy declined to stake his career on the hazards of an encounter with British warships in the waters of the Channel or Atlantic merely to make the world—his oyster—safe for the plutocrats of the Directory. With her antiquated feudalism, corroding commercial habits and loosening colonial ties, Britain, he maintained, was doomed. Her trade with Europe had dried up with the collapse of her allies and their alignment with France. If her commerce with Asia could be cut also, her bankers and oligarchs would face ruin, and her starving people would rise in revolution and join the new order. Invasion would be unnecessary.

So Bonaparte assured his political masters. The way to injure England was by an expedition to the Levant and a threat to India where France could avenge herself for her lost colonies. "We shall change the fate of the world," he told Talleyrand. To the inner few to whom he confided his dreams, he announced that he was about to conquer an eastern empire surpassing the fables of antiquity. He would not only destroy England's hegemony in the Orient but found another, far vaster, in its place. In the East, he informed his brother Lucien, there were six hundred million men. Compared with Asia, Europe was "a mere mole-hill." He would not only become its dictator but its prophet. He would found a new religion.

The road to the East was open. By his Italian conquests he had driven the English battleships from the Mediterranean and secured a line of stepping-stones stretching along the Dalmatian and Ionian coasts towards Egypt. It would be child's play to seize that sandy, fabulous land in the name of its remote Turkish Sultan and "free" its effete people from the despotism of its Mameluke "aristocrats." It would merely be another repetition of the familiar Revolutionary technique of conquest.

In February 1798, therefore, Bonaparte requested the naval authorities at Toulon to hold up the warships ordered for Brest and assemble transports. Three weeks later he drew up detailed plans for an Egyptian expedition. Thereafter, as always when he directed, events moved swiftly. On April 12th engineers, openly wearing French uniforms, landed at Alexandria and began to prepare for the reception of military forces and collect information about the desert roads to Suez, the navigation of the Red Sea and British dispositions in the Indian Ocean. Already French agents were stirring up trouble in the great Indian state of Mysore, and its ruler, Tippo Sahib, had sent ambassadors to the Jacobin governor of Mauritius to invite a Franco-Arab army to India.

Rumours of these preparations, which had been secretly going forward ever since Bonaparte's recent overthrow of the Venetian Republic, had been slowly filtering through to England. In January Captain Sidney Smith had smuggled a message out of Paris, where he was imprisoned, reporting that France had designs on Egypt and the Levant. But in its preoccupation with invasion and Ireland, Pitt's Government paid little attention to such warnings. It had more urgent dangers to consider. With every available ship concentrated in the Channel and off the Irish coast and with Jervis—now raised to the peerage as Lord St.

Vincent—blockading a superior force in Cadiz, nothing could be spared for the Mediterranean. A Britain expecting invasion in Sussex could not police the Levant. Since the Mediterranean was now a French lake, information from that quarter was in any case notoriously unreliable and took weeks of perilous travel to reach England.

Yet, by a strange combination of coincidence and daring, in the crucial spring of 1798 the British Government weakened its naval defences at home and sent a fleet back into the Mediterranean. It did so without much thought of defeating Bonaparte's grandiose eastern designs, of which it was either ignorant or sceptical. Its object was rather to prompt the European Powers to revolt against the Jacobin yoke. For, knowing that his country could not contend for ever alone against the armed Revolution, Pitt was again endeavouring to build up a Coalition. It seemed the surest way of saving Britain.

Already there were signs that this was no empty hope. Prussia still refused to rouse herself from selfish sloth; Russia under her half-mad Emperor Paul remained a remote and inscrutable factor. But, jockeyed at the council table at Rastadt from her ancient leadership of Germany and insulted by upstart Jacobins, Austria was once more growing restive. In March Chancellor Thugut instructed his ambassador Starhemberg to ask if Britain would aid his country against "a fierce nation irrevocably determined on the total subversion of Europe." And he suggested the return of a British fleet to the Mediterranean.

At the beginning of April Pitt, therefore, raised the question in Cabinet. The first Lord, Lord Spencer, and the naval authorities were wholly unfavourable. With thirty Spanish battleships at Cadiz and thirty French ones at Brest, and with the seven Dutch survivors from Camperdown still at the Helder, Britain would need at least seventy capital ships to justify the risk of detaching even the smallest force to the south. At the moment, though several new ships were nearing completion, she could only dispose of fifty-eight, twenty-four off Cadiz and the remaining thirty-four in home and Irish waters. The dispatch of a battle squadron to the Mediterranean, the Junior Sea Lord reported, might be attended by dreadful consequences.

These professional counsels failed to dispirit Pitt. His instinct, which was in accord with that of his country, told him that the moment had come to change to the offensive and that the only real security lay in doing so. Something of his father's spirit and genius for war seemed to have entered into him that spring. He saw clearly that St. Vincent's position off Cadiz would soon be untenable unless the European situation was radically changed in England's favour. As always when his mind was resolved, he carried the Cabinet with him. The increased risk of invasion was not too high a price to pay to bring Austria and her satellite Naples back into the war.

Accordingly on May 2nd, 1798, Cabinet instructions were sent to St. Vincent to detach part of his fleet for a sweep in the Mediterranean. They were accompanied by a private letter from Spencer. "When you are apprised," he wrote, "that the appearance of a British squadron in the Mediterranean is a condition on which the fate of Europe may at this moment be said to depend, you will not be surprised that we are disposed to strain every nerve and incur considerable hazard in effecting it." And the First Lord went on to suggest that, in the event of St. Vincent not commanding it in person, it should be entrusted to the junior flag officer on the station, Sir Horatio Nelson.

By a strange coincidence, on the day that this letter was written Nelson had left St. Vincent's fleet for the Mediterranean. Only a month before he had sailed from England after a long and painful convalescence from an all-but fatal wound, got in a desperate attack on Teneriffe in the previous summer. Within three days of reaching the blockading fleet off Cadiz he had been ordered by St. Vincent to proceed with three battleships and five small craft to Toulon to report on the preparations and destination of a powerful French fleet. His mission was not to fight but to obtain information. For, despite French attempts at secrecy and Bonaparte's studied delay at Paris, news of immense concentrations in Provençal and Italian ports had reached St. Vincent. At Toulon and Marseilles, at Genoa, Civita Vecchia and in Corsica hundreds of transports were assembling, troops embarking, and battleships, frigates and corvettes moving into position for some great venture.

As early as April 24th, only twelve days after the Directors in Paris had signed the formal order for the Egyptian expedition, *The Times* printed circumstantial details of the force. Three days later the same paper reported its destination to be either Ireland or Portugal. But the possibility of Egypt does not appear to have been seriously canvassed in London. For the moment the obvious danger to the empire was not to its circumference but its heart. It never seems to have occurred to the Cabinet that France's impending blow could fall elsewhere. If the new armada in the south was not, like those at Brest, Cadiz and the Texel, intended for the British Isles, it must be bound for the Two Sicilies to forestall any new Coalition and so safeguard the French rear during the hazards of an invasion. By far its most likely destination was Ireland. This was the firm conviction both of the Irish Government and of Pitt. The dispatch of part of St. Vincent's fleet to the Mediterranean seemed an anticipation of an encounter which must otherwise be fought off the Irish coast.

For here in the island which she had conquered, misgoverned and never understood, proud England was faced that spring with disaster. Four million Catholic Irish were united in resolve to fling off the yoke of ten million English, Scots and Welsh, themselves engaged in a life and death struggle with more than forty million Frenchmen, Spaniards and Dutchmen. In the third week of May the long-expected rebellion broke out, and from Wexford to Enniscorthy the whole south-east of Ireland was in flames. On the 30th the Lord Lieutenant believed the situation to be beyond repair. Two days later the Government in London received intelligence that the French fleet had left Toulon, bound, it was believed, for Ireland.

Yet it was not for Ireland, where on Vinegar Hill 30,000

victorious rebels awaited their long-promised coming, that the French had sailed. Instead of seizing the greatest chance he was ever to know for striking England to the heart, Bonaparte was receding into the Orient for his own personal glory. A moral flaw in her rule of a subject people had placed England at her foe's mercy. A still greater flaw in her foe caused the chance to be neglected. Had the logic of Jacobin philosophy resulted in the rule of a selfless patriot like Carnot such a blunder could never have been made. But it had led inevitably—as Burke had foretold—to a dictatorship of a scoundrel like Barras and a military adventurer like Bonaparte. For their failings France had to pay dear.

· · · · · · · · ·

The opportunity which the Corsican missed now passed to another. In his public actions Nelson was swayed by only one thought—love of country. "In my mind's eye," he told Hardy, "I ever saw a radiant orb suspended which beckoned me onwards to renown." But by renown he meant not glory for its own sake but for the good of his country. For all the failings of an ardent nature he was essentially a moral man. Born in a Norfolk parsonage, he was a child of the Church of England. From the influence of its homely piety he had passed at the age of twelve to the rough life of the Navy. Its leading principle—that of unquestioning duty—had been transformed in the crucible of his imagination into a source of passionate inspiration.

Without influence he had risen by sheer merit to the rank of post-captain before he was twenty-one. He impressed everyone with whom he came into contact professionally with the sense that he was no common being. But his greatest success was with those under his command. He was a man who led by love and example. There was nothing he would not do for those who served under him. There was nothing they would not dare for Nelson.

The exigencies of peace after the American war and what seemed to his superiors in that mediocre time the inconvenient excess of his zeal for the Service had deprived him in 1787 of employment. For five years he led the life of a poor half-pay officer, eating out his heart ashore, farming his father's glebe and fretting under the tedium of a respectable but ill-assorted marriage. They were years in which his career seemed finished and in which he and his friend Collingwood in like retirement told each other that they despaired of chance ever drawing them back to the seashore.

The outbreak of war found Nelson bombarding the Admiralty with requests for a ship, though it were only a cockle boat. They gave him a sixty-four, and since then—save for a winter's sick leave after the loss of his arm—he had been on continuous service in the Mediterranean, cheerfully fulfilling every mission entrusted to him and, by his anxiety to excel in the execution of duty, winning a reputation for almost foolhardy gallantry. For four years he had toiled and waited for his hour until the discernment of Jervis and the chance of battle at St. Vincent brought him on to a wider stage. Then in his first independent command as a flag officer he had tasted defeat—albeit glorious defeat—at Teneriffe. He had returned to England physically shattered, with the hope of ever serving again almost vanished.

Now, nearing his fortieth year, he was again in command, with his reputation a little uncertain as of a man too reckless for his age. His countrymen, slow to recognise intellect, knew his courage and ardour but had little conception of the quality of his mind. They had yet to realise its infinite capacity for taking pains, its knife-like penetration, its brilliant clarity. Its very lucidity, reducing every scheme and command to elemental terms such as a child could understand, tended to deceive them. They thought of him as a simple sailorman. They never conceived of him, till his miraculous deeds enlightened them, as the supreme embodiment of the genius of their country.

After many years of apprenticeship, he was now to be pitted against the most dazzling genius of his age—himself the embodiment of that great and terrifying explosion of human energy which patient England was struggling to hold in bounds. Nelson's success or failure was to depend on his ability to guess and anticipate the thought of his adversary. To that test he brought qualities of an almost unique order: immense professional knowledge and experience, the fruits of life-long application and discipline, selfless devotion to duty, inspired courage, a great heart and the imagination which can mobilise the evidence of the present and past to predict the future. His was that strange combination of brooding patience, study and intense concentration with a mercurial temperament that rose like lightning out of storm and, in the hour chosen of destiny, lighted the path to victory. Once he was convinced that a course was right, nothing could shake his constancy to it and the burning tenacity of his purpose.

. . . .

On the 8th of May, 1798, Nelson left Gibraltar with three ships of the line and five frigates, sailing at dusk to conceal his eastward course from watching eyes. Nine days later, cruising in the Gulf of Lyons, one of his frigates captured a French corvette from Toulon whose crew under examination disclosed that the famous General Bonaparte had arrived in the port from Paris, that thousands of troops were embarking and that fifteen battleships of the line were waiting to sail.

Had it not been for the usual confusion and corruption of the Revolutionary ports they would have sailed already. Nearly 40,000 picked troops, more than three hundred transports and fifty warships had been assembled. This huge armada was laden not only with horse, foot, artillery and stores of war but with engineers, architects and professors of every science and art, "from astronomers down to washerwomen." It was equipped for colonisation as well as for conquest. It was commanded by a brilliant galaxy of talent, for under Bonaparte's triumphant banner sailed Kléber, Desaix, Davout, Lannes, Murat, Bessières, Marmont and Junot, while Brueys, with Ganteaume, Decrès and Villeneuve, directed the fleet.

On the 19th, the main division of the expedition with Bonaparte aboard weighed from Toulon, coasting north-eastwards along the Riviera shore in the direction of Genoa to gather its consorts. Nelson did not see it sail for he was still some way from the port. On the following night his flagship, the *Vanguard*, suffered disaster, her newly commissioned crew losing main and mizen topmasts and foremast in a sudden gale. For two days she was battered by the waves off the Sardinian coast and was only saved from total wreck by the cool daring of Captain Ball of the *Alexander*, who took her in tow and persisted in spite of intense danger to his own ship in bringing her under the lee of San Pietro Island.

Here on May 24th, while British soldiers and Irish patriots were fighting in the village streets of Meath and Kildare, Nelson wrote to his wife to tell her of his setback. "I firmly believe that it was the Almighty's goodness to check my consummate vanity." In four days of herculean labour the *Vanguard* was rigged with jury-masts and made fit for sea. Then with his three battleships Nelson sailed for the secret rendezvous where his frigates, scattered by the storm, were to have awaited him. But when he reached it on June 4th the frigates were not there. Next day, still waiting, he received momentous tidings. For Hardy in the dispatch brig *Mutine* arriving from Cadiz brought news not only of the errant frigates which, despairing of the *Vanguard's* plight, had gone to Gibraltar, but of Nelson's appointment to the command of a fleet. The opportunity for which he had waited so long had arrived.

It had come at a strange moment. Bonaparte had sailed a fortnight before and had gone no one knew where. A few days after Nelson had left Cadiz St. Vincent had received Spencer's instructions about sending a fleet into the Mediterranean. Though the Spaniards, under orders from Paris, made as if about to put out of Cadiz, and though a concerted movement of United Irishmen threatened a new outbreak of mutiny in the fleet, the old admiral never hesitated. On May 19th he dispatched Hardy with Nelson's commission. On the 21st, without even waiting for the arrival of the promised reinforcements from England, he sent his ten finest battleships and captains—the élite of the fleet—under Troubridge to join Nelson.

On June 6th Troubridge found his new commander. It was characteristic of Nelson that he refused to transfer his flag from the storm-battered *Vanguard*. His other two battleships were beyond the horizon searching for the newcomers. He did not wait for them but left the fifty-gun *Leander* to bid them follow. His orders were couched in the broadest terms. He was to pursue the Toulon fleet and attack it wherever found. Since Britain had no base in the Mediterranean and necessity dictated, he was not to stand on ceremony with neutrals. Should they out of terror of the French refuse to grant him supplies he was to compel them at the cannon's mouth.

His instructions gave him little clue as to Bonaparte's destination. They mentioned Naples, Sicily, Portugal and Ireland, but made no reference to Egypt. He had no reliable information as to the strength of the French battle fleet though he believed it to consist of fifteen or sixteen ships of the line. He knew even less of its whereabouts. Having no frigates he could not comb the seas for intelligence. He had only the light of his intellect to follow and the strength of his will. "Be they bound to the Antipodes," he assured Spencer, "your Lordship may rely that I will not lose a moment in bringing them to action."

Following the course of the French he skirted the Genoese Riviera and Italian coast. The seas were strangely empty, for the French control of the Mediterranean had banished most of its former commerce. Day after day no sail appeared on the blue horizon. Once a convoy of distant Spanish merchantmen was sighted—plunder that might have made his captains rich with prize money and bought him some fine estate in England with white Jane Austen house and trim lawns and deer park. But his mind was set on his purpose and he let them pass unmolested. He dared not lose an hour.

On June 14th, while far away the fate of Ireland trembled in the balance and the rebel leaders in the green-bannered camp on Vinegar Hill waited for the tidings of French sails, Nelson obtained second-hand news from a passing ship that ten days earlier a great fleet had been seen to the west of Sicily. He accordingly sent the *Mutine* ahead to Naples with a letter begging Sir William Hamilton, the British ambassador, to urge the king and his English-born Prime Minister, Acton, to shake off their subservience to the dreaded Jacobins and strike while the iron was hot. On the 17th he arrived off the port to learn what he had already suspected: that the French had gone to Malta and were either about to attack or had already attacked that island strong-hold.

In a fever of excitement he wrote again to Hamilton. The Neapolitan king, who hated the French, whose sister-in-law had died on the scaffold in Paris and who had secretly implored British aid, had a unique opportunity to strike a blow which should save his throne, liberate Italy and shatter the dark clouds that hung over Europe. The most formidable of French generals and the flower of the French army were at his mercy. For though Nelson had with him a matchless instrument, it could only do the work of a battle fleet. To destroy the enemy, if at Malta, he needed fireships, gunboats and bomb vessels; to annihilate their transports, if at sea, he must have frigates. The Court of the Two Sicilies, if it would take its courage in its hands, could supply both.

But though the timorous Italians sent good wishes and a secret promise of supplies, they would dare no more. Nelson must beat the French before they would stir, even though their inertness robbed him of all chance of victory and themselves of survival. Without wasting time, though still bombarding Hamilton with letters, he pressed through the Straits of Messina and, crowding on all sail, hurried down the coast of Sicily, heading for Malta where he hoped to catch the enemy at anchor. On the 22nd at the southern point of Sicily off Cape Passaro the *Mutine* fell in with a Genoese brig and learnt from her master that the French had captured Malta from the Knights of St. John—which was true—and—which was not true—had sailed again on the 16th eastward bound.

With the instinct of genius, though his instructions had given him no inkling of it, Nelson had already divined Bonaparte's intention. A few days earlier he had written to Spencer, "If they pass Sicily, I shall believe they are going on their scheme of possessing Alexandria and getting troops to India—a plan, concerted with Tippoo Sahib, by no means so difficult as might at first view be imagined." His instructions had cautioned him against allowing the French to get to the west of him lest they should slip through the Straits of Gibraltar. But he reckoned that with the prevailing westerly winds Bonaparte's vast and unwieldy armada had little chance of beating back to the Atlantic. Egypt on the other hand would be an easy run for it. If it left Malta on the 16th, it must already be nearly at Alexandria.

Nelson therefore decided to act. He called a council of his captains, but its result was a foregone conclusion. Men like himself in the prime of life—their average age was under forty—they were little given to hesitation. They endorsed his opinion that all the probabilities—the seizure of Malta, the reported equipment of the expedition, the direction of the wind and the enemy's point of sailing—pointed to Bonaparte's having gone to Egypt. The safe course was for the British to await events where they were: guarding the Two Sicilies, keeping the weather gauge and making sure that the enemy could not get to westward. A lesser man than Nelson, playing for his professional career and safety from official censure, would have taken it. But to have done so would have been to abandon that for which he had set out: the annihilation of the French fleet and transports. With the stake nothing less than the future of the world, he at once set course for Alexandria.

· · · · · · · ·

But the French had not sailed from Malta on the 16th. They had appeared off the island on June 9th and summoned its international custodians, the Knights of St. John, to surrender. The scene had been carefully set: the Maltese had no stomach for their rich and obese masters' cause, the island was swarming with French agents and traitors, and the Knights, comfortably set in their ways and undermined by subtle propaganda, were divided as to the advisability of resistance. After three days' discussion they surrendered, and Bonaparte, whose besieging armada would otherwise have fallen an easy prey for Nelson on the 22nd, took possession of Valetta—"the strongest place in Europe." Here he remained for nearly a week, helping himself to the accumulations of seven centuries of luxurious and cultured living. Then, leaving a strong garrison behind him to hold the strategic half-way house to France, he sailed on the 19th for Alexandria after making arrangements to dispose of the booty.

So it came about that Nelson's look-outs on June 22nd saw the sails of French frigates on the far horizon. But Nelson did not stop to investigate them for he guessed that they could not belong to Bonaparte's main fleet which, according to his own information, had left Malta six days before. Had he possessed any frigates of his own, he would soon have discovered his error. He refused, therefore, to be deflected from his quarry and kept on his course. Shortly afterwards darkness fell, and during the night, which was hazy, the British line of battle, swift, compact and intent, passed unknowing through the converging track of the French expedition. The sound of the British minute guns firing through the mist caused the French admiral to sheer away to the northward in the direction of Crete. Had dawn come half an hour earlier it would have revealed him and his helpless transports. But by sunrise on the 23rd the last French sails were just below the horizon.

That was one of the decisive moments of history. A long train of events had brought the two fleets to that place at that hour, of which the most important were Bonaparte's dynamic ambition and Nelson's zeal for duty. Had they clashed the result would have been certain: the élite and cadre of the Grande Armée would have found a watery grave seventeen years before Waterloo and its terrible chieftain would either have shared it or become a prisoner of the English. For superior though they were on paper—in size and gun power though not in numbers—the French battleships would have been no match on the open sea for the British. Old and shamefully neglected during their long-enforced sojourn in port, destitute of marine stores and crowded with useless soldiers, they could never have withstood those lean, stripped, storm-tested dogs of war from St. Vincent's fleet. Their crews, drawn from the lawless dregs of the Revolutionary ports, had had little training in gunnery or manœuvre. Nelson's knew exactly what to do. Thanks to the Cabinet's bold resolution, to St. Vincent's discipline and self-abnegation, above all to Nelson's inspired fixity of purpose, the blundering, persistent patience of Pitt's England seemed on the afternoon of June 22nd, 1798, about to be rewarded. Bonaparte, epitomising the Revolutionary weakness for desperate gambling, had staked everything on Britain's not being able to send a fleet to the Mediterranean. And now at the moment that he was reaching out to grasp the prize of the Orient, a British fleet crossed his path. . . .

Crossed it and vanished. The Corsican's star had proved too strong and bright for the clumsy purpose of England. But Bonaparte's good fortune did not only lie in his star. With all his genius, he could not understand why his admirals trembled so at the thought of encountering a British fleet in mid-ocean. He had 40,000 soldiers with him: he had only to close and let them board the English corsairs. With England's many dangers nearer home there could not be many of them. He had never seen the destructive power of a British man-of-war in action: could not, battle-scarred though he was, conceive it. Not destiny—which had still to obliterate his bright name—but an error of Britain had saved him. Lack of frigates alone robbed Nelson of a victory that should have been Trafalgar and Waterloo in one. Again and again St. Vincent had pleaded with the Admiralty for more frigates: pleaded in vain. He had had to send his brilliant subordinate into the Mediterranean with too few, and these—now vainly seeking him—had failed him. Treasury parsimony, the unpreparedness of a peace-loving people, above all the needs of restless, ill-treated Ireland had all contributed to this fatal flaw. It was to cost Britain and the civilised world seventeen more years of war, waste and destruction.

. . . .

So it came about that on the 23rd the two fleets, having converged, passed out of reach of one another, Brueys with his momentous freight edging cumbrously northwards towards the greater security of Crete, Nelson with every inch of canvas spread direct for Alexandria hoping to catch Bonaparte before he could disembark. "We are proceeding," wrote Captain Saumarez of the *Orion*, "upon the merest conjecture only, and not on any positive information. Some days must now elapse before we can be relieved from our cruel suspense." On the sixth day Nelson reached Alexandria and to his unspeakable chagrin found the roads empty. No one had seen anything of Bonaparte's armada, though the sleepy Turkish authorities were making languid preparations to repel it and threatening to decapitate any belligerent who dared to land in their country. Still believing in his false information that the French had left Malta on the 16th, it never occurred to Nelson that they had not yet covered the distance. Without waiting he at once put to sea again, steering for the Syrian coast in hope of news of a landing at Aleppo or an attack on the Dardanelles.

As early on June 29th the British sails dropped over the eastern horizon, watchers at Alexandria saw the French rise over the western. Hampered by its lack of skill, vast size and triangular course, Bonaparte's expedition, averaging only fifty miles a day, had taken just double the time of its pursuer. Once more, cruelly crippled by his lack of frigates, Nelson had missed an epoch-making victory by a few hours. With nearly four hundred vessels the French had crosssed the Mediterranean and had not lost a ship. With the superb arrogance of their race and revolutionary creed they boasted that the British had not dared to measure their strength against them. But, though he had still no idea how narrow had been his escape, Bonaparte wasted no time before disembarking. On the 1st of July he landed and issued a grandiloquent proclamation in the style of Mahomet calling on the Faithful to rise against the Mamelukes. On the 5th he stormed Alexandria, putting all who resisted to the sword. A fortnight later, advancing at his habitual speed across the desert, he routed the main Egyptian army under the shadow of the Pyramids. On the 22nd he entered Cairo. Another nation had been overwhelmed.

Meanwhile Nelson, fretting with impatience and full of remorse for the kingdom of the Two Sicilies, had sought in vain for his elusive quarry in the Gulf of Alexandretta. Thence, skirting the shores of Crete, he beat back against westerly winds to Syracuse. Years later he told Troubridge that in his mortification he believed he had almost died through swelling of the vessels of the heart. To St. Vincent, to whom he wrote to ease his mind, he declared that the only valid objection he could conceive against the course he had taken was that he should not have gone such a long voyage without more certain information. "My answer is ready—'Who was I to get it from? . . . Was I to wait patiently till I heard certain accounts? If Egypt was their object, before I could hear of them they would have been in India. To do nothing, I felt, was disgraceful: therefore I made use of my understanding and by it I ought to stand or fall. I am before your Lordship's judgment (which in the present case I feel is the tribunal of my country) and if under all the circumstances it is decided that I am wrong, I ought, for the sake of the country, to be superseded."

Already in England men who knew nothing of the circumstances were saying that he should be. The news of his appointment had been greeted with a clamour of tongues: Collingwood wrote from Cadiz that the resignation of two senior admirals, furious at being passed over, had interrupted all intercourse of friendship in St. Vincent's fleet, which was in consequence in a most unpleasant state. Their friends and many others naturally said that Nelson had blundered. A man not yet forty was not fit to command a fleet on so important a service. Tempers were short in England in the summer of 1798: the long suspense of the spring and the reaction when no invasion came were beginning to fray men's nerves. The Irish rebellion, suppressed after four anxious weeks by General Lake's victory at Vinegar Hill, was still simmering. It was known that Bonaparte was at large and that Nelson had failed to find him. He might by now be in Naples or he might be sailing towards Ireland. All that was certain was that Nelson had missed him, had bungled his mission. There were demands for his recall and for the resignation of the ministers who had appointed him.

On July 19th, with his water nearly exhausted, Nelson reached Syracuse, having in his own words gone a round of six hundred leagues with an expedition incredible and being at the end of it as ignorant of the enemy's situation as at the beginning. "The Devil's children," he wrote, "have the Devil's luck!" His only thought was to be off again. He suffered agonies when the governor of the port, standing on his neutrality, refused to admit more than four ships at a time for revictualling. "Our treatment is scandalous for a great nation to put up with," he wrote to Lady Hamilton, "and the King's flag is insulted. . . . If we are to be kicked in every port of the Sicilian dominions, the sooner we are gone the better. . . . I have only to pray I may find the French and throw all my vengeance on them."

But when the tactful offices of the Hamiltons at the Neapolitan Court had secured an open welcome and ample supplies for the fleet, the essential magnanimity of the man returned. He reproached nobody but himself. "Your Lordship," he wrote to St. Vincent, "deprived yourself of frigates to make mine the first squadron in the world. . . . But if they are above water, I will find them out and if possible bring them to battle. You have done your part in giving me so fine a fleet, and I hope to do mine in making use of them."

On the 25th he was ready for sea. Disregarding the protests of the Neapolitan Prime Minister, who wished him to stand a passive sentinel over the Two Sicilies, he sailed again, this time

—since all intelligence showed that the French were not to the west of him—towards the Morea. With all canvas spread the great ships sped on their search—*Culloden*, *Theseus*, *Alexander* and *Swiftsure; Vanguard, Minotaur, Defence, Audacious, Zealous; Orion, Goliath, Majestic, Bellerophon.* The sea was empty, for their journeying had filled the French authorities in every port of southern Europe with dread. They sailed in order of battle, in three compact divisions in case the French should be encountered at sea: two to tackle Brueys's battle fleet and the other to do the work of the missing frigates and destroy the transports.

Every day throughout the long chase the men were exercised at their guns and small arms. Whenever the weather permitted the captains went aboard the *Vanguard* to discuss with the admiral the precise function which each was to fulfil in battle. In the "school for captains" on Nelson's quarter-deck they unconsciously entered into his mind till each of his ideas—lucid, precise and devised against every eventuality—became as natural to them as to him. Long linked by the comradeship of sea and Service, these rough, weather-beaten men, with their wonderful professional skill, were distilled into a single instinctive instrument of war in the alembic of Nelson's mind and spirit. They became what in his love he called them—a band of brothers.

The keynote of the fleet's readiness for battle was a minute, imaginative attention to detail: the sure hall-mark of a great leader. "No man," Mahan has written, "was ever better served than Nelson by the inspiration of the hour; no man ever counted less on it." Every ship was ready day and night for action: every man schooled in an exact part. Five thousand wills and bodies moved to a single purpose infinitely diversified in individual function. It was a living discipline that wasted nothing, of muscle, mind or matter. Everything was prepared because everything was foreseen. Thus in the *Alexander* Captain Ball had every spare shroud and sail constantly soaked in water and rolled tight into hard non-inflammable cylinders.

On the 28th, three days after leaving Syracuse, Nelson obtained news of the French from some Greek fishermen in the Gulf of

Koron. A month before a great fleet had been seen spread far over the seas, sailing south-eastwards from Crete. With the wind in the west for the past month it was evidence enough. Bonaparte must have gone to Egypt after all. Once more all sail was set for Alexandria.

A little before noon on August 1st, 1798, the Pharos of Alexandria became visible and soon after the minarets of the city and the masts of merchantmen in the port. But of the French fleet there was no sign. Sending the *Swiftsure* and *Alexander* in to investigate more closely, Nelson sadly turned eastwards along the coast as he had done a month before. Dinner was a meal of gloom on every ship: "I do not recollect," wrote Captain Saumarez of the *Orion*, "ever to have felt so utterly hopeless as when we sat down. Judge what a change took place when, as the cloth was being removed, the officer of the watch came running in saying, 'Sir, a signal is just now made that the enemy is in Aboukir Bay and moored in a line of battle.'" In an instant everyone was on his feet and every glass charged. As Saumarez came out of his cabin on to the quarterdeck, the crew broke into exultant cheers.

At the masthead of the *Goliath*, which was leading the fleet with the *Zealous*, the straining eyes of Midshipman Elliot, scanning the low Egyptian shore in the hot haze, had caught the first sight of those heavenly masts. Fearing to hail the quarterdeck lest keen ears in *Zealous* should hear and gain the credit, the exultant boy slid quickly down a backstay and ran to Captain Foley with his tidings. But before the fluttering signal, "Enemy in sight," could reach the masthead, *Zealous* had guessed the meaning of the scurry and cluster of flags on the deck of her sister ship and had been before her. As the signal reached each crowded ship, a "wave of joy" ran through the fleet. Nelson, whose inflexible will had equalled Bonaparte's, had run his quarry to earth at last. "If we succeed," cried Captain Berry voicing his unspoken thought, "what will the world say?" "There is no *if* in the case," replied Nelson, "that we shall succeed is certain; who will live to tell the story is a very different question."

Fifteen miles east of Alexandria the French battle fleet lay at anchor in a great bay guarded by shoals to eastward and by the batteries of Aboukir Castle at its western end. There were sixteen ships in all, thirteen of the line with the *Orient*, Brueys's giant flagship, in the centre of the line. They lay as close inshore as the sandbanks allowed, forming for nearly two miles a line of thousands of guns with 160 yards between each ship. At the head of the line, guarding it from approach from the west, lay Aboukir island crowned with mortars.

At half-past two, about the same time as the English sighted their prey, the French look-outs saw the English sails. As his van was so strongly protected and as to attack his centre or rear his assailants would have to face the concentrated fire of his whole line Brueys felt convinced that there would be no battle that day. It was to his advantage that it should be postponed. His ships were bigger than the British and more heavily gunned, but many of his men were ashore, discipline was lax and the decks were cumbered with stores and booty. Only the most reckless of foes would be likely to attack him in so strong a position with equal or inferior force. By the time they could reach the bay and negotiate the sand-banks it would be almost dark. It would be insanity for them to attack at night. Like most ordinary commanders, Brueys was a static man and he imagined that he had to do with static men like himself.

But the British squadron never paused. It came on out of the west with all sails set. For Nelson at his journey's end was as eager to do that for which he had come as Bonaparte had been to land and take possession of Egypt. His sufferings and anxiety were over at last. He viewed the obstacles, his flag-captain noted, with the eye of a seaman determined on attack. He saw the strength of the French centre, where Brueys had concentrated his greatest ships, and of its rear where the next strongest were gathered. But he also saw the weakness of the van if he could bring his fleet round inside the island and pass between it and the leading ships. And though he had no chart of the shoals except a rough plan taken from a prize, "it instantly struck his eager and penetrating mind that where there was room for an enemy's ship to swing, there was room for one of his to anchor."[1]

It had always been Nelson's plan, discussed on innumerable occasions with his captains, should he find the enemy at anchor to throw the whole weight of his strength on a part of their line and crush it before the rest could come to their aid. Only by doing so could he win the annihilating victory which it was his purpose to achieve: the ding-dong battles of the past two centuries, in which every Englishman laid himself alongside a Frenchman and battered away till one side tired and drew off, could not give it him. There was only just time to work round the island and the shoals before night fell: three of his thirteen capital ships—the *Swiftsure* and *Alexander* reconnoitring Alexandria and the *Culloden* towing a prize—were some miles away and could not reach the scene of battle before darkness. There was no opportunity for consultation or elaborate signals, but there was no need for them. Every captain knew what was in his admiral's mind. At five-thirty he flew the signal to form line of battle in order of sailing, and silently and imperceptibly without slackening their majestic advance the great ships slid into their appointed places. The *Goliath*, whose look-out midshipman had revenged himself on his rival in the *Zealous* by anticipating Nelson's signal while it was still fluttering to the masthead, took the lead. The flagship dropped back to the sixth place where the admiral could exercise tactical control of the battle, seeing how his leading ships fared and using his position to vary the disposition of the remaining five.

In the hour of suspense Nelson gave two other orders. In order to guide the latecomers and avoid the danger of Briton firing on Briton, every ship was directed to hoist four lights at the mizen peak. And on reaching her allotted station she was to anchor by the stern instead of by the head and so place herself in immediate fighting posture. By this simple precaution the enemy was denied the opportunity of raking each British ship as her bows swung round into the wind.

[1] Capt. Berry's account.

Having rounded the island and "hauled well round all dangers," the ships, avoiding the direct approach, shortened sail and hugging the coast worked their way to windward of the van— the weakest, because in his belief the securest, part of Brueys's position. The sun was just setting—"and a red and fiery sun it was"—as they went into the bay. Down below the men were stripping to their trousers, opening the ports and clearing for action: an officer commanding at the guns jotted down the following conversation:

Jack: "There are thirteen sail of the line and a whacking lot of frigates and small craft. I think we'll hammer the rust off ten of them, if not the whole boiling."

Tom: "We took but four on the first of June, and I got seven pounds of prize-money. Now, if we knock up a dozen of these fellows (and why shouldn't we?) damn my eyes, messmates, we will have a bread-bag full of money to receive."

Jack: "Aye, I'm glad we have twigged 'em at last. I want some new rigging damnably for Sundays and mustering days."

Tom: "So do I. I hope we'll touch enough for that, and a damned good cruise among the girls besides."

It had been Nelson's plan to anchor one of his ships alternately on the bow and quarter of each of the leading Frenchmen. But whether by an eleventh-hour suggestion of the admiral or by his own inspiration Captain Foley of the *Goliath*, who was the only officer in the fleet with a French chart, rounded the head of the enemy lines and, sounding as he went through the shallow waters, attacked it from the shoreward side. It was a feat of superb seamanship. Relying on the proximity of the sandbanks the French had never conceived such a thing possible and, feeling themselves safe, had not even taken the trouble to clear the port batteries, which were carelessly cluttered up with stores. *Zealous*, *Orion*, *Theseus* and *Audacious* followed *Goliath*. As each leviathan swept past the undefended flank of the leading French ships she swept them in turn with a fire that left them helpless and broken.

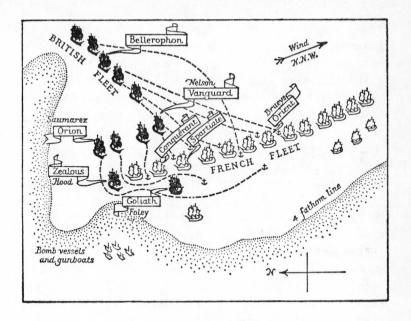

The Battle of the Nile

Within ten minutes all the *Guerrier*'s masts were gone, and within ten minutes more the *Conquerant*'s and *Spartiate*'s.

Meanwhile Nelson led the *Vanguard* and the remaining ships against the other side of the French line. By seven o'clock, within half an hour of the commencement of the action, the five leading seventy-fours were being raked by eight English ships of similar size and greatly superior to them in gunnery while their consorts to leeward watched helpless and inactive. The British ships, the *Majestic* and *Bellerophon*, over-shooting their mark in the growing darkness, engaged the French centre, the first losing her captain in a swift interchange of broadsides with the *Heureuse* and then passing on to engage the *Mercure*, while the second audaciously placed herself alongside Brueys's flagship, *Orient*—a vessel of nearly twice her size.

Wrought to the highest tension by their long, tenacious pursuit, the British fought, as Berry put it, with an ardour and vigour impossible to describe. The French also fought with great gallantry. Captain Dupetit Thouars of the *Tonnant*, after losing both arms and a leg, had his dying trunk placed in a tub on the quarterdeck where he refused to strike his colours though every mast was gone and every gun disabled. But the British were fighting with the certain conviction of victory and, every man knowing what to do in all emergencies, with an order and freedom from confusion absent in the Republican ships. Early in the engagement, when the issue was already a foregone conclusion, Nelson was struck on the forehead by a piece of flying iron from the *Spartiate*'s langridge. Flung to the deck and blinded by the strip of bleeding flesh that fell over his solitary eye, he was carried below thinking himself a dying man. Here in the crowded cockpit he lay in intense pain, insisting on taking his turn at the surgeon with the other wounded men and constantly calling with what he believed to be his dying breath for news of the battle. Once he bade Berry hail the *Minotaur*, anchored ahead of the *Vanguard*, that he might thank Captain Louis for his conduct before he died. Already three enemy ships had struck and three more were disabled, and with his brain wandering a little he endeavoured to dictate a dispatch to the Admiralty. His secretary was too overwrought to write, so the blinded man took the pen himself and with trembling hand traced the words: "Almighty God has blessed His Majesty's arms . . ."

By now the British reserve was entering the fight. The *Culloden*, the finest ship in the fleet, had met with disaster, her brave Captain Troubridge, in his anxiety to arrive in time, having taken the island too close and stuck on the tail of the shoal. Here he remained all night in full view of the battle and in a state of agitation impossible to conceive, suffering the pounding of the sea and struggling to clear his vessel. But he served as a beacon for the *Swiftsure* and *Alexander* hurrying up from the west. The two great ships, furiously fired at by the battery on the island, rounded the reef safely in the haze and darkness and swept down on the centre of the French line, guided by the flashes of the guns and the lanterns gleaming through the British gun ports. In both vessels absolute silence was preserved, no sound being heard but the helmsman's orders and the shout of the leadsman calling the depths.

At one moment a dark shape loomed up in front of the *Swiftsure*. It was the *Bellerophon*, dismasted after her duel with the *Orient*, drifting out of the fight with a third of her crew dead or disabled. Only Captain Hallowell's flawless discipline prevented her from being swept by the *Swiftsure*'s guns before her identity was revealed. But, despite the suspense and the spasmodic fire of the French, not a shot was fired. At 8.3 p.m. precisely the *Swiftsure* dropped into the *Bellerophon*'s vacant berth two hundred yards from the French flagship. At 8.5, anchored and with her sails clewed up, she opened out with a tremendous broadside. A few minutes later Captain Ball in the *Alexander* followed suit.

It was about nine o'clock that Hallowell, still fresh to the fight, noticed flames pouring out of one of the cabins of the *Orient*. He at once directed every available gun on the spot. The fire spread quickly owing to the way that oil, paint and other combustibles had been left about the French flagship. As the great vessel, the finest in the Republican navy, blazed more fiercely, every British ship in the neighbourhood trained her guns on her. Down in the hold of the British flagship Nelson heard of the impending fatality and insisted on being led up on deck to watch: as soon as he saw her imminence of doom he ordered the *Vanguard*'s only undamaged boat to be lowered to rescue the survivors. With the fire racing downwards towards the *Orient*'s magazine, the ships about her closed their hatches or drifted away to avoid the explosion. Only *Swiftsure* and *Alexander* remained firing grimly up to the last moment, with long lines of men with buckets stationed to extinguish the outburst when it came.

At a quarter to ten the *Orient* blew up with a terrifying detonation. The shock could be felt by French watchers at Rosetta ten miles away, and down in the magazine of the

Goliath the boys and women at their blind, monotonous task of passing up the powder thought that the after-part of their own vessel had exploded. The whole bay was lit as brightly as day by the expiring flame of the great ship as she rose into the air. After she vanished silence fell on the combatants: then after some minutes the guns opened out again. As they did so the moon rose dazzling in her Egyptian beauty over the wreckage and slaughter.

Yet though the night was still young the battle was losing momentum. With the great admiral who had conceived it dazed and disabled by his wound, the soul was gone out of it. Five of the French ships had already struck: another, the 80-gun *Franklin*, was failing fast. But the victors after sailing and fighting all day were exhausted. They would fire for a time and then desist: all night the battle flared up and then died away. "My people was so extremely jaded," reported Captain Miller of the *Theseus*, "that as soon as they had hove our sheet anchor up they dropped under the capstan bars and were asleep in a moment in every sort of posture." After the surrender of the *Franklin* the second lieutenant of *Alexander* approached Ball to tell him that, though the hearts of his men were as good as ever, they could do no more and begged him to let them sleep for half an hour by their guns. Nelson's slightly disjointed messages speeding through the night were received rather than obeyed: in that confused interminable nightmare of weariness nothing was ever quite carried through to an end.

As it began to grow light the magnitude of the victory became apparent. At 5.27 a.m. Captain Hallowell noted that six enemy battleships had struck their colours; on board his own ship "carpenters were busy stopping the shot holes, . . . people employed knotting and splicing the rigging." At six he heard the minute guns of the *Majestic* firing as she buried her captain. The whole bay was floating with charred wreckage and dead bodies, mangled and scorched. By this time it was light enough to see that three other battleships were at the victors' mercy, dismasted hulks aground or drifting. Only Villeneuve's three spectators in the rear remained uninjured. Presently these slipped their anchors and began to bear out to sea. But one of them, the *Timoleon*, in her haste to be gone ran on to the sandbanks. Her crew swam ashore and made off inland, a cloud of smoke revealing that her captain had fired her. Alone of the thirteen French ships the *Guillaume Tell* and the *Généreux* with two frigates, escaped into the blue of the Mediterranean. For a while *Theseus*, the only British ship sufficiently undamaged to carry sail, pursued them till a signal from the admiral recalled her.

In the first aftermath of battle Nelson and his men could scarcely conceive the fullness of what they had done. All day on August 2nd they were engaged in fishing naked prisoners from rafts and floating wreckage—sullen, downcast fellows, very different from the merry Frenchmen some of the older sailors remembered capturing in the American war before the Tricolour had supplanted the Lilies. More than two thousand unwounded prisoners were taken and nearly fifteen hundred wounded: that night Nelson dined half a dozen wounded French captains in his cabin. Brueys, the first admiral in France, had been cut in half by a British cannon ball before the *Orient* blew up. Two thousand more of his men had been killed or drowned, nine of his thirteen battleships captured, two more destroyed. Nothing like it had been known since the day when the Duke of Marlborough had entertained a French marshal and two generals in his coach after Blenheim.

For it was not so much defeat that the French had suffered as annihilation. Though superior to their assailants by thirty per cent. in men and twenty per cent. in weight of broadside, and fighting in a chosen position in a dangerous bay with the head of their line protected by shore batteries, they had been overwhelmed by the skill and ferocity of the attack. In a few hours they had literally been blown out of the water. And the price paid by the victors had been scarcely 200 men killed and 700 wounded. It was an astonishing testimony to the intensity and accuracy of British gunfire, to Nelson's leadership and to the new school of close fighting he had initiated. Above all, it revealed, in the hands of an inspired commander, the quality of British discipline. In his general order thanking his men Nelson, recalling the mutinies of the previous summer, emphasised this point. "It must strike forcibly every British seaman how superior their conduct is, when in discipline and good order, to the riotous behaviour of lawless Frenchmen." Nothing so deeply impressed the same lawless Frenchmen, many of them professed atheists, as the religious service which was held on the morrow of the battle on the splintered, bloodstained decks of the British flagship. It struck them as an extraordinary thing that six hundred men—the roughest of the rough—could be assembled for such a purpose amid the scene of so much carnage and profess their mild faith with such order and quietness.

The battle was evidence also of the inadequacy of Revolutionary France's administration and the selfishness of her general. Because of the corruption prevailing everywhere after nine years of social scramble, her great ships—triumphs of the marine builder's art—were neglected and rotten, short of essential stores, and their crews ill-fed and discontented at the long arrears in their pay. These handicaps to French courage and *élan* had been increased by Bonaparte's theft of skilled gunners and seamen for his land operations and by his utter disregard of the needs of the fleet since his landing. Only a week before the battle Brueys had urged that its security depended on an immediate return to Toulon to refit. This, though he afterwards endeavoured to conceal the fact, Bonaparte had forbidden. Wishing to retain the fleet for his private purposes, he ignored expert advice and jeopardised the existence of the force on which French mastery of the Mediterranean depended. For so long as the Republican battle fleet was in being, the incursion of the British into that, to them baseless, sea could be only temporary and precarious.

With its destruction the whole position had changed in a night. On August 1st the French, as masters of Egypt, Corfu and Malta and—save for Naples—of the entire southern shore of Europe from Cadiz to the Turkish frontier, held the Mediter-

ranean in their grip. By the morning of the 2nd they were themselves immobilised in all the lands and islands they had crossed its
waters to conquer.

II

Yet though the subsequent recapture of Malta and Nelson's
destruction of the Danish fleet under the guns of Copenhagen
in 1801 left Britain complete mistress of the seas round Europe,
her attempt to rouse the continent against the hegemony of
France failed. At the end of 1799, abandoning his marooned army
in Egypt and evading the British cruisers, Bonaparte escaped
to France, overthrew its Government and again struck down
Britain's allies. Faced by a stalemate and exhausted by nine
years of war, in the autumn of 1801 the two nations—the one
supreme at sea, the other on land—patched up a peace.

It was short lived. The British had needed it to trade; Napoleon—as he now styled himself—in order to prepare to conquer
the world. By the spring of 1803 he was ready. Emperor now
of the French and absolute ruler of western Europe, he assembled
a vast army on the Channel shore and mobilised the fleets of
France, Spain and Holland to break the British blockade. As
part of his Grand Design for invasion the French Mediterranean
fleet was to escape from Toulon, cross the Atlantic and ravage the
West Indian sugar islands—Britain's richest possession—and, by
causing a panic on the London Exchange, force the Admiralty to
weaken its watch on Brest and the Western Approaches in order
to rescue them. Then, doubling back to Europe, its commander,
Villeneuve, was to join hands with the blockaded Spanish
squadrons at Cadiz and Ferrol and, either sweeping up the
Channel or round Scotland, gain possession of the Straits of
Dover for long enough to enable the Grande Armée to land in
Kent. But though in the spring of 1805 Villeneuve carried out
the first part of his mission, Nelson, divining his intention with
the instinct of genius, followed him so closely that the sugar
islands were saved, while the First Lord of the Admiralty, old

Lord Barham, ignoring the panic in the city and refusing to lower his guard, concentrated such strength in the Western Approaches that Villeneuve and the Combined Franco-Spanish fleet, unable to enter the Channel, were forced to take refuge at Ferrol. Had the British admiral, Sir Robert Calder, who intercepted them off Finisterre possessed the same offensive spirit as Nelson they would almost certainly have been destroyed.

On August 18th, after having ascertained that Villeneuve had not returned to the Mediterranean, Nelson anchored off Portsmouth in the *Victory*. Having chased him for 14,000 miles and failed to find him, he was depressed and anxious about his reception. But the waiting crowds on the ramparts were cheering, and all the way to the capital the enthusiasm continued. Without knowing it the tired, ailing admiral had become a legend. Forgotten during his long vigil off Toulon and all but reviled when the French fleet escaped from that port, his dash to save the West Indies had caught the country's imagination. Once more, as in the old days before his passion for Lady Hamilton and his parting from his wife had sullied his fame, he was "our hero of the Nile"—the wonderful admiral whose name had swept England's foes from the seas. The unexpected popularity was like sunshine to him. As he walked down Piccadilly the people flocked about him: it was affecting, wrote an eye-witness, to see the wonder, admiration and love of every one, gentle and simple; "it was beyond anything represented in a play or a poem of fame." The West India merchants voted him thanks for having saved their possessions; but for his modesty, thought the *Naval Chronicle*, he was in danger of being turned into a demigod.

The popular enthusiasm was partly the outcome of intense strain. For months the country had been expecting invasion. The grand army was encamped on the other side of the Straits of Dover, and Boulogne was full of waiting barges. When in July the combined Franco-Spanish fleet had been reported making for the Channel, the Volunteers were called out, all leave was stopped, and at one moment of supreme alarm the beacons had been lit in the North. Walter Scott, holiday-making in Cumberland, had galloped a hundred miles that day to attend the muster at Dalkeith.

·　·　·　·　·　·　·　·

To Pitt and Barham, therefore, the news of Nelson's return was something more than a hero's homecoming. It was the chance to resume the offensive. Believing that the country's best hope of salvation lay in attack, they had sent out Calder, like Drake, to destroy the Combined Fleet off the Spanish coast. He had failed, and they and their admirals had temporarily fallen back on the defensive. Now, by so swiftly bringing the Mediterranean Fleet back to the Channel, Nelson had given them the strength not only to defend the Western Approaches but to counter-attack.

Everything depended on their doing so. For the enemy had effected a concentration at the most decisive point on England's life-line. Whether Villeneuve was still in Ferrol or at large in the Bay, he lay athwart the sea route to the Mediterranean and the Indies. He threatened not only England's shores but the merchant fleets by which she lived. The outgoing East India "trade" was detained in Plymouth: the Lisbon-Oporto, long overdue, could not leave the Portuguese ports.

Out in the Atlantic two other homecoming convoys were in danger: the sugar fleet from the West Indies which Nelson had saved in June, and, somewhere between St. Helena and the Soundings, a fabulously rich fleet from China and India. Sailing in its solitary escort was the retiring Governor-General's brother, the young "Sepoy general", Sir Arthur Wellesley, who had done such wonderful things against the Mahrattas. The threat to the trades hamstrung the Navy as well as the City, for until the press-gangs could seize their crews the Admiralty could not man the new battleships which Barham had been fitting out in such haste.

Till Villeneuve could be removed from his central position on the Spanish coast England's sea communications were paralysed.

And on these depended not only her trade, but the fortunes of Europe. At that moment transports were waiting to sail for Odessa to bring a Russian army into the Mediterranean to co-operate with a British force just dispatched to Malta under Lieutenant General Craig to liberate Italy. At Cork 5000 troops, formerly destined for India, were waiting to sail under Sir David Baird on a still more momentous mission. During the summer they had been hastily allocated to the West Indies until Nelson's dramatic voyage had saved those islands. They were now embarked under secret orders to re-capture the Cape of Good Hope, the half-way house to India. Ever since its restoration to the puppet Batavian Republic by the Peace of Amiens the Government and City had been haunted by the fear of its occupation by the French. During the past year Napoleon's renewed intrigues in the Levant and the presence of his cruisers in the South Atlantic, combined with bad news from India, had intensified the fears of Leadenhall Street; all through the summer of 1805, Castlereagh had been urging Pitt to safeguard his communications with the East by repeating his coup of 1795 before it was too late. And events were now so critical that even a few days' delay might prove fatal.

During the last week of August it became known in London that Villeneuve had left Ferrol with thirty sail of the line. No one could say for certain where he had gone or what was happening to Calder. But the French admiral was now thinking only of safety, and Calder never saw the Combined Fleet. The honour was all Collingwood's. Since Nelson had left him he had been blockading Cadiz and its half-dozen Spanish three-deckers with three seventy-fours, fully expecting to have "a rattling day of it" soon. "A dull superiority," he told a friend, "creates languor; it is a state like this that rouses the spirits and makes us feel as if the welfare of all England depended on us alone." Yet even Collingwood, whose officers would have been astonished to hear such sentiments from their taciturn, prosy-looking commander, had scarcely bargained for the ordeal before him. For on August 20th—the day that Nelson reached

London—there appeared out of the north twenty-nine French and Spanish battleships. It was the great fleet on whose movements all the world was speculating, from Napoleon pacing his watch-tower at Boulogne to Pitt in his map-lined room and Cornwallis in his cabin off Ushant.

Since leaving the Bay on the 15th Villeneuve had never paused. Hurrying down the coasts of Galicia and Portugal, glimpsed momentarily by excited British frigates, he stopped only to capture and burn a solitary merchantman. Collingwood's "three poor things with a frigate and a bomb" off Cadiz seemed utterly at his mercy. But, though sixteen capital ships were detached to destroy him, Collingwood evaded them. Resolved not to be driven through the Straits without dragging his pursuers after him and keeping just out of gunshot, he tacked whenever they tacked and finally, when their patience tired, followed them back to Cadiz. There, with French and Spanish masts clustering in the harbour "as thick as a wood," he calmly resumed the blockade, signalling like Duncan before him to an imaginary fleet over the horizon. It was an uncomfortable position—"a squeeze," as he called it in a letter to his wife—but it failed to perturb this formidable Northumbrian. "I hope I shall have somebody come to me soon," he wrote, "and in the meantime I must take the best care of myself I can."

He did not have long to wait. Bickerton, watching Cartagena three hundred miles to the east with four ships of the line, abandoned the blockade on hearing the news and hurried to his aid. Calder, learning from a frigate that Villeneuve had left Ferrol with thirty battleships, gave chase to the southward. "It is a noble and most animating scene," wrote Captain Codrington of the *Orion* to his wife, "which I wish you could witness: eighteen sail of the line and but two frigates under every sail they can possibly set." By the 29th they, too, were off Cadiz.

After seven months Napoleon's Grand Design had ended in humiliation and frustration. Only the prudence or timidity of his admiral had saved his fleet from a fate as awful as that of the Spanish Armada. His army, like Parma's before it, was marooned on the shores of the Channel with all hope of a crossing gone. The blockade had been resumed. The Cadiz squadron was back in its port and the Toulon and Ferrol squadrons blockaded with it. Only Allemand's squadron was left at large. The initiative was again in British hands.

.   .   .   .

On the evening of September 2nd the *Euryalus* frigate brought the news from Cadiz. As she heaved to off the Needles Captain Blackwood went ashore to hire a chaise and four in Lymington. At five in the morning he stopped for a few minutes at Merton to see the most famous man in England. He found him already up and dressed. Like all the rest of the world Nelson had been eagerly awaiting the tidings he brought. "Depend on it, Blackwood," he said, "I shall yet give Mr. Villeneuve a drubbing." A few hours later he was receiving his charge at the Admiralty. At his first return Barham, who, scarcely knowing him, had distrusted his brightly-coloured reputation, had sent for his journals. But a few hours' perusal had resolved the old man's doubts. Nelson might be a junior admiral and unorthodox, but he was complete master of his calling. His right to return to his command—now of such supreme significance—was indisputable.

Nelson received the summons with quiet gladness. "I hold myself ready to go forth whenever I am desired," he wrote to George Rose, "although God knows I want rest. But self is entirely out of the question." His friends had never seen him so cheerful. In those last quiet days at Merton and in London, taking farewell of all he loved, he radiated hope and inspiration.

The sun had come out that autumn after the long cold winds of the summer. And the news that poured into England with that mellow September sunshine matched its splendour. Not only was the Combined Fleet held in Cadiz, but the home-coming convoys and, with them, the City's wealth and credit were saved. And on the 5th came still more glorious tidings. For six days before, it was learnt from a captured schooner, Napoleon's troops at Boulogne had broken camp and marched off in haste

"because of a new war with Russia." After more than two years
of suspense England was no longer in imminent danger. Pitt's
plans for raising the siege of his country had triumphed.

.   .   .   .

All that Napoleon had thought impossible had come to pass;
Pitt had forced him from the Channel by setting Europe at his
back. As early as August 13th, while still intent on crossing the
Channel, he had told Talleyrand that he would be in Vienna by
November to deal with the Russians if they dared to show
themselves. Ten days later his last hopes of crushing England
had been dashed. From Decrès came a long, heart-broken letter,
assuring him that Villeneuve had gone to Cadiz and beseeching
him, in that event, not to order him back to the Channel but to
regard it as a decree of Fate. At the same time news reached
Boulogne of Craig's arrival at Malta and of a Sicilian request for
the withdrawal of French troops from Naples. The link between
Pitt's plans and Russian and Austrian preparations was complete. The Emperor saw it all. Austria would temporise till the
winter rains and mud, and then by the spring he would have to
face 100,000 Russians in Germany, armed by Pitt, and 40,000
English and Russians in southern Italy.

He had been tricked. "Once I raise my camp on the ocean," he
had written, "I shall not be able to stop myself; my plans of
maritime war will have failed." Yet if Pitt had momentarily
filched the initiative, it could be regained. Speed, secrecy, surprise and ruthless resolution could do what they had done
before. "My mind is made up," Napoleon told Talleyrand, "I
shall invade Germany with 200,000 men and shall not halt till I
have reached Vienna, taken Venice and everything Austria has
in Italy and driven the Bourbons from Naples. I shall stop the
Austrians and Russians from uniting. I shall beat them before
they can meet. Then, the Continent pacified, I shall come back
to the camp on the ocean and start to work all over again for
peace at sea."

.   .   .   .

While Napoleon was planning under the chestnuts of St. Cloud, Nelson was bidding farewell to England. Much of his brief respite while the *Victory* was being made ready for sea he spent at the Admiralty, drawing up plans for his mission. Barham, who by now had completely surrendered to his fascination, had offered him forty ships of the line and *carte blanche* to choose his officers. "Choose yourself, my Lord," the admiral replied, "the same spirit actuates the whole profession. You cannot choose wrong."

Many saw him during those last days on his native soil. Haydon watched him going into Dollond's near Northumberland House to buy a night glass—a diminutive figure with a green shade over one eye, a shabby, well-worn, cocked hat and a buttoned-up undress coat. Charles Lamb, who had formed a prejudice against him and thought him a mountebank, passed him in Pall Mall "looking just as a hero should look." The little admiral "with no dignity and a shock head" had captured the hearts of his countrymen at last: the challenging eye, the curving lip, the quick moods, the marks of exposure and battle struck deep into the popular imagination that autumn. Among those who met him was a soldier waiting for an interview in the Secretary of State's ante-room: the famous admiral, conspicuous by his empty sleeve and eye-patch, at first tried to impress him by his histrionic address. But after a few minutes, sensing something in his expression, Nelson left the room and, ascertaining from the porter that he had been talking to the young victor of Assaye, Sir Arthur Wellesley, returned and spoke of public affairs with such good sense and knowledge that that most unimpressionable of men confessed that he had never had a more interesting conversation.

Yet the real Nelson lay deeper than either the charlatan or the statesman or than that half-hero, half-baby whom Lord Minto saw on his last day at Merton attending on the heart-broken Lady Hamilton as she swooned before her astonished guests. The real core of the man was his absolute self-surrender. "I have much to lose and little to gain," he wrote to his friend Davison, "and I go because it's right, and I will serve the country faithfully." The shy, austere Prime Minister, who shared the same unselfish love, showed his recognition of it when, on the admiral's farewell visit to Downing Street, he waited on him to his carriage —an honour he would not have paid a Prince of the Blood.

At half-past ten on the night of Friday, September 13th, after praying by the bedside of his child, Nelson took his leave of Merton. "May the great God whom I adore," he wrote in his diary, "enable me to fulfil the expectations of my country." Then he drove through the night over the Surrey heaths and Hampshire hills to Portsmouth. He spent the morning at the George Inn transacting business, and at two o'clock, accompanied by Canning and George Rose, who were to dine with him, went off to the *Victory*. Near the bathing machines, which he had chosen in preference to the usual landing stage, a vast crowd was waiting to see him go. "Many were in tears," wrote Southey, "and many knelt down before him and blessed him as he passed. . . . They pressed upon the parapet to gaze after him when his barge pushed off, and he returned their cheers by waving his hat. The sentinels, who endeavoured to prevent them from trespassing upon this ground, were wedged among the crowd; and an officer, who had not very prudently upon such an occasion ordered them to drive the people down with their bayonets, was compelled speedily to retreat. For the people would not be debarred from gazing till the last moment upon the hero—the darling hero of England!"

On the following morning, Sunday the 15th, the *Victory* weighed, with the faithful Blackwood in attendance in the *Euryalus* frigate. It was from "a herbless, weather-worn promontory" on the Dorset coast that a day later Anne Garland in Hardy's tale saw through an old coastguard's perspective glass a great ship with three rows of guns and all sails set passing the meridian of the Bill like a phantom. All the way to the Scillies adverse weather continued; it was not till the 21st that the *Victory* cleared the Soundings. Then with a northerly wind she ran swiftly across the Bay and down the Portuguese coast. By

September 25th Nelson was off Lisbon, sending an urgent warning to the British consul to conceal his coming from the public, and another to Collingwood to refrain from hoisting colours on his arrival. "For I hope," he wrote, "to see the enemy at sea."

In the fleet they were waiting for him a little wearily. After the excitements and disappointments of the summer the prospect of another winter of close blockade was having a depressing effect. "These French rascals," Captain Fremantle wrote, "will never come out and fight but will continue to annoy and wear out both our spirits and constitutions. . . . Here I conclude we shall remain until Doomsday or until we are blown off the coast, when the Frenchmen will again escape us." Some pinned their hopes on a peace through Russian mediation: few saw any prospect of ever seizing the elusive shadow, victory. To make matters worse, the acting Commander-in-Chief shunned society and seldom communicated with any one. He himself confessed in his letters home that he was worn to a lath with this perpetual cruising: his sole comfort his dog Bounce and the thought of his home in Northumberland—"the oaks, the woodlands and the verdant meads." For it was only when the guns began to sound that Collingwood grew inspired. "Is Lord Nelson coming out to us again?" asked Captain Codrington. "I anxiously hope he may be, that I may once more see a Commander-in-Chief endeavouring to make a hard and disagreeable service as palatable to those serving under him as circumstances will admit of and keeping up by his example that animation so necessary for such an occasion. . . . For charity's sake send us Lord Nelson, oh ye men of power!"

On September 28th the prayer was answered. As the *Victory* joined the fleet the captains hurried aboard to greet the admiral, forgetting everything in their enthusiasm. Their reception, Nelson told Lady Hamilton, caused the sweetest sensation of his life. "He is so good and pleasant a man," wrote Captain Duff of the *Mars*, a newcomer to his command, "that we all wish to do what he likes without any kind of orders." Codrington, who was also serving under him for the first time, spoke of the joy throughout the fleet; every one felt that his work would be appreciated and that nothing but the best would be good enough for such a commander. Soon every ship's company was busy painting in black and yellow bands after the old Mediterranean pattern and endeavouring to make her what the delighted Codrington called "a dear Nelsonian—in all things perfect."

For Nelson's task, as he made the fleet aware, was to transform it into an instrument fit to do the service for which the country was waiting. Less than a third of its twenty-nine battleships had been with him in the Mediterranean. Of the remainder most, for all their staunch virtues and wonderful skill, fell a little short of that flawless discipline, training and spirit which he expected of those who sailed with him. If he was to annihilate a superior enemy he knew he had to crowd into a few brief weeks, and perhaps only days, the teaching of years. And he had to school the captains not of a mere squadron but of the Navy itself, a third of whose fighting strength was now gathered under his command.

But Nelson in those autumnal days of 1805 was a man exalted. On the two days after his arrival—the first of them his forty-seventh birthday—he entertained his flag officers and captains to dinner, and, as he laid before them his plans for destroying the enemy, an electric current ran through them. "Some shed tears," he told Emma afterwards, "all approved. It was new, it was singular, it was simple! And from admirals downwards it was repeated—'It must succeed.'" Some who listened at the long table were strangers: others were old friends like Collingwood who had shared with him "a brotherhood of more than thirty years." But all were welded that night into one by the magic of the Nelson spirit and ritual: the gleaming silver and mahogany, the stately music, the cheerful, courtly hospitality, the friendliness and consideration, the sense that ran through all of sharing in a great adventure. Jealousy, sulking, backbiting—maladies that long confinement in overcrowded ships easily bred—could not survive in such an atmosphere. "We can, my dear Coll, have no little jealousies," Nelson wrote to his Second-in-Command. "We have only one great object in view, that of annihilating our enemies and getting a glorious peace for our country."

Consciously or unconsciously Nelson in those last weeks off Cadiz was fashioning a tradition and a legend that was to be of priceless service to England. He reminded the Navy that, whatever the bonds of authority, leadership was not a mere matter of transmitting orders but of evoking the will to serve. Building on all that was best in the great naval tradition in which he had been nurtured and discarding all that was bad, he established an ideal of discipline that was as revolutionary an advance on the dead, unfeeling authoritarianism of the past as the teachings of Rousseau, and far more practical. It was founded, not on a corporate abstraction, but on the individual who alone, as he saw, embodied the principle of life. Its ideal was liberty in a framework of discipline—a liberty that worked and was grafted, in the English mode, on nature. Captain Codrington testified how pleasant it was, after Lord Nelson's arrival, to be given constant change of scene and occupation, freedom of choice and method and yet to know precisely how far one might go.

It was this which, as an officer said, double-manned every ship in the line. Nelson was essentially a humanitarian who, wooing men to duty, trusted them and had the imagination to see into their hearts. By his reckoning the best disciplinarian was he who most loved and understood men, who remembered that they were human beings and treated them accordingly. One of his first acts was to order that the names and families of all killed and wounded should be reported to him for transmission to the chairman of the Patriotic Fund and that an account of every man's case should accompany him to hospital. In this spirit he allowed Sir Robert Calder to return in his own flagship to England to face his court martial, thus depriving the fleet of one of its precious three-deckers at the very moment that he was fretting for every gun to annihilate the enemy. "I much fear I shall incur the censure of the Board," he wrote to the Admiralty, "but I trust that I shall be considered to have done right as a man to a brother officer in affliction—my heart could not stand it." It would have been idle for authority to complain; such tenderness and consideration were an essential part of Nelson's success. He could not discard them without ceasing to be Nelson.

All the while that he was inspiring others with cheerfulness and resolution Nelson's own heart was aching for the home which he had barely seen and for the woman and child from whom he had so long been parted. On the second night after he entertained his captains to dinner he was seized by a painful and dreadful spasm. "The good people of England will not believe," he wrote, "that rest of body and mind is necessary to me." To comfort Emma, he told her that the brief days of happiness at Merton were only a foretaste of greater happiness: "Would to God they were to be passed over again, but that time will, I trust, soon come, and many, many more days to be added to them."

Even as he wrote he knew that what he had come to do precluded the likelihood of return. To secure his country and make her victory certain—whether now or in the more distant future— he had to destroy the great concentration lying before him in the inner harbour of Cadiz. The chance would probably never occur again and, when it came, a few brief hours of opportunity would be all he could hope to snatch from the gods of wind and tide. In that day with a force of less than thirty ships of the line— a few more, perhaps, if the promises given him in England could be made good—he would have to shatter, burn and blast a superior enemy fighting with the courage of desperation. Before him in Cadiz were perhaps thirty-five or thirty-six sail of the line including the three most powerful ships in the world. At Cartagena, two days distant, were six more. And to maintain his fleet on that inhospitable coast he was under the necessity of sending it in detachments to provision and water in the Straits: almost his earliest act had been to dispatch a first instalment of six battleships under Rear-Admiral Louis, thus reducing his fighting strength to twenty-three. "I am very, very, *very* anxious," he wrote to George Rose, begging for reinforcements. "It is, as Mr. Pitt knows, annihilation the country wants and not merely a splendid victory of twenty-three to thirty-six—honourable to the parties concerned but absolutely useless in the extended scale to bring Bonaparte to his marrow bones. Numbers only can annihilate."

For the menace created by the union of the French and Spanish fleets still remained—a standing challenge to England's strained resources. To keep the Grand Fleet throughout the winter on that exposed and treacherous shore was almost impossible. Yet at the least easing of the blockade the enemy might escape either in a body through the Straits, so imperilling the whole Mediterranean position, or in detachments into the Atlantic to harry trade and the colonies. Though Nelson did not know that before leaving Boulogne Napoleon had prescribed commerce-raiding as the future task of his battle-fleets, he was well aware of its dangers; one of his last acts before leaving England had been to draft a plan for establishing protective cruiser-lines along the Portuguese coast. Already Allemand with a three-decker and four other battleships was roving at will across the home terminals and the Bay. On the day the *Victory* sailed from Portsmouth he had all but run down Baird's and Popham's transports two hundred miles to the west of Lisbon; later, venturing into the Soundings, he had captured the *Calcutta*, whose captain had been forced to sacrifice himself to save his convoy. After evading an angry lunge from Cornwallis, Allemand had transferred his activities to Nelson's communications off the Portuguese coast. A division of the Channel Fleet under Captain Strachan had sailed on September 29th to find him.

Still graver, in Nelson's view, was the risk of Villeneuve running for the Mediterranean. His statesman's instinct warned him that Napoleon, having failed to cross the Channel, would again as in '98 turn eastwards and try to conquer the world by breaking the ring of British sea power at its weakest point—in the Levant. His first step must be the great island off the toe of Italy which, still nominally ruled by the weak king of the Two Sicilies, was menaced by St. Cyr's army in the Calabrian ports. When Nelson left England no news had been received of Craig's arrival at Malta or of the long-awaited Anglo-Russian landing in Southern Italy: France and Russia were still nominally at peace and Austria, though mobilising, had not declared war. But the explosion might occur at any moment, and Nelson knew that when it did Napoleon would try to forestall the Allies at Naples. That he would use Villeneuve and his great concentration at Cadiz to further his purposes seemed certain.

To prevent it and to forestall any sudden dash by Ganteaume to join Villeneuve, Nelson withdrew his inshore squadron from before Cadiz. Instead he moved his fleet fifty miles out into the Atlantic where he could both guard against a surprise from the north and control the entrance to the Straits without the risk of being prematurely blown through them. The task of watching the enemy he left to Blackwood's frigates and a linking division of his faster seventy-fours, which maintained hourly communications by flag and gun signals. By withdrawing over the horizon he hoped to tempt Villeneuve out: everything, he told Blackwood, must yield to the overriding necessity of "not letting the rogues escape without a fair fight." He even canvassed the possibility of smoking them out with Colonel Congreve's rockets and the American Fulton's primitive torpedoes which Pitt and Castlereagh, under the intoxicating influence of Sir Sidney Smith, had been vainly trying to use against the abandoned invasion flotilla at Boulogne. Barham had been urging his colleagues that these vaunted inventions, if worth anything at all —which he doubted—had far better be tried on the enemy's battleships at Cadiz than on discarded barges. Yet though in his anxiety for an early decision Nelson repeatedly begged Castlereagh to hurry out the rockets, he pinned his chief hope on the pressure of famine. Thirty thousand seamen and troops were a heavy drain on the resources and communications of Cadiz, and the prescient Collingwood had instituted a strict blockade of the coast. Nelson, confirming his orders, implored the authorities at home to support him and ignore the protests of neutrals and vested interests.

Unknown to the British, Villeneuve was already preparing for sea. On September 27th he had received Napoleon's orders to sail for Cartagena and Naples. Anxious to recover his relentless master's esteem, he had at once ordered his captains to make ready. But on October 2nd, just as they were about to sail to "strike down England's tyrannical dominion of the seas," rumours reached Cadiz of Nelson's arrival and of his plan to attack with infernal machines. Immediately the port was in a tumult; the order to sail was suspended and all hands were diverted to arming a harbour guard of gunboats. At a Council of War on October 7th, though an easterly breeze offered a chance of entering the Straits before the British could engage, it was resolved, after heated debate, to disobey Napoleon's orders. The French and Spanish admirals were brave men, but they had no wish to commit suicide. And to sail with Nelson in the offing, they reckoned, was suicide.

. . . .

With Villeneuve's failure to use the east wind, hopes of a fight fell very low in the fleet off Cadiz. Only Nelson, buoyed up by some inner sense of impending events, remained convinced that the enemy would put to sea. And on the very day that Villeneuve and his admirals were debating Napoleon's orders, Nelson's belief became a certainty. For the *Royal Sovereign* arrived from England after a refit with news that war had broken out in Europe and that Craig's army was on the point of leaving for Italy. The British fleet, after securing the enemy in Cadiz, was ordered to cover his landing. Nelson now knew that Villeneuve or his successor would sail and what course he would take. The fate of Sicily, of the Mediterranean, of Pitt's offensive and, in the last resort, of England would be decided by a naval engagement at the mouth of the Straits.

For that ordeal—now imminent—Nelson summoned up all his art. Ever since he had learnt on that early September morning at Merton that Villeneuve had taken shelter in Cadiz he had been pondering how to destroy him. "I will try to have a motto," he told Rose before he left England, "or at least it shall be my watchword—Touch and take!" He had never been content with the classic conception of a naval victory: an ordered cannonade in long laboriously formed lines of battle in which the French, receiving an attack from to windward, were always able to withdraw, occasionally leaving a few prizes in British hands. A disciple of the great eighteenth century pioneers who had first had the courage to defy the Admiralty's Fighting Instructions and break the formal line of battle, and a lifelong student of naval tactics, Nelson had long wrestled with the problem of how to transform limited into decisive victory. As a commodore at Cape St. Vincent, and then in his first independent command at the Nile, he had pointed the way. But never till now had he directed a major fleet in battle in the open sea.

On October 9th, two days after his new orders reached him, he issued instructions to his flag officers and captains. He had already outlined them verbally in those two dramatic evenings in the *Victory*'s cabin. He now committed them formally to writing. The problem, as he postulated it, was to bring such crushing force against a portion of the enemy's line as to overwhelm it and to do so in time to destroy the remainder before night fell. "Thinking it almost impossible," he wrote, "to bring a fleet of forty sail of the Line into a line of battle in variable winds, thick weather or other circumstances . . . without such a loss of time that the opportunity would probably be lost of bringing the enemy to battle in such manner as to make the business decisive, I have made up my mind . . . that the Order of Sailing is to be the Order of Battle." In other words not only was the classical line of battle to be discarded in the heat of the fight, as it had been in earlier engagements, but it was never to be formed at all.

The spirit of the offensive was implicit in every line of Nelson's Memorandum. So was his genius. It was, as Thursfield wrote, "the last tactical word of the greatest master of sea tactics the world has ever known, the final and flawless disposition of sailing-ships marshalled for combat." Attack was to be made in two main divisions, one of which was to immobilise the enemy's van by a feint while the other broke and destroyed his rear and centre. No time was to be wasted in manœuvring for position, for, with the brief October days and the uncertain winds of that region, none could be spared; instead the approach was to be made by whatever course would most quickly bring the fleet to gunshot of the enemy's centre. Then one division under Collingwood was to break the enemy's line at about the twelfth ship from the rear, while the other, under Nelson's immediate command, after keeping the enemy's van in the maximum uncertainty as to its intentions by hovering to windward till it was too late to succour the rear, was to fall on the centre. "The whole impression of the British fleet," Nelson wrote, "must be to overpower from two or three ships ahead of their Commander-in-Chief, supposed to be in the centre, to the rear of their fleet. . . . I look with confidence to a victory before the van of the enemy can succour their rear." Their flagship was to be taken, and the battle was not to be regarded as over so long as a single enemy ensign remained flying.

It was characteristic of Nelson that within the broad framework of his orders the maximum freedom of action was reserved both for himself and Collingwood. From the moment pursuit was joined the latter was to have complete control over his own division. No hard and fast tactical rules were laid down, for the precise conditions in which the enemy would be found could not be foreseen. "Something," Nelson wrote, "must be left to chance; nothing is sure in a sea fight." Individual captains were to look to their particular Line as their rallying-point. "In case," he added, "signals can neither be seen or perfectly understood, no captain can do very wrong if he places his ship alongside that of an enemy."

During the days that followed the issue of his Memorandum Nelson's main anxiety was lest the foe should escape through the Straits before his cruisers could warn him. As usual he was short of frigates: the last French fleet, he told the Admiralty, had slipped through his fingers that way and he was resolved that this one should not. Fortunately he had an apt disciple in the thirty-four year old frigate captain, Henry Blackwood. Much of his time, "working like a horse in a mill" to complete the last detail of preparation, was spent in coaching this daring and vigilant officer. "Those who know more of Cadiz than either you or I do," Nelson wrote to him, "say that after these Levanters come several days of fine weather, sea breezes westerly, land wind at night; and that, if the enemy are bound into the Mediterranean, they would come out at night, run to the southward and catch the sea breezes at the mouth of the Gut and push through whilst we might have little wind in the offing. In short, watch all points and all winds and weather, for I shall depend on you."

Nelson was confident of his ability to defeat the enemy. "I will give them such a shaking," he told Blackwood, "as they have never yet experienced; at least I will lay down my life in the attempt." But he was growing increasingly anxious lest the re-inforcements promised from England should not arrive in time to achieve complete annihilation. Louis with six of his battleships was still in the Straits, and he had now been forced by the needs of Malta and the Russians to send them farther eastward with a convoy past Cartagena. Others, however, despite the menace of Allemand to his supply lines, were straggling in as fast as Barham could dispatch them from the dockyards, and on the 13th the *Agamemnon* showed over the horizon with his old flag-captain, Berry, in command. "Now we shall have a fight," Nelson cried, rubbing his hands. The newcomer brought the immediate strength under his flag to twenty-seven of the line including seven three-deckers.

Yet the ships in Cadiz harbour continued to lie at their moorings, and Nelson began to wax impatient. "I don't like to have these things on my mind," he told a friend in England. On the 17th the wind veered into the east again: the Combined Fleet could not have finer weather for sea. But still there was no sign of life from the bare forest of masts beyond the low thin strip of the isthmus.

Yet within the port, unknown to the blockaders, the enemy was stirring. On October 11th, four days after the Council of War had decided not to fight, news arrived that Rosily was on his way to take over command and was already at Madrid. The idea of being superseded with the stigma of cowardice upon him was more than Villeneuve could bear. He knew that Louis was in the Straits: he did not yet know that reinforcements had arrived from England, for Nelson had been careful to conceal them. He therefore estimated British capital strength at 23 to his own 33, with an equal number of three-deckers on either side. Of these one, the Spanish *Santissima Trinidad*, carried 130 guns, and two others 112 guns against the 100 guns of the largest British ships.

Reckoning that an occasion so favourable would never come again, Villeneuve ordered the Fleet to sea. He would pass the Straits or perish. "There is nothing," he assured his captains, "to alarm us in the sight of the English fleet; they are not more brave than we are, they are worn by a two years' cruise and they have fewer motives to fight well." Having brooded so long over the thought of Nelson, he had formed a surprisingly accurate idea of what he would do. "The enemy," he wrote in his Fighting Instructions, "will not trouble to form line parallel to ours and fight it out with the gun. . . . He will try to double our rear, cut through the Line and bring against ships thus isolated groups of his own to surround and capture them. Captains must rely upon their courage and love of glory rather than upon the signals of admirals who may be already engaged and wrapped in smoke. The captain who is not in action is not at his post."

The chivalrous Spaniards, aware that more than half their crews had never been to sea, protested but, for the honour of their flag, agreed to sail. Villeneuve was now inexorable. Just as the injured Calder had taken his flagship home to Portsmouth to appease his honour, the French admiral to vindicate his took his whole fleet into the jaws of destruction.

At six o'clock on the morning of Saturday, October 19th, the *Sirius*, Blackwood's nearest frigate inshore, gave the longed-for signal. "Enemy have their topsail yards hoisted." An hour later the first ships were reported coming out of harbour. At half-past nine Nelson received the news fifty miles out in the Atlantic. At once the signal was hoisted for a "General Chase," followed soon afterwards by "Prepare for Battle." All day the British fleet stood towards the Straits under a clear sky with a north-easterly wind, intending to catch Villeneuve at the entrance to the Gut. Though during the afternoon the wind began to drop, the enemy's fleet was reported at sea. "How would your heart beat for me, dearest Jane," wrote Codrington to his wife, "did you but know that we are now under every stitch of sail we can set, steering for the enemy."

Yet by one o'clock on the morning of the 20th, when the fleet began to close on Gibraltar, there was no sign of the foe. Dawn broke on an empty solitude of thick, squally sea and cloud, with the fine weather of the previous day gone and, with it, Codrington's dream of a general engagement, a glorious victory and a quick return to England. "All our gay hopes are fled," he wrote, "and instead of being under all possible sail in a very light breeze and fine weather, expecting to bring the enemy to battle, we are now under close-reefed topsails in a very strong wind with thick rainy weather and the dastardly French returned to Cadiz." To add to the general disappointment there was no sign of Louis, whom Nelson had hoped to find in the Straits, that officer being now far away to the east, receding, to his own intense chagrin and that of his crews, in the direction of Malta.

Yet just as Nelson was about to beat back to his old station for fear of being driven by the south-wester through the Straits, word came from the frigates that Villeneuve was still at sea to the northward and that a group of his ships had just been sighted in some confusion off Cadiz lighthouse. The Combined Fleet's seamanship had proved unequal to the task of getting out of harbour in a single tide, but the ships were still coming out. Nelson, therefore, after giving orders to wear and stand to the north-west, called Collingwood aboard for consultation. But, though he listened to his eager advice to attack at once, he refused to do so. For, if he was to gain the victory on which he counted, he knew that he must let his foe get farther away from port. He dared not trust his courage with a bolt-hole.

Later in the day, when the British fleet had reached a point some twenty-five miles to the south-west of Cadiz, there was an improvement in the weather, and visibility became clearer. At one moment, owing to the continued confusion of the enemy's ships—it was not till midday that they were all clear of harbour—there was an alarm that they were trying to get to the westward. But Nelson, with his strong strategic grasp, refused to believe it, especially as the wind was steadily shifting into the west. He continued on his course, watching the enemy over the rim of the horizon through the eyes of his frigates. During the afternoon he spent some time on the poop talking to his midshipmen; "this day or to-morrow," he remarked, "will be a fortunate one for you, young gentlemen." Later he entertained some of them at dinner, promising that he would give them next day something to talk and think about for the rest of their lives.

.   .   .   .

October 21st dawned calm and splendid. There was a faint wind out of the west-north-west and a heavy swell rolling in from the Atlantic towards Cape Trafalgar and the Gut of Gibraltar. The British Fleet, having wore to the northward a couple of hours earlier to reach a commanding position before Villeneuve's weather beam, was about twenty miles off the Spanish coast; the enemy nine miles away to the south-east still steering towards the Straits. The supreme moment of Nelson's life had come. The whole horizon, clear after the low clouds of yesterday, was filled with Villeneuve's ships.

Having summoned the frigate captains aboard, Nelson a little after six gave the signal to form order of sailing in two columns—his original idea of a third being abandoned owing to his reduced numbers—and to bear up and sail large on an east-north-easterly course, so taking the fleet towards the enemy's line of retreat. Shortly afterwards the signal, "Prepare for Action" was made. An hour later the admiral's prescience was justified, for Villeneuve, realising his adversary was more powerful than he had supposed and fearful of meeting Louis in the Straits, abandoned his course for the Gut and gave the order to wear together and form line of battle on the port tack in inverse order. But, though by doing so he brought Cadiz under his lee, he was too late to avoid an engagement. The Spanish captain, Churruca, watching the signal through his telescope, snapped his glass to with a curt, "Perdidos!"

Yet the enemy's movement added to Nelson's difficulties and the complexity of the attack. Not only was the Combined Fleet sailing in inverse order, but his own line of approach to it must now bring the shoals of Trafalgar and San Pedro under his lee. And the heavy ground swell and his seaman's instinct warned him that, though at the moment the wind was dropping, a gale from the Atlantic was imminent. When Blackwood came aboard at eight o'clock to congratulate Nelson on his good fortune, he found him, for all his cheerful spirits and calm bearing, deeply intent on the enemy's direction and formation. The admiral's thoughts were running, not on victory which he knew was by now inevitable, but on the possibilities of the foe's escaping. He told Blackwood to be ready to use his frigates in the latter stages of the fight to complete the work of destruction and not to think of saving ships or men. For his end, he kept stressing, was annihilation, not prizes.

By this time the British fleet was approaching the enemy from windward, sailing to the eastward in two almost parallel lines at an oblique angle to his northerly course. Being in great confusion during and after its manœuvre, the Combined Fleet was moving at a far slower pace, the van being forced to wait for the laggards, while the British leaders, with studding sails set on both sides, were forging ahead leaving their own stragglers to follow as best they could. For both Nelson and Collingwood were resolved not to waste a minute of the all-too-short day, but to bring their ships to the attacking point by the shortest possible course.

There was little need for signals, for almost everything had been determined in advance. Collingwood's Lee division which, in accordance with the admiral's memorandum, was to attack the enemy rear, was on a port line of bearing steering to cut the line at a point from twelve to sixteen ships ahead of the last ship. Nelson with the Weather division was steering a slightly more northerly course towards the centre and—since the enemy's line was moving as well as his own—aiming at a point some two miles ahead of his leading ship. It was a wonderful sight, and Codrington in the *Orion* called up his lieutenants to see it: the Combined Fleet straggling like a forest of canvas across five miles of sea, its bright, many-coloured hulls and the scarlet and white *Santissima Trinidad* towering up in the midst. Many of the enemy ships were doubling each other in their confusion and, instead of forming a straight line of battle, were tending to move in a wide crescent with its arc to leeward. By comparison the two British divisions, though strung out a little in their haste, looked, with their black and yellow painted hulls, grim and forbidding.

About nine o'clock, with the fleets still several miles apart, Nelson made an inspection of the *Victory*. Dressed in his threadbare, storm-stained admiral's frock-coat with the stars of his four Orders sewn on the left breast and accompanied by the frigate captains, he made the tour of the low, half-lit decks and the long curving lines of guns. The crews, stripped to the waists, waited with the alert silence of the Navy's age-long ritual, but here and there a whispered aside or a legend chalked on a gun revealed their mood. Walking swiftly, Nelson occasionally stopped to speak to the men at their quarters, repeating the old counsel that they were to hold their fire till they were sure of their object. Once he tapped a powder monkey on the shoulder and warned him to take off his shirt lest a spark should set it alight. Only when he reached the quarter-deck ladder to the poop did the pent-up emotion of the ship's company break in a great cheer. He stood there for a moment, with his emaciated figure and lined face, looking down on his men.

The wind was gradually failing and shifting into the west, and the pace of the British Fleet slackened from three to two knots. But it was still gaining on the French and Spaniards who, from their thickening line and resolute bearing as they forged, closehauled, slowly to the north-north-west, clearly meant to make a fight of it. Nelson from the poop watched them grimly, then observed, "I'll give them such a dressing as they've never had before!" Blackwood, seeing that the flagship from her leading position would be unduly singled out for attack, suggested the propriety of letting one or two ships go ahead as was usual in line of battle. With a rather grim smile Nelson assented and ordered the *Temeraire* and *Leviathan* to pass the *Victory*. But, as the *Victory* continued to carry every stitch of sail she possessed and as neither Captain Hardy nor Nelson would consent to shorten it, her consorts made little headway. Finally, as the *Temeraire* vainly struggled to pass, Nelson called out to her through his speaking-trumpet, "I'll thank you, Captain Harvey, to keep in your proper station!" Thereafter the *Victory*, like the *Royal Sovereign* in the Lee line, continued in indisputed possession of the lead. The order of sailing remained the order of battle.

About an hour before the time when the opposed lines seemed likely to converge, Nelson left the poop and retired to his dismantled cabin. Here Pasco, the flag-lieutenant, coming in with a message, found him on his knees composing the prayer which was part of his legacy to England:

"May the Great God whom I worship grant to my Country, and for the benefit of Europe in general, a great and glorious Victory; and may no misconduct in any one tarnish it; and may humanity after Victory be the predominant feature in the British Fleet. For myself, individually, I commit my life to Him who made me, and may His blessing light upon my endeavours for serving my Country faithfully. To Him I resign myself and the just cause which is entrusted to me to defend."

Afterwards he made a codicil to his will, committing his child and Lady Hamilton to his country's keeping, and got Blackwood to witness it. Elsewhere, while the crew of the French flagship was taking a solemn oath to die with Villeneuve to the last man, other Britons were indulging in home thoughts; Captain Duff of the *Mars* scribbled a line to tell his wife that he was praying that he would behave as became him and still have the happiness of taking her and his children in his arms. Meanwhile, with the rich diversity of England, Codrington of the *Orion* was sitting down to a leg of turkey, and Cumby, the first lieutenant of the *Bellerophon*, was piping the ship's company to dinner, "thinking that Englishmen would fight all the better for a comfortable meal."

Shortly after Nelson reappeared on the poop, land was sighted. At first, since the fleet had been sailing for several days on a dead reckoning, it was thought to be Cadiz, and the admiral, fearful lest the enemy should escape, signalled that he would go through the end of the line to cut off their retreat. A few minutes later it was identified as Cape Trafalgar, and he reverted to his original plan. The *Victory* was now closing towards the centre of the enemy's van where the *Santissima Trinidad* and the French flagship, *Bucentaure*, towered up among their fellows. There was no desultory firing at long range, and it became plain that the enemy was holding himself in for a grim fight.

After signalling to make "all possible sail," Nelson remarked to Pasco that he would amuse the fleet with a signal. "I wish to say Nelson confides that every man will do his duty." After a brief consultation about the capacity of Popham's code, this was altered to "England expects." Soon after it had been hoisted, and j ist as the first ranging shot from the *Fougueux* ploughed up the water in front of the *Royal Sovereign*, No. 16—"Engage the Enemy more closely"—was seen flying at the *Victory*'s masthead where it remained till it was shot away.

The advance was over: the battle about to begin. The British fleet had been brought in accordance with the terms of Nelson's memorandum "nearly within gunshot of the enemy's centre." The time had now come for the Lee division to fall on his rear while Nelson prevented the van from coming to its aid. Judging that the disproportion of force and the enemy's inversed sailing order justified a modification of his original instructions, Collingwood decided to cut the line at the sixteenth instead of the twelfth ship from the rear. He thus set his fifteen battleships to engage not an inferior but a superior force. But he relied on British gunnery and discipline to give him the necessary ascendancy. Nelson approved, for as the *Royal Sovereign* bore down under a hail of fire on the great black hull of the *Santa Ana*, he cried out, "See how that noble fellow Collingwood carries his ship into action!" His Second-in-Command, who, a few minutes before had been muttering, "I wish Nelson would stop signalling: we know well enough what we have to do," was now feeling the exaltation which always came to him in the hour of danger. Munching an apple like the countryman he was and pacing the quarterdeck as the shot splashed the water all round him, he remarked, "Now gentlemen, let us do something to-day which the world may talk of hereafter." What seemed to give him most delight was the resolute bearing of the French. "No dodging and manœuvring," he wrote afterwards in ecstatic recollection. "They formed their line with nicety and waited our attack with

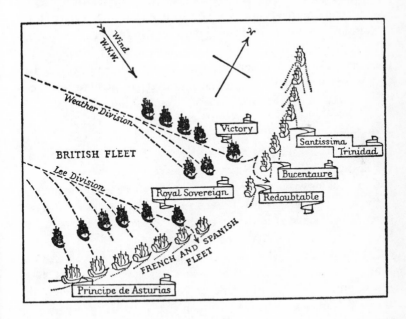

Trafalgar

great composure. Our ships were fought with a degree of gallantry that would have warmed your heart. Everybody exerted themselves and a glorious day they made it."

The fight between the Lee division and the enemy's rear began just before midday. At eight minutes past twelve, after enduring the fire of six French and Spanish ships for nearly a quarter of an hour, the *Royal Sovereign* broke the line, discharging as she did so one broadside into the bows of the *Fougueux*. Then she ran alongside the latter, with the muzzles of the guns almost touching, and simultaneously engaged the *Indomitable* to leeward, evoking from the watching Nelson a slap of the thigh and a shout of "Bravo! Bravo! what a glorious salute!"

Five minutes later Collingwood's second ship, the *Belleisle*, followed the *Royal Sovereign* through the gap and ran aboard the *Fougueux*. Thereafter she took on seven ships in turn as they drifted by and, with her colours still flying at the stump of her shattered mainmast, ended by capturing a Spanish seventy-four. Within a quarter of an hour eight of Collingwood's fifteen ships were in action, all breaking the line but the *Mars*, which lost her captain, Duff, at the first impact. At one moment no less than five enemy ships, fighting with the utmost gallantry, were pounding away at the *Royal Sovereign*, while Collingwood with his customary frugality helped one of his officers to take up an old studding-sail from the gangway hammocks and roll it up. But the terrific intensity of the British fire soon told: in three and a half minutes the *Royal Sovereign* discharged three broadsides. No ship, Collingwood had told his men, could stand up to three in five minutes, and he was proved right. "A glorious day for old England!" he was heard to shout as the French rear began to crumple, "we shall have one apiece before night."

By now it was half-past twelve, and the *Victory* had opened fire on the enemy's centre. For the first half hour Nelson had been performing his essential task of containing and deceiving the French van while the Lee division did its work. He had been steering to close with the *Santissima Trinidad*, the eleventh ship in the line, meaning to break through between her and the

Bucentaure, two ships in rear. But while he did so he retained his option of ranging up to the enemy's advanced ships, keeping their flag-officer, Rear-Admiral Dumanoir, in a state of impotent uncertainty till the last possible moment. At one time he made a feint of hauling out towards them, eliciting from Codrington the tribute, "How beautifully the admiral is carrying his design into effect!" Then, when it was too late for Dumanoir to save the rear, he turned again to starboard and opened fire on the cluster of great ships in the centre which he had marked as his special prey. At this point he threw prudence to the winds and, bearing up so as to pass under the lee of the *Bucentaure*, ran straight at the enemy's line, bringing down upon the *Victory*'s bows the fire of hundreds of guns.

Because of the obtuse re-entering angle at which the enemy's van was sailing, Nelson's approach, instead of being oblique like Collingwood's, had of necessity far more of the perpendicular in it than normal discretion allowed. But, having served his primary purpose, his object was now to get as quickly alongside the enemy as possible and complete the work of destruction before it was too late. He did so regardless of his own safety and left the rest of his division to scramble into the fight as best it could. For, with the short October afternoon beginning to run, there was not a second to be lost. As Blackwood left him to warn each captain to take whatever course he thought fit to get quickly into action, Nelson wrung his hand and bade him farewell. "God bless you, Blackwood," he said, "I shall never speak to you again."

When Villeneuve saw the British flagship's sudden turn he knew that his hour had come. Never, he wrote after the battle, had he seen anything like the irresistible line of the British approach, but the final charge of the *Victory*, closely supported by the *Neptune* and *Temeraire*, was something he could not have conceived had he not actually witnessed it. It unnerved him. In sudden desperation he hoisted the signal for every ship not engaged to get into action without delay but failed to give the specific order to Dumanoir to tack and come to the aid of his encircled rear and centre. As a result the latter, still uncertain,

THE FIRE AND THE ROSE

continued to stand to the northward until it was too late to effect the course of the battle.

At 12.40 p.m. the *Victory*, within musket-shot of the French flagship, put her helm to port and steered for the stern of the *Bucentaure*. The line was at this point so close that the *Redoubtable*'s jib boom was actually touching her leader's taffrail. Puzzled, the flag-captain asked the admiral which of the two ships he should run down, only to receive the reply, "Take your choice, Hardy, it does not much signify which." As the *Victory* passed astern of the *Bucentaure* her mainyard, rolling with the swell, touched the vangs of the Frenchman's gaff: then with a terrific explosion her port broadside opened, while the forecastle carronade, raking the crowded deck, swept down a hundred of his crew. A moment later she ran aboard the *Redoubtable* and broke the line. Behind her the *Temeraire*, *Neptune*, *Leviathan* and *Conqueror*, supported by *Brittania*, *Ajax* and *Agamemnon*, followed in quick succession.

By one o'clock the centre as well as the rear of the Franco-Spanish line was a mass of flame and billowing smoke. For nearly a mile between the two British flagships the ridge of fire and thunder continued. Codrington who, taking advantage of Nelson's order, had hauled out of line to starboard to reach the fight by the shortest route, calmly reserving his fire as he did so till he found an object worthy of it, described "that grand and awful scene"—the falling masts, the ships crowded together, the broadsides crashing into blazing timbers at point blank range as rival boarding parties vainly sought an opportunity. For this was a sea battle of a pattern never previously attempted—more terrifying and more decisive. In the *Victory*, her mizen top-mast shot away, her wheel broken, and her sails torn to shreds, the decks were swept continuously by rifle fire from the *Redoubtable*'s tops, while every now and then a broadside from the *Bucentaure* or the *Santissima Trinidad* struck home with terrific force. A single shot killed eight marines on the poop: another, narrowly missing Nelson, flung his secretary, a mangled heap spurting blood, at his feet. "This is too warm work, Hardy," he said, "to last long." Down in the crowded cockpit the scene of horror was so awful that the chaplain, Scott, could bear it no longer and stumbled up the companion-ladder, slippery with gore, for a breath of fresh air. There, "all noise, confusion and smoke," he saw Nelson fall.

As they bore him down, his shoulder, lung and spine shot through and his golden epaulette driven deep into his body, the admiral covered the stars on his breast with his blood-soaked handkerchief lest his men should see and be discouraged. "They have done for me at last, Hardy," he said. In the cockpit, gasping from pain and exhaustion, he told the surgeon in broken sentences that he was past help. Five minutes later, as he lay there in the blinding darkness, the *Bucentaure*'s last mast fell, and Villeneuve, "a very tranquil, placid, English-looking Frenchman, wearing a long-tailed uniform coat and green corduroy pantaloons," sought for someone to whom he might surrender. A marine officer with five men from the *Conqueror* went aboard the French flag-ship to take him, while the British admiral was being stripped of his clothes and covered with a sheet that the surgeon might probe his wound. As each French and Spanish ensign fluttered down, rounds of cheering broke from the *Victory*'s gundecks, faintly audible amid the cries and groans of the cockpit. "It is nonsense, Mr. Burke," Nelson whispered to the purser who bent over to fan him and give him water, "to suppose that I can live. My sufferings are great but they will soon be over."

By five minutes past two, little more than two hours after firing began, the action in the centre was all but done. Eight French and Spanish ships had been beaten out of the fight by five British, and, despite the heroism of their officers and crews, three after suffering appalling losses had been forced to surrender. About the same time, the *Santa Ana* struck to the *Royal Sovereign* in the Lee division. Half an hour later the number that had yielded had increased to five, while seven more were isolated and doomed. To the north the ships of the French van were struggling, with the aid of rowing boats, to get round on the starboard tack, but remained cut off from the battle by the rear ships of

Nelson's division entering the fight from windward. About this time, after repelling a last despairing attempt to board by the survivors of the shattered *Redoubtable*, Hardy went below in response to the admiral's repeated enquiries. He found him in great pain and weakness but with a mind still intent on the progress of the battle. "I hope none of our ships have struck, Hardy," he said when he had been told of his captures.

"No, my Lord, there is no fear of that!"

"I am a dead man, Hardy. I am going fast; it will be all over with me soon. Come nearer to me. Pray let my dear Lady Hamilton have my hair and all other things belonging to me."

About three-thirty the fight flared up again as Dumanoir's squadron stood down to rescue the last French and Spanish ships resisting in the centre and rear. But the *Victory*, calling a few undamaged consorts around her, barred the way. As her starboard guns opened fire, Nelson, clinging vainly to life, murmured, "Oh, *Victory*, how you distract my poor brain!" Within twenty minutes the counter-attack had failed, and three more prizes had fallen to the British Weather division. On this Hardy again went below and congratulated the admiral on his victory, telling him that fourteen or fifteen enemy ships had surrendered. "That is well," whispered Nelson, "but I had bargained for twenty." Then the prescient mind of the great sailor, reverting to the thoughts of the morning and that steady, ominous swell out of the west, began once more to range ahead. "Anchor, Hardy, anchor!" he cried with a sudden spasm of energy. Afterwards he begged the captain not to throw his body overboard, bade him take care of Lady Hamilton and his child and, with some flash of childhood's tenderness battling against the delirium of pain, asked him to kiss him.

After Hardy had left, the admiral began to sink fast. His voice became very low and his breathing oppressed. His mind now seemed to be running on his private life. "Remember," he told the chaplain, Scott, who was rubbing his chest to ease his pain, "that I leave Lady Hamilton and my daughter Horatia as a legacy to my country." "I have *not*," he said a minute later,

" been a *great* sinner, doctor." But towards the end he reverted to the battle, now dying around him. " Thank God," he kept repeating, " I have done my duty." The last words he said were, " God and my country."

About the same time Dumanoir called off his four last un-captured ships and hauled out of the fight. A quarter of an hour later the Spaniard Gravina, mortally wounded, hoisted the signal to retire and withdrew towards Cadiz with ten crippled ships, leaving the remainder in the victors' hands. As he did so, Nelson's spirit passed and became "one with England and the sea."

CHAPTER 7

Retreat to Corunna

" Slowly and sadly we laid him down,
 From the field of his fame fresh and gory;
 We carved not a line and we raised not a stone,
 But we left him alone with his glory."

Charles Wolfe

TRAFALGAR MADE BRITAIN'S mastery of the seas absolute.
Napoleon's victories at Austerlitz, Jena and Friedland made his
mastery of Europe as complete. Yet by his very military ascendancy—as Castlereagh predicted in a remarkable speech in
parliament—Napoleon was creating a power which one day
might help to free the continent. Through sheer necessity the
British Army had begun to climb out of the forty years' pit of
defeat and neglect into which it had fallen after the great days of
Minden and Plassey. The officer who bought his promotion like
his uniform in Bond Street and commuted by two hours' daily
bullying on the parade ground for a life of drinking bumpers on
—and under—the messroom table, was gradually being replaced
by the ardent lad who had grown up to hate Bonaparte and view
his profession as an opportunity for glory. The crimping house
with its sordid tale of mercenary cruelty had yielded to the flash-
ing, devil-may-care recruiting-sergeant, parading in his ribbons
and finery before the gaping militiamen and extolling the glories
of his corps. By the time Trafalgar had cleared the seas for the
free movement of British land forces a new spirit of martial pride
was running again through the half-brutalised ranks. The scarlet
and gold regiments of England not only looked smart: they felt

smart. "If our commanders are well-chosen," wrote Lord Paget "(and there are some very good ones), the British Army is in a state that will astonish friend and foe."

Much of this improvement had been due to the administration of the Duke of York, who since 1795 had reorganised Army training, supervised the appointment of officers and established a Royal Military Academy and a Staff College to promote uniformity of method throughout the Service. Still more was due to bitter experience. The British Army had been driven from the continent by a revolutionary technique of war. The mechanical models of drill and discipline on which it had formed itself had largely failed in action. It had to adapt itself to new methods or accept permanent exclusion from Europe.

But the mainspring of all reform had been the *corps d'élite* of light infantry which had been formed at Shorncliffe Camp under the first soldier in the Army, Sir John Moore. Born in November, 1761, the son of a Glasgow doctor, Moore had seen hard fighting in America, Corsica, the West Indies, Ireland, Holland and Egypt, becoming a brigadier at thirty-four, major-general at thirty-six and lieutenant-general at forty-three. Handsome and athletic, with broad shoulders and generous, penetrating eyes, there was something in his glance and bearing that warmed the coldest nature. He seemed made to inspire confidence and courage. "Every one," wrote the Duke of York's Military Secretary, "admires and loves him."

This great soldier was at once realist and idealist. So clear was his perception of what was wrong and so passionate his resolve to set it right that he sometimes expressed himself with a vehemence that alarmed the timorous. "My feelings were so strong and my indignation such," he wrote on one occasion, "as to bring tears to my eyes and for moments to stop my speech." When his normal good humour and love of friendly banter were in abeyance, there was a touch of pedantry in his virtue, not uncharacteristic of his uncompromising northern race. Towards corruption and injustice he was merciless. "Soldiers are flogged for drunkenness," he once observed, "I could not look them in the face if I was not to punish it equally in officers." The chilling contempt with which he turned on those who behaved unworthily was, like the love he inspired, still remembered fifty years after his death.

Yet it was not Moore's frown that made men follow him but his example and inspiration. He expected of others only what he demanded of himself. An ambitious man, he applied to his life, at a time when wire-pulling was the bane of the service, the unflinching principle that a soldier should not choose his lot but go wherever he was ordered. In the field he shared the lot of the meanest private; at the siege of San Fiorenzo he slept every night in his clothes on a bed of straw. Though a poor man, he on more than one occasion advanced the money to enable a deserving officer to obtain promotion. His simplicity and directness shrivelled up meanness and shabby conduct. Fearless, he shamed fear in others. "I ordered them to leap over it," he wrote in his diary after an engagement, "and upon their hesitating showed them the example of getting over it myself."

When Moore received his first command the Army was at the lowest point of its history. Its discipline was based on mechanical parades and mass firelock exercises, copied in the letter rather than the spirit from Frederick the Great's Prussia and increasingly divorced from the realities of war and human nature. It was enforced regardless of humanity and common sense; soldiers were treated as automata to be bullied and flogged into an unthinking obedience. Moore, faced by a triumph of the natural courage and enthusiasm of the Revolutionary armies, went back to nature to defeat them. He did not discard the traditional discipline of the British Service; he humanised it. Against the *élan* of the armed *sans-culottes*, so resistless when confronted only by the "stiff solidarity" of the old monarchial armies of the continent, he opposed an equal enthusiasm based on common-sense discipline and careful training.

His opportunity to remodel the Army arose out of the need for light infantry. The French had won their battles with a horde of highly individualised skirmishers and sharpshooters going ahead of their dense, half-disciplined columns and firing from every side into the rigid Teuton lines whose only reply were machine-like volleys, imposing on the parade ground but ineffective against such invisible and fast-moving targets. By the time the columns came into range or the cavalry charged, the defenders were already demoralised, and the rather sketchy discipline of the former—strengthened by successive victories—was seldom tested. An antidote for the *tirailleur* had had to be found. At the outset the British, being almost without light infantry, had relied on hired German Jägers who were little more than armed game-keepers and foresters. The exigencies of West Indian warfare, like those of American warfare two decades before, caused General Grey and his successors, Abercromby and Moore, to train special companies as protective and reconnaissance screens. The need for more of these being acutely felt during the brief invasion of Holland in 1799, the Duke of York had ordered the formation of an experimental rifle corps at Horsham to which fifteen regiments were ordered to send officers and men for courses of instruction. Trained in Windsor Forest by two brilliant leaders, Colonel Coote Manningham and Lieutenant-Colonel William Stewart, these were formed in the spring of 1801 into the 95th Regiment of the Line—a rifle corps with distinctive green uniform and dark buttons and accoutrements. Disbanded at the end of the Revolutionary War, they were re-formed when the war clouds regathered, armed with the new Baker rifle—a weapon of high precision compared with the smooth-bore musket of the heavy infantry—and in October, 1802, consigned to Shorncliffe Camp for special training under Sir John Moore. Here, facing across the Channel towards Napoleon's cantonments, they formed with the 14th Light Dragoons and the 52nd and 43rd Regiments—both reconstituted as light infantry—the spearhead of the force designed to repel invasion. For the next three years, until they passed overseas, they were trained by Moore in an amalgam of disciplined team-work and individual initiative un-matched even among Napoleon's finest veterans. With the archers of Crécy and Agincourt and the Brigade of Guards, they formed England's peculiar contribution to the art of land warfare.

Moore's goal was the "thinking fighting man." In the reconstituted 52nd—his own regiment—officers, themselves taught their drill in the ranks, were encouraged to get to know their men as individuals, to bring out the best of which each man was capable and teach him to think for himself. Wherever possible, he was to be shown the why and wherefore of things; to comprehend his duty instead of merely obeying it blindly out of fear or mechanical routine. Punishment, particularly of the "curse, hang and flog" kind that robbed a man of dignity, was discouraged. Its place was taken by a discipline of example and encouragement. In an army notorious for inability to fend for itself in the field, every man of the Light Brigade—taking a leaf from the self-reliant French—was taught to cook and tailor and to take pride in living sparely against the day when he would have to depend solely on himself. Troops were trained for war under war conditions; when they marched, they bivouacked by the roadside instead of in town or village. The formal brass, feather and pipeclay review so dear to military pedants was abandoned for the field-day—an exercise in which war conditions were reproduced as closely as possible. Everything was made to serve the one great end of reality: the defeat of Napoleon's invincibles.

In all this Moore worked with nature instead of against it. In the quick march which he and his assistants devised for the light infantryman, the constrained and rigid movements of the Prussian march were abandoned for a free and natural rhythm whose object was the maximum of speed with the minimum of fatigue. By being taught to move quickly men became habituated to thinking quickly. In the same way the art of fire was taught, not as an automatic contribution to a blind mechanical volley, but as a highly individualised application of the qualities of judgment, observation, vision and skill. Its object, Moore's pupils were told, was "to inflict death upon the enemy rather than to confound, astonish and intimidate." Armed with a rifle capable of great accuracy up to 300 or even—in the hands of a master—500 yards, the rifleman was taught, first at the butts and then in the field, to judge and use cover and varied ground, to fire always to kill and never to waste a shot. He was trained not as a machine but as a craftsman, the consciousness of whose skill—the best guarantee for his survival on the battlefield—gave him courage and self-confidence. So also the care of the rifle was strictly inculcated, and distinguishing green and white cockades awarded for marksmanship.

Above all, Moore's men were schooled in that art which, though repeatedly forgotten under the shock of successive inventions and weapons, is in all ages the ultimate arbiter of war: the combination of fire and movement. The essence of light infantry work was movement, whether in search of information or in the protection of the heavy infantry of the Line. And fire was taught as the concomitant of movement, so that at all times and in all places movement—with its manifold dangers—should be covered by accurate, well-timed and economical fire. A rifleman in battle was the instrument of an orchestra in which every change of position, whether of individual or unit, was, wherever possible, protected by co-ordinated fire, directed at the precise spot from which any interference with that movement might come. The Light Brigade's special system of drill was directed to this end. Taught to the recruit by word of mouth in close order on the parade ground, it was subsequently carried out in extended order by bugle, horn and whistle. It aimed at combining the action of highly individualised and rapidly-moving men and units, working together to destroy or outwit the enemy.

At the back of every rifleman's mind Moore instilled the principle that the enemy was always at hand ready to strike. Whether on reconnaissance or protective duty, he was taught to be wary and on guard: to explore country, gather information, watch and question travellers and inhabitants, investigate and map-out roads, paths, fords and bridges. It was the pride of a light infantryman never to be caught napping; of a light infantry regiment or company never to have an outpost or piquet surprised. When attacked, the latter were taught how to fall back without giving away the position of their main body; rules carefully devised, but always elastic and capable of infinite adjustment, were laid down for setting and relieving sentry lines and patrols by day and night, for defending approaches to villages, bridges and road junctions, for utilising hedges, woods and orchards and every incline of the ground for cover and fire. The British army of the future was to be encompassed at all times and places by an invisible screen of marksmen, watching the enemy from behind every bush and stone, each one an alert and intelligent individual acting in close but invisible concert with his comrades.

The leaven of Moore's training had only just begun to permeate the heavy, unthinking mass of the old Army when the opportunity came to test it and him. Even his Light Infantry regiments were still recruited from the national rag-tag-and-bobtail: penniless, drunken Irish peasants, village bad-hats, slum bullies and pimps, balloted Militia ploughboys with a penchant for drink and roving. But in 1808 the British soldier was summoned from the barrack-square to the battlefield by Napoleon's invasion of his satellite, Spain, and by the passionate reaction of the Spanish people to his treachery and their appeal to Britain for help. In July of that year a small British advance-guard under Sir Arthur Wellesley landed in Portugal and by its victory at Vimeiro succeeded in expelling the French from that country. Moore himself followed with reinforcements at the end of August, but, owing to the distrust felt of him by the politicians—who resented his outspokenness—only as a subordinate to two senior officers with a tithe of his ability and fighting experience. But their sudden recall, and that of Wellesley, in September to face a Court of Enquiry in London unexpectedly presented him with the greatest command held by any British general since Marlborough.

The decision to throw the whole weight of the nation's military effort into Spain was taken as a result of the surrender on July 23rd of a French army to the ragged patriots of Andalusia.

When the astonishing news of the capitulation of Baylen reached him, the Secretary for War, Lord Castlereagh, urged the dispatch of a British Army to northern Spain to enable the men of Asturias and Aragon to strike at the enemy's communications. With this object he at once began collecting transports, and by September 3rd had completed preparations for sending 14,000 infantry, 4000 cavalry and 800 artillerymen under Lieutenant-General Sir David Baird to Corunna. Three weeks later the Cabinet decided to add to them 20,000 of the 30,000 troops already landed in Portugal and to place the whole under the command of Sir John Moore.

The decision was based on a sound instinct: that a major test was imminent in Spain and that every available man would be needed. With hatred for his rule growing from Vistula to Ebro, Napoleon could not afford to admit defeat; when his troops abandoned Madrid, French funds fell from 94 to 70. He made no attempt to conceal the fact that he was preparing revenge. "The hideous leopard," he told his soldiers, "contaminates by its presence the peninsula of Spain and Portugal. Let us carry our victorious eagles to the Pillars of Hercules. . . . No Frenchman can enjoy a moment's repose so long as the sea is not free."

Yet Britain's military preparations were founded on an illusion. Ministers, and to a still greater extent the public to whom they were responsible, supposed that Spain was a modern, homogeneous State whose strength could be measured by its size and historic prowess. Palafox's defence of Saragossa stirred the popular imagination; the tale of the brave girl who, standing on her kinsfolks' heaped corpses and the ashes of her home, continued to train her gun on the invader, was in every mouth. The patriotism and the courage of the Spaniards became for the moment an article of British faith.

On the face of it, there seemed reason for confidence in Spain. Within a few weeks of Baylen the French had been expelled from every part of the peninsula save Navarre and Barcelona. Madrid had been reoccupied by Castaños on August 23rd,

Saragossa relieved of all danger a week earlier; Joseph Bonaparte had abandoned Burgos and withdrawn as far as Vittoria without a fight. By the end of August a bare 60,000 French troops stood behind the Ebro in the extreme north-west corner of the peninsula they had hoped to conquer. Forty thousand of their comrades remained behind as prisoners or corpses.

British belief that the French had met their match in the Spaniards was more than shared by the latter. They did not merely suppose they could smash Napoleon: they knew it. "They have no idea," wrote *The Times* correspondent from Corunna, "that it is possible for them to be beaten; their rage is unbounded when the name of Bonaparte is mentioned, but their hatred of the French is mixed with contempt." All the fierce hereditary pride of their race had been re-kindled. A spontaneous popular outburst had thrown off both the French invader and the corrupt government that had obscured their national glories. Once more, as in the days of Charles V and Philip II, they were the greatest nation in the world. They took no thought for the morrow, but gave themselves up to unbridled rejoicing.

What this valiant and ancient people failed to see was that in overturning a corrupt Administration and scaring a few French generals they had not solved their real problem. They had merely exchanged, with Napoleon's help, a bad government for no government at all. Their grandees, poisoned by the same sterile pride and servile attendance on an idle Court that had ruined the aristocracy of France, were without backbone or political experience; for generations they had hardly been free to leave Madrid without the king's permission. Some of them, as a result of the former French alliance or because they feared anarchy, sympathised with the enemy or were suspected by the people of doing so. The lesser nobles, the provincial gentry and ecclesiastics, who, with the urban mobs, had taken the lead in raising the standard of independence, were mostly narrow provincials whose sympathies were bounded by their own mountain skyline. They were without the slightest capacity for administration or for co-operating with any one whose views differed from their own. They shared to the full the national contempt for compromise and the strong national sense of personal pride. Within a few weeks of the French retreat several of the provincial Juntas were almost at open war and were threatening to employ their respective armies not against the enemy but each other. All competed for British arms and money, demanding fantastic quantities of both and doing their utmost to prevent their neighbours from getting any. Only with the utmost difficulty, and under pressure from England, could they be got to join in setting up a Supreme Junta. Nor, thereafter, did they pay it the slightest respect.

To local jealousies and vanity was added what a warm British admirer called the "apathy and confidence of the Spanish character." Every Spaniard seemed ready to postpone public business to an indefinite to-morrow. The need for application, perseverance and discipline was universally ignored. It was imagined that victories were made by instinctive courage, armies by popular enthusiasm, strategic combinations by eloquence. Ragged hordes of armed peasants and students trailed about the countryside, undrilled and unsupplied, discussing with all the fervour of their race the grand operations which were to overthrow the greatest soldier of all time. There was no supreme command, for no provincial Junta would allow the army to be commanded by any general but its own. Yet in imagination and boastful talk—to which the whole nation seemed prone—this leaderless force, exaggerated in numbers and untrained for war, was not merely to drive the veterans of France from their strongholds in the north, but by a series of intricate converging operations over a three-hundred mile front, to encircle and annihilate them. Afterwards it was to advance to Paris and dictate peace.

With such confidence in their prowess the Spaniards were in no mood to take advice from British generals. They did not need amateurs to teach them how to make war. They took the money, arms and ammunition they proffered, but for the rest ignored the foreign heretics who until so recently had been their enemies. So long as the British remained at a distance, a warm and truly Spanish eloquence was extended to them; the moment they set their clumsy and unhallowed feet on Spanish soil or tried to interfere with the Spaniard's imperious preference for his own way, they became objects of loathing and suspicion. Any discipline, save of its own choosing, was anathema to this stark, passionate people. Thus the released Spanish prisoners from England, who had been feasted, clothed and armed by their former captors, mutinied on the way home and carried off the British ship in which they were sailing.

.   .   .   .

It was in such circumstances that at the end of the first week of October, 1808, Moore received his mission. Leaving 10,000 troops to defend Portugal, he was to proceed with the remaining 20,000 to northern Spain, where he would be joined by another 17,000 under Sir David Baird. He was to support the Spanish armies in their attempt to encircle the French and, in the event of a Supreme Commander being appointed by the Junta, to place himself—with reservations—under his orders. He was to convey his troops into Spain by land or sea as he thought best. A correct and friendly personal letter from Castlereagh assured him of every assistance.

The army heard of the appointment with satisfaction. A new spirit began to run through the dusty camp of Queluz; the men knew instinctively that the unaccountable inertia of the past six weeks was at an end. The new general appeared everywhere, inspecting regiments, reorganising magazines and stores, dismissing fraudulent contractors and talking to every one he encountered. Men suddenly began to work with a will.

Yet some of those to whom the Commander-in-Chief spoke noticed an underlying gravity in his expression. Ministers might write of going into Spain like going into Hyde Park, but Moore as a practical soldier knew the difficulties. He could not effect his junction with Baird by sea because, without previously establishing magazines in the barren Galician hills, it would be impossible to march so large an army through the passes to Castile in time to succour the Spaniards. And though Ministers talked about the impending envelopment of the French—"a sort of gibberish," Moore privately noted, "which men in office use and fancy themselves military men without knowing how far it is susceptible of being carried into practice"—he was painfully aware that the problem was not, as people in England supposed, whether he could reach the Ebro in time to share the triumph of the Spanish armies but whether he could unite his own forces behind them before Napoleon launched his attack. His one chance of doing so in time—for he was convinced that Napoleon would strike before winter—was to march his men across the Portuguese highlands to Salamanca and join forces with Baird in the Castilian plain at Valladolid or Burgos.

For such a march—more than three hundred miles across mountains rising in places to 4000 feet—Moore had neither maps nor magazines. His commissariat and Staff were both raw, and, owing to the Treasury's failure to supply bullion, it was impossible to obtain enough carts and draught animals. His men had therefore to carry the bulk of their equipment. And though he sent his engineers ahead to prospect, he was unable in the time at his disposal to discover whether any of the roads were fit for heavy artillery. The Portuguese seemed certain that none were, and, with the torrential autumn rains daily expected, Moore dared not risk it. He therefore dispatched all his guns save half a dozen light six-pounders by the Elvas and Badajoz highway to Madrid together with his transport park and an escort of 4000 troops, including his entire cavalry force, under Lieutenant-General Sir John Hope. Only when they had gone too far for recall, did Moore discover that his allies had misinformed him.

On October 16th, while the foxhunters in England were riding out in their autumnal glory, the army turned its face towards Spain. "A more glorious set of fellows," wrote young George Napier, "never was seen." They wanted only experience in continental warfare. Their equipment was still incomplete, but Moore could wait no longer. "The regiments are already marching," he wrote to Pitt's niece, Lady Hester Stanhope, "I pray for good weather. If it rains, the torrents will swell and be impassable, and I shall be accounted a bungler. I wish you were here with us, in your red habit *à l'Amazone*."

For the next three weeks the troops pressed across the mountains into the north-east. The sand and olive trees of the Tagus plain, the crash of the muskets on the paving stones, the gloomy, stinking streets and high, shuttered houses, with barbers strumming on guitars in the doorways and loafing crowds in long brown cloaks and three-cornered hats, gave way to primitive hill villages where the corn was threshed by trampling bullocks and mules and the blow-flies swarmed over the middens in the central square. The roads became goat-tracks and ravines; every few minutes a cart would sink into a hole or overturn on a stone. Presently there were precipices and gullies over which the six-pounders had to be hauled on ropes by sweating, cursing infantry-men.

After the first week the rains came down: not ordinary rain such as Englishmen knew, but cascades of huge globular drops which soaked every one to the marrow and drew clouds of steam from the dripping columns. There was no shelter save for a rare mountain farm or peasant's hut, swarming with fleas and rank with the stench of the communal vessel round which the family and the livestock slept. Every mile the way grew more rocky and bleak. Occasionally a ruined Moorish castle on a conical hill guarding a defile would relieve the monotony. But still the army pressed on, climbing ever higher into the cold, dripping clouds. As it approached the Spanish frontier, all sign of human habitation vanished, save once in a glimpse through clouds, a solitary convent nestling in a bunch of trees on the bosom of the mountain, a vast abrupt vale, and below, revealed in that apocalyptic second, the whole system of the waters. Then the swirling mist closed down again, and there was nothing to be seen but the bleak, rocky, wretched road with a black hill on one side and a precipice on the other, both lost in impenetrable, icy cloud. It made a young officer with a touch of the poet feel as if he were travelling on the bare outside of the world, "bordered by the chaotic beginning of things."

With the crossing of the frontier in the second week of November spirits rose. First impressions of the new country were greatly in its favour; the houses were cleaner and the farms better stocked, the proud, courtly people more handsome and hospitable, the landscape more romantic. Ensign Boothby, who had gone ahead of the right flank of the army to Alcantara, where Trajan's viaduct over the Tagus reminded him of "the bridge of Sin and Death striding over chaos," was greeted by the alcalde in his scarlet cloak and treated to the fandango by girls whose graceful pride, as they snapped their fingers and alternately raised and lowered their heads, awed alike their rustic partners and the watching redcoats. Later he was entertained in a capital house with curtains and clean beds by "a fine, black, animated Spaniard" with a most beautiful wife, from whose long, black mantilla, brilliant rolling eyes, Roman nose, sweet mouth, jet black hair and graceful curls he could not take his eyes. The quicker tempo of the land affected the marching columns as they hurried on through sparkling air and cork woods to Salamanca. They felt ready for anything. "We had fought and conquered and felt elated," wrote Rifleman Harris of the 95th; "Spain was before us and every man in the Rifles seemed only too anxious to get a rap at the French again. It was a glorious sight to see our colours spread in those fields. The men seemed invincible and nothing, I thought, could beat them."[1]

. . . .

[1] *Recollections of Rifleman Harris*, 71. See also *Boothby, under England's Flag*, 185-6 *et passim*; *Services Adventures and Experiences of Captain Blakeney*, 22-4, 27-9; A. L. F. Schaumann, *On the Road with Wellington*, 11-63; *Journal of a Soldier of the Seventy-First Regiment*, 50-1; *Oxfordshire Light Infantry Chronicle* (1902), 226.

Meanwhile another British army had entered Spain. On the morning of October 13th, Mr. Crabb Robinson, *The Times* correspondent at Corunna, was startled by the report of cannon and, running to the ramparts, saw more than a hundred and fifty transports sailing in a double line before a gentle breeze; it made him proud to see them. It was Baird with the first 12,000 from England. Unfortunately there was a hitch, for no one had given authority for them to land, and the provincial Junta was either unable or unwilling to do so. In the end a special messenger had to be sent to Madrid to obtain the Supreme Junta's leave. Hookham Frere, however, who landed at Corunna a few days later as British Envoy, was given a tremendous reception. His carriage was dragged through the streets amid vivas, crackers and rockets, he was feasted at a banquet of countless dishes highly flavoured with garlic and treated to a theatrical performance at which Pluto appeared trampling Bonaparte under foot while the whole audience rose and sang "God Save the King" and "Rule Britannia."

But not till October 25th was any reply received from Madrid. It then only gave authority for Baird to land if he insisted and strongly urged that he and his transports should remove themselves to some point on the coast less dangerously near the naval arsenal of Ferrol. Baird, a blunt Anglo-Indian soldier, however insisted, and next day his troops began to put ashore. But his difficulties had only just begun. The authorities objected to their disembarking in any but the smallest detachments and failed to make any arrangements for their feeding. It was not till November 4th that they were all ashore. Even then their progress was painfully slow. As in Portugal, the Treasury had omitted to provide bullion to hire forage wagons and draught cattle. There was not even money to pay the troops.

All this took place in an atmosphere of complete unreality. Nobody in Corunna seemed to have the slightest idea what was happening elsewhere in Spain. The only information that could be obtained from the local leaders was that the French were flying; questioned as to where they were flying or from whom, they took refuge in vague generalities and evasions. Moore was faced by precisely the same difficulties: there was no Spanish Commander-in-Chief or General Staff, and the only authority to whom he could appeal was a Supreme Junta of thirty-four persons, all possessing equal powers and all apparently equally unpractical. So far as they gave their minds to military matters—most of their time was spent in discussing theoretical constitutions and quarrelling with the provincial Juntas about their powers—they were obsessed by a fantastic plan for encircling the French with a converging movement of three almost completely unco-ordinated armies whose numbers in their own imagination they exaggerated as much as their fighting capacity. Any anxiety Moore might feel for the junction of his own forces, now moving across Spain in widely separated columns, he was assured, was entirely needless, since the enemy was securely hemmed in by immensely superior strength. The British Government seemed to share this illusion; misled by the uncritical optimism of its military agents with the Spanish armies, Castlereagh wrote on November 1st that the French were threatened from Saragossa to Bilbao by forces more than twice as large and that Napoleon's reinforcements could never reach them.

The Spanish leaders gave little thought to Napoleon. That he was likely to strike before their schemes matured never crossed their minds. Yet since the disaster at Baylen he had increased the year's levée of conscripts to a quarter of a million and transferred the pick of his veterans from Germany and Italy to Bayonne, using continuous relays of wagons to move them quickly. Within four weeks of leaving the Danube and Elbe they were concentrated on the Spanish frontier.

At the same time the Emperor took steps to safeguard his rear. Putting his jack-boot down on underground patriotic activities in Prussia and browbeating the Austrian ambassador, he summoned his ally, the Czar Alexander, to Erfurt. Here at the end of September, amid servile princes and splendid pageantry, he secured a promise of Russian military aid against any uprising in the east. Then he hurried back home to Paris and told his Legislative Assembly that he was on his way to Spain to crown his brother in Madrid and plant his eagles on the towers of Lisbon. As his berlin drove southwards, the long columns of the Grand Army were already pouring along the trunk road to Vittoria. By November 1st, 1808, 120,000 troops were already on the Ebro.

Had the Spanish armies, though outnumbered, acted on the defensive, they might have been able to hold the French until the arrival of Moore's troops. But, having wasted three months in controversy, they chose the moment of the Grand Army's appearance for their long-advertised attack. On the last day of October Blake with the Army of Galicia, advancing without the slightest support from his colleagues, walked into Ney's lines at Durango. Here his troops, half naked and starving, were trounced and driven back to Bilbao. "Intractable as swine, obstinate as mules and unmanageable as bullocks," as a disgusted British officer wrote, they were "cut up like rations or dispersed in all directions like a flock of sheep."

A week later Napoleon reached Vittoria. He found himself in the centre of a horseshoe, with a compact force of the finest troops in Europe facing three widely separated bodies of peasant levies whose total numbers were inferior to his own. He struck immediately. In two successive days Blake was routed again at Espinosa, only escaping annihilation by a precipitate flight over the Cantabrian mountains, and the Army of Estremadura—theoretically in reserve—was utterly shattered at Gamonal village north of Burgos. On November 9th Burgos was a busy military base, supposedly far behind the lines and swarming with cheerful Spanish soldiers. A day later it was a deserted city full of untidy corpses and sacked houses while around it the French cavalry hunted Count Belvedere's men over the Castilian plain. Belvedere himself—a youth of twenty completely unaccustomed to command—fled with his Staff to Aranda, 60 miles in the rear. The Spanish centre had ceased to exist. On the 13th the French occupied Valladolid—the intended rendezvous of the British army—while the Supreme Junta was still debating the possibility of their being able to advance at all.

. . . .

Such was the state of affairs on November 13th when Sir John Moore, having covered 250 miles of mountain track in just over three weeks, was met at Ciudad Rodrigo by an urgent summons from Belvedere. "The Spaniards," he noted dryly, "seem to think that everybody should fly but themselves." Two days later

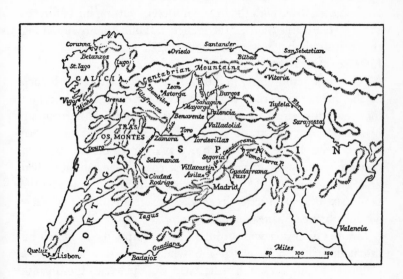

Spain 1808-9

at Salamanca he heard the news of Gamonal. He had arrived too late. Valladolid, sixty miles to the north-east, was already in French hands; without so much as a Spanish piquet between, his army was threatened with destruction before it could assemble. Baird, who had been expected at Astorga by November 14th, was still detained by the rains at Lugo nearly a hundred miles to the north-west; his 5000 horse under Lord Paget had only landed

at Corunna on the day Moore reached Salamanca. Hope, with
the artillery, was a hundred miles away to the south on the far side
of the Guadarramas. A more depressing position for a commander it was scarcely possible to conceive. Behind on Moore's
only line of retreat were the barren, rain-soaked mountains
through which he had come and a countryside in which he had
no hope of maintaining himself.

Yet the very folly of the Spanish generals that had betrayed him
came to his aid. For Castaños and Palafox, wholly regardless
of the fate of their colleagues, proceeded to advance on Napoleon's eastern flank with the insane notion of cutting him off from
France. The result was that the French, not unnaturally supposing
the British to be in retreat to Portugal, switched their main
forces eastwards from Burgos towards the Ebro. Meanwhile
Moore, being completely in the dark as to what either the French
or the Spaniards were doing—for no one troubled to send him
information—remained where he was, resting and regrouping
his army and trying to obtain intelligence. By November 18th
he knew that Blake had been routed at Espinosa on the 10th and
that the chance of a junction with Baird was even slighter than
he had supposed. It did not add to his comfort to receive on the
same day a cheerful letter from Castlereagh predicting an early
advance by the Spanish armies.

Moore's dilemma was pitiful. The assumptions on which his
instructions had been issued and which were still held by the
Cabinet no longer existed: they had vanished with the Spanish
armies of the North and Centre. The fog of war had descended
over the Castilian plain ahead, and he had no cavalry with which
to penetrate it. The Ebro was nearly three hundred miles away
and the whole French army lay between him and it.

Yet so long as Castaños was fighting there, it would be craven
to abandon the Spaniards to their fate. Because his first duty was
to preserve his army—his country's only one—Moore had sent
Baird and Hope discretionary powers to fall back on Corunna
and Lisbon should they find their way barred by overwhelming
force. But until the attempt to assemble his forces had been made,

he felt he had no option but to remain where he was. To Hester Stanhope, perhaps his dearest friend on earth, he wrote that he was in a scrape and that she must be prepared for bad news, though his troops were in good spirits and eager to make a fight for it. "Farewell, my dear Lady Hester," he added, "if I extricate myself and those with me from our present difficulties, I shall return to you with satisfaction; but if not it will be better I shall never quit Spain."

It was in this resolve that Moore on November 28th sat down to reply to an urgent letter from Baird. Five days earlier the latter at Astorga, a hundred and twenty miles to the north, had heard of the disasters of Espinosa and Gamonal and the French capture of Valladolid. Armed with Moore's discretionary power to fall back on Corunna, he had at once ordered a retreat. "It certainly never could be the intention of the British Government," he wrote, "that we should engage in the defence of the country, unaided and unsupported by any Spanish force." But Moore at once recalled him. "I see my situation," he informed him, "in as unfavourable a light as you or any one can do. But it is our business to make every effort to unite here and to obey our orders and the wishes of our country. It would never do to retreat without making the attempt. If the enemy prevent us, there is no help for it, but if he does not, I am determined to unite the army. When that is done we shall act according to circumstances. There is still a chance that the presence of so large a British force may give spirits to the Spaniards."

But late that night Moore learnt that the last Spanish army had ceased to exist. Riding five hundred miles in six days, a member of the British mission at Castaños's headquarters arrived from the capital to report that on November 23rd that general and Palafox had been routed at Tudela. The British were now the only undefeated force in northern Spain.

Around them was a population without the slightest outward trace of the fervid Iberian patriotism so extolled at home. The peasants continued their ceaseless labour in the fields. The townsmen, wrapped in their brown winter cloaks, lounged about in their hundreds in the sunshine, "apathetic, indifferent, gloomy and sunk in utter idleness." They seemed unmoved alike by Moore's appeals for help and the menace of the foraging cavalry which rode at will over the countryside. "After leading us into a most dreadful mess through their deceitful and mendacious promises," a Hanoverian officer wrote, "they run away and say: 'Now try to get out of it as best you can!' The people here have the cool effrontery to look upon the English troops as exotic animals who have come to engage in a private fight with the French, and now that they are here all that the fine Spanish gentlemen have to do is to look on with their hands in their pockets. They do not regard us in the least as allies who are prepared to shed their blood for Spain; they simply look upon us as heretics. In our billets it is as much as we can do to get a glass of water."

Under the circumstances there seemed nothing for it but to get out as quickly as possible. During the night Moore wrote again to Baird, ordering him to return to Corunna, re-embark in his transports and proceed to the Tagus. His own retreat through the Portuguese highlands to Lisbon would begin as soon as Hope's column, now at Villacastin seventy miles to the south-east, could reach him. He ordered it to proceed by forced marches to Alba de Tormes and thence to Ciudad Rodrigo on the Portuguese border where he proposed to join it. So long as Castaños's army remained in the field, he wrote, there had been hope, but now he could see none.

Till his guns and cavalry arrived Moore's position was one of acute danger. He had no idea how many troops Napoleon had with him on the Castilian plain: he knew that they could not be less than 80,000 to his own 17,000; he suspected that they were far more. To increase his troubles, protests began to arrive from Hookham Frere at Madrid urging him, in the name of the patriots, to stand firm, and repeating the old, familiar fables of impending Spanish victories. To support them came two Castilian generals—creatures of fantasy—who, declaring that 20,000 of their troops were barring the mountain road to

Madrid, outlined fresh projects for the annihilation of Napoleon.

Yet at that moment the Emperor was in the suburbs of Madrid. As soon as he had learnt of the rout of the Spanish armies on the Ebro, he had marched on the capital. In his path was the snow ridge of the Guadarramas, where 12,000 Spaniards, hastily dispatched from Madrid, were holding the narrow and all but impregnable Somosierra defile. But once again the impact of cavalry proved fatal to undisciplined troops. Under cover of a mountain mist Napoleon launched the Polish lancers of the Imperial Guard against the guns at the head of the pass. The defenders fled in confusion, leaving the road to Madrid open. On December 1st Napoleon's advance guard appeared before the city.

Next evening Moore learnt what had occurred from his aide-de-camp, Colonel Thomas Graham, who arrived from the capital just in time to give the Spanish generals the lie. As an exposé of their projects the news was conclusive. On the other hand, it temporarily relieved the British army of danger. Either because he was unaware of its position or because he viewed it with indifference, Napoleon had vanished over the mountains to the south. Two days later Hope, who had shown the greatest calm, initiative and judgment in a most trying situation, arrived with his precious guns and cavalry at Alba de Tormes, a day's march from Salamanca. For the first time since he left Lisbon Moore had a balanced fighting force under his immediate command.

On the morrow, December 5th, 1808, just as he was preparing to retreat at leisure on Portugal, further tidings arrived from the Spanish capital. The populace had risen once more, refused to admit Napoleon and appointed new leaders who were preparing to resist to the death. Madrid was to become a second Saragossa. The brave and generous British were urged to hasten to its aid.

In Moore's heart there flickered once more a faint spark of hope. He had little belief that Madrid could withstand the French assault; like Napoleon he knew the power of artillery. Nor was he in any doubt of the peril of remaining a day longer in northern

Spain, now that his guns were safe. The odds against him—though he could not tell how great—were enormous. But he had been sent to save Spain, and, though her leaders had shown themselves worthless, her people, he was beginning to see, might be worth saving. A connoisseur in human virtue and courage, he saw—with a flash of poet's insight—that, under all its absurdities and fantasies, this strange, moody, mercurial race had bottom. The hardy, sober, industrious peasants who went about their daily affairs with such astonishing indifference when the French were at their doors, and who never gave them a thought till they were riding down the village street, were true men after all. Again and again during Moore's stay at Salamanca British officers were caught in villages overrun by the tide of French cavalry. Yet though every Spaniard in the place knew of their presence, not one was ever betrayed.

Such a people, resolved to save itself, might still be saved. If British action could give them the will to fight on, Moore saw that it was his duty to give it. Deep down he knew that there was something more precious even than his country's only army: her honour. If he could use the fine instrument he had made—even if in doing so he should break or lose it—to create in Spain a permanent focus of resistance to Napoleon, he would have done what he had been sent to do. For the first time since he crossed the frontier his path became clear.

One thing the Spaniards needed above everything else: that of which in their brief hour of triumph they had been so prodigal—time. While Madrid held out, the southern provinces and Portugal were still free from the invader. Within a few weeks the winter would fall with its fierce winds from the mountains and the snowdrifts blocking the passes; if Napoleon's tempestuous advance could be held till then, the patriot leaders at Sevile, Valencia and Cadiz and the British and Portuguese at Lisbon might still be able to form new armies before the spring. To relieve Madrid, as the leaders of the populace demanded, was far beyond Moore's power: he could not, with half his little army and the bulk of his cavalry still in Galicia, cross the Guadarramas into the plains of New Castile. That would be to walk into the lion's den.

Yet a plan was taking shape in his mind. If he could join forces with Baird, he might strike eastwards with 35,000 men at Napoleon's communications with France. At the very moment that his contemptuous enemy thought he was retiring on Portugal, he would advance in the opposite direction. By doing so he would secure the support—for what it was worth—of the remnants of Blake's defeated army which La Romana had rallied on the Asturian border. Startling as such a move might seem, Moore saw what far-reaching effects it might have. Unable to feed his army on the wintry tableland of central Spain, the conqueror of Europe would be forced to recross the Guadarramas in the December snows and deal with the threat to his life-line. Then the British army would become the quarry and have to run for its life over the mountains. But in the meantime Spain would have been given a respite—and a second chance.

Moore acted quickly, for speed was the essence of what he had to do. On the evening of December 5th he wrote two letters— one to Castlereagh, informing him of his intentions, and the other to Baird, recalling him to Astorga while warning him to be ready for an immediate retreat into Galicia. "Madrid still holds out," he told him, "this is the first instance of enthusiasm shown. There is a chance that the example may be followed and the people be roused. . . . I mean to proceed bridle in hand, for, if the bubble bursts and Madrid falls, we shall have to run for it."

Four days later, while Moore was waiting for Baird to retrace his steps, his aide-de-camp, Colonel Graham, returned to headquarters with the tidings that Madrid had capitulated. On the very day after the patriot leaders had dispatched their appeal to Moore they had entered into negotiations for surrender. Nor did they trouble to inform him that they had done so. On December 4th the Emperor had entered the capital. The way was open to Lisbon and Cadiz.

But Moore came of a stubborn race. He had made up his mind

to harass Napoleon's communications, and, though Spain now seemed doomed, he meant, while his adversary's back was turned, to effect his junction with Baird and do what damage he could before he had to run for it. One of his officers, scouting to the north-west, had discovered that the French, in their southward surge, had evacuated Valladolid; they were obviously still unaware of his presence on the edge of the Castilian plain. He was free to advance to it and assemble his army where he had originally planned. His troops, who made a fine show parading in the noble square of Salamanca in the December sunshine, were now thoroughly rested after their march; strict discipline had been reestablished and, careless of the future, they only asked to be led against the enemy. The weather had suddenly grown cold; at night the frost was so intense that a Highlander of the 71st had his powdered pigtail frozen to the ground as he slept. But the days were clear and exhilarating, and the ground had dried up.

On December 11th the advance began. But three days later, when the army was half-way to Valladolid, a sheaf of captured documents was brought into Moore's headquarters at Alaejos. A French officer, carrying dispatches from Napoleon's Chief-of-Staff to Marshal Soult near Burgos, had been murdered in a roadside village for insulting the postmaster. His papers came into the hands of the British skirmishing cavalry. They showed that Napoleon had far greater forces in Spain than had been supposed —well over 300,000 men—and that, all resistance in the centre of the country having collapsed, he was advancing towards Badajoz and Lisbon. But their most valuable disclosure was that Soult, unaware that the British were in his path, was moving westwards across the Carrion with 18,000 men, while Junot was marching on Burgos in support.

It was the most useful information that Moore had received from his allies since he entered the country, and it reached him characteristically, not from their rulers but through the rude and obscure. It revealed both his danger and his opportunity. If Baird continued his march on Carrion and Burgos unsupported by the rest of the army fifty miles to the south, he would be overwhelmed. But if the British united promptly and fell on Soult's lines on the Carrion before Junot arrived, it would be Soult who would be overwhelmed. With La Romana announcing his readiness to move from Leon against the marshal's right flank, Moore had a chance of confronting an isolated group of the French army with forces twice as large. If he could only be quick enough he might, before retreating to the sea, present his country with a resounding victory.

He therefore gave orders to change his march from north-east to north so as to join Baird at the earliest moment. On December 15th, with the latter's advance guard at Benavente, he crossed the Douro in two columns at Zamora and Toro. The snow from the mountains was beginning to fall and the violence of the wind was such that the men could hardly stand. But nothing could halt Moore's pace; already his cavalry screen had made contact with Soult's patrols around Tordesillas and he knew that the alarm must soon be raised. Rifleman Harris of the 95th dropped under his load in the streets of Zamora like one dead; "we staggered on," he wrote, "looking neither to the right nor to the left." In his haste Moore was trying discipline high; the Spaniards still barred their houses and hid their food; the wintry plain was treeless and fuel unobtainable. But the troops were sustained by the thought of a fight; it was believed that Soult—the Duke of Damnation as they called him after his Dalmatian title—was flying before them and that they were near the end of the chase which they supposed had been going on ever since they left Lisbon. They were rough, unlettered men who knew nothing of strategy. But fighting the French was in their blood.

By December 20th the British forces had met, the infantry around Mayorga, the cavalry at Melgar Abaxo. The men surveyed each other curiously; those from Corunna, fresh from good quarters and rations, with bright jackets and shining accoutrements, those from Portugal gaunt, wayworn and rugged, with faces burnt dark by the sun. Next day they pushed on together towards Sahagun. Here at dawn on the 21st, after Lord Paget's cavalry had tried to surround a brigade of French horse,

500 men of the 15th Hussars charged and routed 700 French dragoons, capturing 13 officers, including two colonels, and 144 other ranks. Later, while the British marched into the town, Soult, now thoroughly alarmed, halted his advance and withdrew his outposts behind the Carrion.

. . . .

Though Moore could not know it, news of his move had reached Napoleon. Busied with edicts for reconstituting Spain, the Emperor had assumed that the British were in retreat before his vanguard down the Madrid-Lisbon road. The capture of some stragglers from Hope's division at Talavera had confirmed this impression. But on December 19th, just as he was about to set off from Madrid for Badajoz, Napoleon learnt the truth. The swaggering islanders, instead of retiring on their ships, had marched out of Salamanca eastwards and were already half-way across his lines of communication.

Napoleon retrieved his error with characteristic speed. Halting his westward march, he ordered an immediate concentration on the Castilian plain north of the Guadarramas. Leaving the Badajoz highway for Salamanca, his advance guard was to sever Moore's communications with Portugal. Ney was recalled from Aragon to support Soult, thus giving a respite to Saragossa, now facing a second siege. Soult himself was to act on the defensive and decoy the British on to Burgos. Meanwhile the flower of the Grand Army was to cross the Guadarramas under Napoleon's personal command and fall on Moore's flank at Tordesillas and Valladolid. Everything was to give way to the destruction of the arch-enemy.

But the price was the postponement for another year of the conquest of the Peninsula and the crossing of the Mediterranean. Napoleon knew that Austria was rearming, that his exactions and conscriptions in Germany were rousing a Teuton hornets' nest and that the example of Spain was awakening dangerous hopes in every corner of Europe. With Russian revenues dwindling under the pressure of the British blockade, he dared not rely on the

Czar's friendship. Once more the islanders with their meddling and stupidity had spoilt his best-laid designs. "All the evils, all the plagues which can afflict the human race," he wrote to Josephine, "come from London!"

Only one thing could retrieve the situation: the complete destruction of the British army. And that, thanks to Moore's temerity, was imminent. "The day we succeed in seeing these English," Napoleon wrote as he hurried north from Madrid, "will be a day of jubilee. Ah! that these 20,000 were 100,000 so that more English mothers might feel the horrors of war!" That night, while Moore's troops were resting and repairing their boots, the Grand Army began to ascend the Guadarrama. It was bitterly cold, a blizzard was blowing and the track was thick with snow. Three times the officers of the advance-guard reported that the pass was impracticable in such weather. But nothing could shake Napoleon's purpose: linking arms with two of his generals, he marched with the leading files till the summit was reached. It almost seemed that night as though the Revolution incarnate was hunting the soul of England over the mountains.

By December 23rd, Napoleon was at Villacastin, only 60 miles south of Valladolid where—unaware of the last minute alteration in the British march—he supposed Moore to be. Actually the latter was at Sahagun—40 miles further north—issuing orders for an attack on Soult's lines across the Carrion. "Sir John dines with General Paget," wrote a subaltern, "and battle is the word!" Advancing through the night, the troops were to fall on the French at dawn, following up with an assault on the enemy's main position at Saldana on Christmas Day. "The movement I am making," Moore reported to Frere, "is of the most dangerous kind; I not only risk to be surrounded at any moment by superior forces, but to have my communications intercepted with the Galicias. I wish it to be apparent to the whole world that we have done everything in our power in support of the Spanish cause and that we do not abandon it until long after the Spaniards had abandoned it."

Yet by a strange irony the unseeking soldier who was staking so much to keep his country's word was at that moment being reviled by ignorant amateurs as a timid procrastinator who had sullied England's honour by looking on while the Spaniards were overwhelmed. "I can't bear to think of it," wrote a grand lady; a retired ambassador at Brighton spoke with scorn of the British commander's readiness to get out of the way. Even Hookham Frere, flying with the Junta to Sevile, bombarded Moore with petulant notes charging him with an inactivity that had brought indelible disgrace to England and ruin to her ally. So outrageous did this brilliant man's letters become that his friend Canning was forced to remind him that the force he was seeking to commit to adventures in the Spanish hinterland was his country's only army; another, he was told, she had not to send.

.   .   .   .

On the evening of December 23rd, 1808, while Walter Scott at Ashestiel was writing that little could be hoped of a general who was always looking over his shoulder, Moore's men set out on their momentous march. They were in the highest spirits, telling each other that now they would beat the French to death and have their ease. "Every heart," wrote Captain Sterling, "beat high, every breast was buoyant for victory." As each column moved off into the snowlit night the regiments broke into cheers. Then they marched in silence, though some, remembering that it was the eve of Christmas, spoke of friends in England and of the yuletide feast.

But a little after midnight the leading files of the Light Brigade heard the sound of galloping on the road behind and saw a dragoon spur furiously past towards General Craufurd at the head of the column. Turning in his saddle, the general, after a glance at the dispatch, gave the order, "Halt!" A few minutes later the troops, grumbling furiously, were retracing their steps. Everywhere, as the orders were received, exultation gave way to gloom; even the best-disciplined murmured. When the First

Foot Guards, drawn up outside Sahagun Convent, were told by Sir David Baird to go back to their quarters and be ready to march in the morning, "nothing could be heard on every side but the clang of firelocks thrown down in despair."

For during the evening of the 24th Moore had learnt, first from La Romana and then from his own cavalry patrols, that Napoleon had recrossed the Guadarramas. At Palencia, only twenty miles to the south of Carrion, billeting officers had arrived with Imperial cavalry; the Emperor himself was reported close behind. Any further advance by the British would be suicidal. A day would be needed to reach Soult, another to beat him and a third to return to Sahagun, and by that time Napoleon's forces would be all round them. There was only one thing to do: to get back to Astorga and the mountain road to Corunna before it was too late.

War is largely a matter of guesswork; a general can seldom see what is happening on the other side of the hill. He must form on imperfect evidence the picture on which his plan of campaign is based and constantly refashion it on better. Yet it is a frailty of the human mind to cling rigidly to conceptions once formed. The hall-mark of a great commander is that, while refusing to allow mere rumour to confuse his dispositions, he is quick on receiving fresh data to abandon a false conception.

On the evidence of Marshal Berthier's captured dispatch Moore had formed a picture of the military situation in northern Spain as it was in the third week of December. On that picture he had acted boldly and decisively. But, just as his stroke was in mid-air, he received new information showing that the picture on which he was acting was no longer true. He did not hesitate. He withdrew his army westwards as quickly as it had come.

By doing so he averted—just in time—what might have been the greatest military disaster in British history. Napoleon was seeking to avenge by a single decisive stroke the Nile, Copenhagen and Trafalgar, Egypt and Vimiero, his lost colonies and the blockade of the Continent. He believed that England, war-weary and politically divided, would never recover from the catastrophe

of her last military hope. Her striking force was within his grasp.
While the Grand Army drove up like a thundercloud out of the
south against Moore's exposed flank, Junot was about to reinforce
Soult on his front and Lefebvre was hurrying up from the south-
west to seize the Galician passes in his rear. Yet, by his sudden
change of direction on December 13th and then by his equally
prompt retreat on the 23rd, Moore still eluded that grasping
hand. As the infuriated beast he had drawn charged down on
him, he stepped quickly aside.

But, unlike a matador, a commander has more to control than
his own body. He has to adjust his movements to his command.
It is courting disaster to ask too much of it. And Moore's men
had been sorely tried. During the past few days they had been
driven forward at a pace only endurable under the conviction
that victory was at hand. In bitter weather and an inhospitable
countryside they had outrun their supplies. Half of them were
young unfledged troops fresh from England; the other half had
been marching, save for one halt, at extreme pressure since the
middle of October. Now, without explanation, they were
ordered to retreat at an even faster pace. Discipline threatened to
crack under the strain.

Moore's problem was twofold. It was to cross the Esla and
gain the mountain defile beyond Astorga before the fastest
mover in the world could cut him off. It was also to hold his
army together as a fighting, manageable unit. He could not
defend any position for long or it would starve or be surrounded.
He could not go too fast or his discouraged and uneducated men
would lose cohesion. His assets were that his best troops were of
his own training and that, by skilful and timely dispositions, he
had left a margin of space and time between himself and the
hunter. His handicaps were that his solitary line of supply was
too congested and ill-found to maintain so large a force in mid-
winter, and that, owing to the habit of his country, his army was
drawn largely from the wastrel and criminal classes.

From Sahagun to Benavente and the Esla was nearly fifty
miles: to Astorga and the Galician defile another thirty. Beyond

that lay a hundred and fifty miles of mountain road to Corunna. There were few towns and villages on the way; the countryside afforded neither food nor fuel. The army was therefore forced to retire in corps by succession. Allowing La Romana with 7000 ragged Spaniards to follow the safest route and that least likely to impede the British retreat, Moore sent off Hope and Fraser on the 24th and Baird on Christmas Day. He himself took the road nearest Napoleon's line of advance with Edward Paget's Reserve division and the Light Infantry regiments he had trained. Lord Paget, Edward Paget's brother, covered the rear with the cavalry.

The advance had been made in frost and snow; the retreat began in a thaw. By day the roads were rivers of slush and mud; at night they became glaciers. All Christmas Day, while Napoleon rested his troops at Tordesillas, the English, soaked and frozen, pressed on. Tired, dispirited men looked in one another's faces and asked whether they were ever to halt again. "By Jesus, Master Hill," demanded an Irishman of the 95th, "where the devil is this you're taking us to?" "To England, M'Lauchlan," came the disquieting reply, "if we can get there."

.   .   .   .

"Should the English pass to-day in their positions," Napoleon observed at Tordesillas, "they are lost." "Put it in the newspapers," he ordered, "and make it universally known that 36,000 English are surrounded, that I am at Benavente in their rear while Soult is in their front." But, imagining them to be still at Sahagun, on the 27th he resumed his northward march towards that town instead of north-westwards to Benavente. So well did Paget's cavalry screen do its work that not till he reached Medina del Rioseco that night did the Emperor discover that Moore had been too quick. By then all but the British rearguard had crossed the Esla which, swollen by the thaw, had become a torrent.

But under the strain of the march, tempers and discipline collapsed. Dejection and shame now showed on every face. The men could not comprehend the leadership that refused to let them stand at bay. Forbidden to loose their anger against the French, they wreaked it on the Spaniards. There was a rumour that the retreat was due to La Romana's refusal to co-operate: the memory of barred doors and sullen scowls was in every heart. The villages on the road were mercilessly ransacked for firewood; "everyone found at home," wrote a private of the 71st, "was looked upon as a traitor to his country." All Moore's remonstrances and rebukes could not stop the rot; his officers were losing control. Wet and cold, with every door in the town shut against them and the army commissaries hastily burning the provisions and stores, the soldiers took the law into their own hands. In the Duke of Ossuna's lovely castle at Benavente— "surpassing anything I had ever seen," declared a Highlander, "such as I have read the description of in books of fairy tales"— they drove their bayonets into the painted walls to hang up their knapsacks and washing, broke up priceless furniture for firewood and ripped up the tapestries for bed-clothes. "What the English soldiers cannot see any purpose in," wrote the German Schaumann, "does not interest them."[1]

Behind the dissolving army the Reserve Division and the Light Brigade remained obedient to their orders. They were facing the enemy and were therefore occupied and cheerful. "We are all well," wrote General Paget, "but a good deal harassed." The riflemen whom Moore had trained at Shorncliffe lay in the path of the oncoming French like cats watching for their prey, and, when their chance came, they did not waste ammunition. On the night of the 28th, after repeatedly driving off Napoleon's Imperial Chasseurs, they filed silently across the bridge over the Esla at Castro-Gonzala while the engineers prepared to fire the mine at which they had been working all day. Yet though the

---

[1] Schaumann, 92-3. "I blush for our men," wrote a Scot who shared their sufferings. "I would blame them, too; alas! how can I, when I think upon their dreadful situation, fatigued and wet, shivering, perishing with cold?— no fuel to be got, not even straw to lie upon. Can men in such a situation admire the beauties of art?" *Journal of a Soldier*, 55.

men were so tired that they could scarcely keep open their eyes, when the drums beat to arms on an alarm every one was at his post in an instant.

The British cavalry, under Lord Paget's confident hand, behaved, too, magnificently. On his arrival at Medina del Rioseco Napoleon, realising that Moore had already crossed his front, swung his columns to the north-west and ordered his cavalry forward through Mayorga and Valderas to drive the British rearguards into the Esla. Hitherto these superb horsemen, drawn from the finest fighting races in Europe, had been accustomed to carry everything before them; in Spain the mere sight of their brazen casques and streaming horse-hair had turned armies into rabbles. But the British and Hanoverian cavalry were quite unimpressed by them. Three brilliant regiments in particular—the 7th, 10th and 15th Hussars—proved, as at Beaumont fourteen years before, that, though inexperienced in the art of manœuvring with large armies, the British in personal encounter could match any cavalry in the world.

By the morning of the 29th the last patrols were across the Esla, and the Emperor, who had brought his headquarters forward to Valderas, ordered his horse to cross the river and discover whether the British were retiring on the wild Portuguese mountains to the west or on Astorga and Galicia. Accordingly 600 Chasseurs of the Imperial Guard under Colonel-General Lefebvre-Desnoëttes forded the swollen river a little above Benavente and appeared before the town just as the British rearguard was preparing to march out to the north-west. Suddenly the narrow streets, where the tired riflemen of the 95th were snatching a few hours' sleep, echoed with the clatter of hoofs, the rattle of sabres and shouts of "Clear the way, Rifles! Up boys and clear the way!" The French general, driving in the piquets of the 18th Hussars outside the town, found that he had caught a tartar. Splendidly mounted, the British 10th Hussars and the 3rd Hussars of the German Legion, forming line as they rode, swept down on the surprised Chasseurs—big fellows with huge bearskin helmets and green uniforms—who, seeing what was coming, wheeled about and galloped for the ford. For a minute or two the race was equal; then a patch of swampy ground on the British left gave the fugitives a few breathless seconds to splash their way through the water. But nearly two hundred, including Lefebvre-Desnoëttes, were taken prisoner or left, sliced and mangled, on the bank or in the blood-stained stream. All the while the exultant riflemen in the town kept cheering like mad: it added much to their excitement when the rumour spread that Napoleon himself was watching from the heights beyond the Esla. Later, as they swung out of Benavente along the Astorga road, the captured French general rode in the greenjackets' midst—a big, sulky fellow in scarlet and gold with a bloody wound across his forehead.

Meanwhile the rest of the army was racing for Astorga as fast as its disorganised state would permit. Any thought of staying in the open plain till Napoleon's forces had had time to deploy was out of the question. Already wastage and sickness had reduced the British effectives to 25,000. There could be no safety for them until they reached the mountain defiles. Even then shortage of provisions and the danger of an outflanking movement through one or other of the converging valleys of that intricate region threatened to force them back to the sea. Moore saw clearly that it was Napoleon's game, not his, to fight a battle. The farther he could draw the Grand Army into the remote, inhospitable mountains of the north-west, the better for the Peninsula. "The game of Spain and England," he wrote to the Junta, "must always be to procrastinate and save time."

But for the moment the question was whether the British could escape Napoleon's converging jaws. Already the threat to their flanks was developing fast. On December 29th, the day Paget's rearguard evacuated Benavente, Soult's cavalry, fanning out to the north, overwhelmed La Romana's disintegrating army at Mansilla. By leaving the bridges over the Esla undestroyed the Spaniards opened the road through Leon and beyond. Meanwhile it was discovered from the captured Chasseurs that other forces were seeking to reach the great mountain defile at Villafranca. As soon, therefore, as he reached Astorga on the 30th, Moore sent officers ahead to watch any attempt either to cut the Corunna road from the direction of Leon or to use the track from Benavente to Orense to work round his southern flank. However bad such cross-country roads might be, he could not forget how often he had been misled about Iberian topography. Nor could he rely on the Spaniards defending their native passes; La Romana, ignoring every entreaty and his own promise, had failed to take his starving army over the Cantabrian range into the Asturias, and was now flying across the British line of retreat towards Orense. For these reasons Moore on New Year's Eve dispatched Major-General Craufurd's Light Brigade towards Vigo to guard the valley of the Minho and his southern flank.

The threat of hunger kept pace with that of encirclement. Owing to the inadequacy of Baird's commissariat only two days' provisions were found at Astorga, while the flight of the Spanish bullock-drivers and their carts made it impossible to bring up supplies from the next magazine at Villafranca. The only course was to cover the fifty miles to that place before the army starved. Shortage of rations further undermined discipline; the natural tendency of the frightened inhabitants to hide what little food they possessed led to illicit house-to-house searches, and these in their turn to orgies in the cellars. The bad characters, who according to one witness numbered from fifty to a hundred in every battalion, came into their own. The national weakness for drink—always accentuated in an army recruited at the ale-house door—found a terrible vent, and hundreds of uncontrollable and armed men roved the streets in delirium. To add to the horror La Romana's troops poured into the town while the British were still evacuating it—a starving, shivering, stinking, typhus-ridden rabble who fell on the homes and chattels of their country-men like a wolf-pack. Their example was eagerly followed by their allies.

The renewed retreat completed the army's demoralisation. In many units the sullen men became openly mutinous. The road into the mountains was knee-deep in snow and ice that became a river of slush by day and froze again at night. Boots, already in tatters, were wrenched off bleeding feet; horses could not stand and died in the snow or slid over frozen precipices. With every gust of wind clouds of snow blew in the men's faces. It was bitterly cold: there was no fuel, no shelter and nothing to drink but snow. "We suffered," wrote a soldier of the 71st, "misery without a glimpse of comfort." All the time La Romana's pitiful scarecrows kept getting in the way, swarming with famished howls through the battered doors of every wayside farm or hut.

At the top of the mountain a great pass ran through a barren waste of snow. All the way through it, for eight or nine miles, the men trudged in angry silence broken only by the groans of the dying by the wayside or the occasional report of a pistol fired at the head of a fallen horse. Afterwards at the village of Bembibre hundreds of troops left the ranks and, burning and plundering, fought their way into the wine vaults. Here, as the old year went out, horrible scenes were enacted. "Bembibre," wrote an officer, "exhibited all the appearance of a place lately stormed and pillaged. Every door and window was broken, every lock and fastening forced. Rivers of wine ran through the houses and into the streets, where soldiers, women, children, runaway Spaniards and muleteers lay in fantastic groups with wine oozing from their lips and nostrils."

Here too on the first day of the New Year came the rearguard, sounding their bugles, hammering on the doors and rousing the insensible men in the cellars and streets with blows from their rifles. Behind them—though still at a respectful distance—came the French cavalry. As the rumours of their approach ran through the plundered town the streets filled with revellers whom all the efforts of their comrades had failed to rouse, reeling, staggering and crying out for mercy. They received none from the French dragoons who, eager to avenge Benavente, slashed at drunkards, cripples, women and infants in arms. Yet even in this pit of shame the stubborn English spirit flickered; during the night and following day with a wonderful persistence many stragglers regained the retreating columns—tattered soldiers with bloodshot eyes and festering wounds and women who had been raped in barns but had fled from their violators to rejoin the colours.[1]

It was this spirit, almost as much as the valour of the Reserve and Light Brigade, that robbed Napoleon of his triumph. "The English are running away as fast as they can," he wrote from Benavente; "they have abandoned the Spaniards in a shameful and cowardly manner. Have all this shown up in the newspapers. Have caricatures made and songs and popular ditties written. Have them translated into German and Italian and circulated in Italy and Germany." For, as his prey eluded him, the Emperor's indignation rose. He hated the British from the bottom of his soul. The man who had plundered half the cities of Europe felt genuine horror at the ill-disciplined rapscallions who had pillaged the wine shops of Benavente. He particularly disliked their barbaric destruction of bridges—one of the principal channels of civilisation.

On New Year's Day, 1809, while pressing forward from Benavente to Astorga to join Soult, Napoleon learnt that Moore had reached the mountains and that his last hope of forcing a battle on the open plain had passed. He at once resolved to leave Spain. As he approached Astorga a courier galloped up with dispatches from Paris. He dismounted, read them in the presence of his troops and paced angrily up and down. Later it became known that momentous tidings had arrived: that Austria was arming for war, that there had been a revolution in Turkey—incited by British agents—that traitors had been plotting in Paris. That night the Emperor handed over command of the army to Soult, and ordered the immediate return of the Imperial Guard to Valladolid. The English were beyond his reach. So for that winter were Portugal and southern Spain.

From this time, though 50,000 Frenchmen with more than fifty guns were still at their heels, the chief threat to the British

[1] Blakeney 49-51; *Journal of a Soldier*, 58-61; Harris, 96; Schaumann, 107-111, 128; A. M. Delavoye, *Life of Lord Lynedoch*, 293; *Diary of Sir John Moore* (ed. J. M. Maurice), 378-84; *History of the Rifle Brigade*, 36, 104.

came not from the enemy but from the weather and their own indiscipline. At Villafranca—a mountain town fifty miles from Astorga and a hundred from Corunna—where the main body of the retreating army arrived on New Year's Day, the troops refused to await the official distribution of rations and sacked the magazines while the commissaries stood by helpless. "Every soldier took what he liked, everything was plundered, carried away and trampled under foot; the casks of wine were broken open so that half their contents were spilt over the floor, and the general fury and unruliness of these hordes of men was such that those officers who attempted to maintain order had to make haste to fight their way out of the crowds, if only to save their lives." Fourteen days' store of biscuits, salt meat and rum vanished in a few hours, and with them all hope of a stand at Villafranca. Later houses were beaten up in search of drink and the disgraceful scenes of Bembibre re-enacted. Almost every sign of a disciplined fighting force disappeared. The artillerymen broke up their ammunition wagons for fuel and threw their contents into the river.

The rot continued until the 2nd when the Commander-in-Chief, who had been marching with the rearguard, arrived to restore order. All stragglers were at once arrested and locked up, and the emaciated, lacerated survivors of the French cavalry charge at Bembibre were paraded round the town as a warning. A man taken in the act of plundering a magazine was shot in the market place: another hanged for breaking into a house, while the troops were made to file past the dangling corpse. Later the army, with some semblance of discipline, marched out towards Lugo, and Moore rejoined the rearguard holding the bridge over the Cua at Cacabelos five miles to the east.

Here also, since the drunken orgy at Bembibre, there had been some loss of discipline. Sir John, whose faith in his army had been almost broken, ordered the division to parade in close column and addressed it in forcible terms. Sooner than survive such conduct, he announced, he trusted that the first cannon-ball fired by the enemy would remove him from the scene of his disgrace.

"And you, 28th"—turning on a famous regiment that had fought by his side in Egypt—"are not what you used to be. If you were, no earthly temptation could tempt one of you away from your colours for an instant." Next morning, some plundering having occurred in the village during the night, Major-General Paget had the culprits paraded in a hollow square and flogged. While the last offenders, who had been sentenced to be hanged, were waiting their turn under the triangles, the French were reported approaching, whereupon the thirty-three-year-old general—most impressive of disciplinarians—turned on his division with, "My God! is it not lamentable that, instead of preparing the troops confided to my command to receive the enemies of their country, I am preparing to hang two robbers?" He then paused. "If I spare the lives of these two men, will you promise to reform?" There was a great shout and the prisoners were taken down.

Immediately afterwards, as if the affair had been staged, the enemy appeared on the skyline in action with the piquets. Battle was immediately joined. It was the tonic the men required. In the fighting the 52nd, the Light Company of the 28th—the "Old Slashers"—and a battalion of the 95th that had not accompanied the other half of the regiment to Vigo covered themselves with glory. The French cavalry were repelled and their leader, General Colbert, killed. "We popped them off whenever they showed their ugly faces," said a rifleman, "like mice in the sun!"

After that there was no further difficulty with the rearguard. That night, after Villafranca had been evacuated, the men marched eighteen miles to Herrerias without losing a straggler. The retreat now bore two faces, one of shame and suffering, the other of glory: the demoralised misery of the main body trudging over the frozen hills, and the splendour of the fighting division that covered its retreat. During the next fifty miles to Lugo the agony of the army surpassed anything yet encountered. Drenched with rain, famished with cold and hunger, ignorant when their torture was to cease, thousands of redcoats toiled up the agonising slope of Monte del Cabiero, leaving behind a trail of dying men, women, horses and mules. Above the howling of the wind nothing could be heard but groans and curses. In the terrible defile beyond Villafranca, where the road ran between enormous precipices round the bends of the raging Valcarso, the men, worn out by their excesses, dropped in shoals. The worst was endured on the high ground near Los Royales and Constantino. On the desolate, wintry height many, through the failure of the commissariat, died of starvation clasped in one another's arms in the snow. "The misery of the whole thing was appalling," wrote Schaumann, "huge mountains, intense cold, no houses, no shelter or cover of any kind, no inhabitants, no bread. The howling wind, as it whistled past the ledges of rock and through the bare trees, sounded to the ear like the groaning of the damned." At one point on that march of death a dying woman gave birth in an overturned bullock cart; an officer of Moore's Staff, finding the living infant whimpering at her frozen breasts, wrapped it in his cloak and carried it away with him. Then "the dark, almost polar night fell" and concealed such sights from men's eyes.

Occasionally, where the mountains permitted, French cavalry patrols swept round the flanks of the rearguard to fall on the stragglers. Yet though they gathered in nearly a thousand prisoners by this means, they always encountered more than they bargained for. The sound of their trumpets borne on the wind had an electrifying effect. However desperate their plight, the pallid British scarecrows would instinctively face about, level their muskets and fire. "I heard them more than once say," wrote a private of the 71st, "as they turned from the points of our bayonets, they would rather face a hundred fresh Germans than ten dying Englishmen." Nothing in all their sufferings so enraged the latter as the failure of the enemy to close. "Why don't they come on like men," cried one, "whilst we've strength in us left to fight them?"

Scenes not dissimilar were enacted in the parallel march on the road to Vigo. Here Brigadier-General Craufurd—the little,

dark, wiry man whom the men of the Light Brigade called
Black Bob—kept his troops in heart and good order by sheer
strength of personality. Wherever suffering or danger was
greatest, he was certain to appear, growling like a worried bull-
dog and bearing a canteen of rum and a small cup which he
offered to his men with oaths and homely counsel. "Many a man
in that retreat," wrote one of them, "caught courage from his
stern eye and gallant bearing. . . . He did not like retreating, that
man. War was his very element, and toil and danger seemed to
call forth only an unceasing determination to surmount them."
Once he caught an officer crossing a stream on a soldier's back:
"Put him down, sir, put him down," he shouted, plunging into
the icy water, "go back, sir, and go through the water like the
others!" On another occasion he halted the brigade and sentenced two men to be flogged by drumhead court-martial,
standing beside them while the sentence was carried out. "If he
flogged two," wrote Rifleman Harris, "he saved hundreds." His
troops looked upon him as the finest soldier in the world and
would have followed him to hell. They walked at his side like
familiars and, whenever he halted to deliver one of his stern
reprimands, half a dozen of them—unshaven, shoeless and savage
—would stand "leaning upon their weapons and scowling up in
his face as he scolded; and, when he dashed the spurs into his
reeking horse, they would throw up their rifles and hobble after
him again."

Such troops and their fellow light-infantrymen of Edward
Paget's rearguard developed as the retreat went on an immense
pride in their powers of endurance. At night they lay down, as
19 year-old Lieutenant Blakeney wrote, in martial wedlock, each
folding to his breast his better half—his musket. For the stragglers and weaklings littering the way they felt nothing but contempt; clodhoppers they called them. At every village along the
line of retreat the angry shout would go up: "Burst open the
door!" and the laggards would be frog-marched into the street
and set marching with kicks and blows. "Now show yer nerve,"
cried the sergeant of the 43rd, throttling his own racking cough;

"if you die to-day, you won't have to die to-morrow. Fall in!"

．　．　．　．　．　．　．　．

At Lugo on January 6th Moore halted his army and prepared to give battle. Despite the wet and dreadful cold the effect on discipline was instantaneous. The men asked only one thing: to be allowed to visit their sufferings and injured self-respect on the enemy. For two days they bivouacked on an icy ridge without shelter and with scarcely any food, hoping against hope that the French would attack. On the third day, as the enemy made no sign and the last provisions were exhausted, the retreat was resumed in a terrible night of sleet and hail. Two more days of suffering and demoralisation followed, during which the French captured another five hundred footsore, starving laggards, though only after the latter, forming square under the orders of a sergeant, had put up a desperate fight. By the second night the march had become not a succession of battalions but a vast, disorganised multitude without respect of regiment, brigade or division; the colours of that famous corps, the Royals, were attended by nine officers, three sergeants and only three privates. During this time the rearguard repeatedly saved the army.

In the course of January 10th the hills were left behind and the main body reached Betanzos on the coastal plain. Here the sun was shining and the orange and lemon trees were in flower; there was ample provision of food, and the famished troops were able to fill their stomachs. Next day, with indescribable feelings, they caught their first glimpse of the sea and the distant masts of ships. A thorough reorganisation having taken place under the supervision of the Commander-in-Chief, the army entered Corunna that night in tolerable formation, the ragged, shoeless scarecrows stumping on frostbitten, bleeding feet through the streets with every commanding officer leading his regiment and every captain and subaltern flanking his section. The highlight was the performance of two battalions of the First Foot Guards, each 800 strong, who marched in perfect formation in column of sections, with drums beating and the drum-major twirling his staff.

Before the retreat Moore had urged the Government to send transports to Corunna or Vigo—a summons which had caused great indignation among the more sanguine Ministers. But not till the night of January 3rd-4th, during the midnight halt at Herrerias after the action on the Cua, had he decided, on receiving his engineers' reports, to embark the main army at Corunna. When, therefore, it arrived, though the bay was filled with hospital and store ships, the transports were still wind-bound at Vigo. There was nothing for it but to wait for them and trust to their coming before Soult, who had lost a day or two on the march, could bring up his reserves and heavy guns.

Nor had the general been well served by his engineers. Corunna was protected on the south by a range of heights. But, like those at Toulon fifteen years before, they were too extensive for the army to hold. Sickness, the detachment of Craufurd's contingent to Vigo and heavy losses on the retreat—at least 5000 had fallen or had been captured—had reduced Moore's infantry to a bare 15,000. The only position on which so small a force could fight a delaying action was an inner ring of low hills completely dominated by the outer heights. Moreover embarkation presented grave risks, since it was almost impossible to get out of the harbour in certain winds. "Figure to yourself," wrote a naval officer, "two or three hundred sail of bad-sailing merchantmen, crammed chock full, and a French army at hand who, possessing themselves of the place, would be enabled from both sides of the entrance to throw shot and shells at leisure at the unhappy transports attempting to work out. Such a situation makes me shudder!" To make matters worse, until the transports should arrive, there was a serious shortage of food; on the day the British marched into the town every provision shop closed its doors.

Therefore, though the soldiers rejoiced at the end of their sufferings and a happy commissary sat over Don Mascosa's mulled wine, smoking cigars and admiring the beauties of the harbour, those charged with the army's safety continued deeply anxious. Some even urged the Commander-in-Chief to ask Soult for a negotiated evacuation. But Moore rejected this proposal and proceeded with his usual energy to make the best of the situation. He at once embarked as many of his sick and wounded as possible in the store and hospital ships and began to fortify the landward approaches to the town. In this he was aided by the townsfolk, who, regardless of their own bleak future, threw themselves, men, women and children, with whole-hearted abandon into digging trenches, strengthening the neglected ramparts and carrying ammunition to the forts and batteries. It was as though, touched by the sufferings of their allies, they had resolved by a single impulse to make amends for all the improvidence and procrastination of the past six months. Among the consequences of the latter was a huge magazine of four thousand barrels of powder, sent out in haste from England at the beginning of the war and since left undistributed and unused. This was fired on the 13th, causing an explosion which broke every window in the town, swept the harbour with a tidal wave and killed a sergeant and two men on piquet more than a mile away.

Moore did not destroy everything that he found at Corunna. From the stores he took arms and ammunition, giving to every man a new firelock and a pouch filled with fresh powder—an instance of the effects of sea power, for the French, with the long mountain road behind them and their powder and arms damaged by exposure, could hope for no such advantage. And Moore needed all the help he could get. The rearguard after its superb performance during the retreat—in which, though continuously engaged, it had lost fewer men than any division in the army—was holding the crossing over the Mero at El-Burgo, four miles east of the town. But, with the enemy massing beyond the river, the position ceased to be tenable after the 13th when a partially masked battery was disclosed commanding the broken bridge. General Paget's small force had no alternative but to withdraw in haste, leaving the French free to cross. A battle under the walls of Corunna could no longer be avoided.

Fortunately on the evening of the 14th the missing transports arrived, 110 sail strong, bringing the total at anchor in the harbour to 250. With them came a squadron of battleships— *Ville de Paris, Victory, Barfleur, Zealous, Implacable, Elizabeth, Norge, Plantagenet, Resolution, Audacious, Endymion, Mediator*—a glorious spectacle, thought an onlooker, had it been possible to forget the service for which they had come. Yet it was one which brought relief to thousands of British hearts. That night Moore, not daring to waste an hour, lest a sudden change in the wind should enable the French artillery to destroy the fleet at anchor, embarked the remainder of his sick, all but eight of his guns and, since the rocky terrain did not admit of their use in battle, the whole of his cavalry. Only a thousand horses could be taken. The remainder, many having foundered during the retreat—not for want of shoes but for nails and hammers—were shot on the beach.

During the morning of the 15th Soult, forcing back Paget's outposts, occupied the heights round the town, overlooking and partially enclosing the inferior British positions on the slopes of Monte Mero. Sharpshooting and cannonading continued all day, about a hundred men falling on either side. Sir John Moore spent the afternoon inspecting his lines, talking as usual to every officer and giving cautions, orders and exhortations. "He looked wistfully at the enemy," wrote young Boothby who rode with his Staff, "apparently wishing with painful eagerness for a battle." Those, Boothby added, who supposed that such wishes were excited by any thought of his own fame did not know Sir John Moore; only that morning in a letter to the admiral he had expressed his anxiety for an engagement as the only means of securing an unmolested embarkation.

Yet possibly another—and not ignoble—thought was in Moore's mind. In his last dispatch, sent off two days earlier, he had told Castlereagh that he could never have believed that a British army could become demoralised in so short a time; its

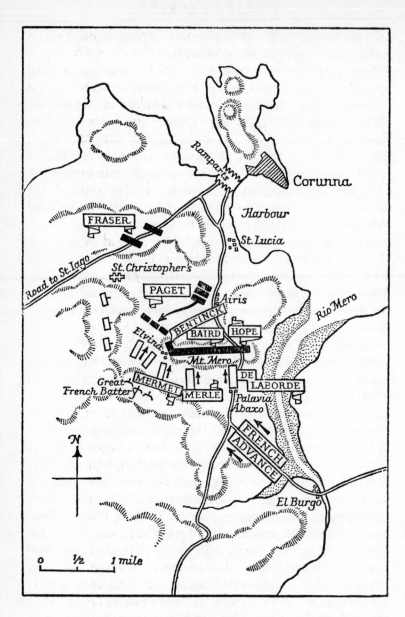

Corunna

conduct in retreat had been infamous beyond belief. Yet he could not refrain from also stressing his unbroken confidence in the valour of his troops; whenever there had been any prospect of fighting, the men had shown their determination to do their duty. In a retreat of nearly three hundred miles, carried out under appalling conditions in the face of a superior foe and without the slightest help from the Spaniards, they had not—for all their insubordination—lost a gun or a colour.

But next day—January 16, 1809—though their drums beat early to arms and a battery of eleven twelve-pounders had appeared during the night on a rocky eminence overhanging the British lines, the French made no move. During the morning, while the last stores and baggage were embarked and Mr. Robinson of *The Times* paid farewell calls in the town, the scarlet lines waited unmolested under a cloudless sky among the Monte Mero rocks and heather. At midday, when it seemed clear that the enemy were not going to attack, Moore gave orders for the Reserve to embark during the afternoon and for the rest of the army to follow as soon as it was dark. Among the white houses of Corunna two miles away Crabb Robinson, going to dine at the hotel, found the table d'hôte packed with departing English officers.

But between one and two o'clock, just after Moore had observed to his secretary, "Now if there is no bungling, I hope we shall get away in a few hours," the French began to move. Soult, supposing that his enemies were breaking formation, had decided to destroy them as they went down to their ships. He had a score of heavy calibre guns to their eight light six-pounders, a superiority in manpower—16,000 or more to their 15,000—and far greater forces coming up over the mountains in his rear. The ground and all the circumstances were in his favour. He waited no longer but launched his troops at a run down the mountain side in three columns, with a cloud of voltigeurs swarming ahead into the valley below the British lines. At the same time the great battery of heavy guns on the rocks opposite the British right opened with terrible effect.

Down by the harbour, as the firing broke out, everything changed. Crabb Robinson looked up from his dinner to find that the redcoated officers had all left. Crowds of people gathered in the streets and on the roofs to hear the musketry and watch the smoke rising like mist from the nearby hills. The Reserve, marching down to the quayside with thoughts set on England, halted to a man as if by word of command at that compelling sound; a few minutes later an aide-de-camp came spurring down the road to recall them. Perhaps the most astonishing transformation of all was that of a fatigue party digging entrenchments near the ramparts under the orders of Lieutenant Boothby of the Engineers. All his efforts had failed to induce the men to lay aside the air of extreme weariness they had assumed. Each shovel of earth approached the top of the bank as slowly as the finger of a clock. Boothby was therefore considerably astonished at their behaviour when an order came for them to join their regiments marching to the field. "They threw down their tools, jumped to their arms, halloed and frisked as boys do when loosed from school, these poor, tattered, half-dead looking devils."

Meanwhile the French had taken all their first objectives. Pouring down the hillside in a torrent, 600 voltigeurs under old General Jardon—a true, foul-mouthed, gallant son of the Revolution, who never changed his linen and always marched on foot with the leading files, carrying a musket—drove the defending piquets out of Elvina village. He was closely followed by General Mermet with the main column. Another phalanx on its right made for the British centre. Behind, the guns of the great battery pounded cannon-balls over their heads into the British lines. Here, on the extreme right of the ridge above Elvina, twenty-six-year-old Charles Napier, commanding the 50th Foot, walked up and down the ranks making his men shoulder and order arms to distract their minds from the round shot, while his piquets fifty yards below disputed with the French skirmishers.

Suddenly above the thunder of musketry and the cries of "En

264

avant, tue, tue, en avant, tue!" of the French column, he heard the gallop of horses and, turning round, saw Sir John Moore. "He came at speed," he wrote, "and pulled up so sharp and close he seemed to have alighted from the air; man and horse looking at the approaching foe with an intenseness that seemed to concentrate all feeling in their eyes. The sudden stop of the animal, a cream-coloured one with black tail and mane, had cast the latter streaming forward; its ears were pushed out like horns, while its eyes flashed fire, and it snorted loudly with expanded nostrils, expressing terror, astonishment and muscular exertion. My first thought was, it will be away like the wind! but then I looked at the rider, and the horse was forgotten. Thrown on its haunches the animal came, sliding and dashing the dirt up with its fore feet, thus bending the general forward almost to its neck. But his head was thrown back and his look more keenly piercing than I ever saw it. He glanced to the right and left, and then fixed his eyes intently on the enemy's advancing column, at the same time grasping the reins with both his hands and pressing the horse firmly with his knees: his body thus seemed to deal with the animal while his mind was intent on the enemy, and his aspect was one of searching intenseness beyond the power of words to describe. For a while he looked, and then galloped to the left without uttering a word."

Here the other two columns were attacking the British line which ran for about a mile along the scrubby ridge to the marshes of the Mero on its left. On the fringe of the latter the easternmost column had driven Lieutenant-General Hope's outposts out of Palavia Abaxo village and was coming on towards the slope at the double. But it soon became clear that the real danger was to Baird's division on the other flank opposite the great battery, and particularly to its extreme right where Lord William Bentinck's brigade—consisting of the 4th, the 50th and the 42nd—was holding a small knoll above Elvina. A further French column, supported at a distance by cavalry, was now surging round the western edge of the ridge into the valley which ran down behind the British position towards the harbour two miles away. To protect the latter the 52nd and the Rifles had been hastily extended, screening the rest of Paget's Reserve which had taken up its position in the suburb of Airis behind the British lines. Though the French were swirling all round the knoll on which he was posted, Lord William—an habitually placid man—was ambling about on an old mule, which seemed as indifferent to the fire as he, and talking to every one with the utmost good humour. "I only remember saying to myself," Charles Napier wrote, "this chap takes it coolly or the devil's in it."

Presently Moore returned and joined the group on the knoll. A round-shot struck the ground close to his horse's feet, causing it to spin round, but he never took his gaze from the enemy. A second shot tore the leg off a 42nd Highlander who started screaming and rolling about, much to the agitation of his comrades. "This is nothing, my lads," Moore called out, "keep your ranks, take that man away; my good fellow, don't make such a noise, we must bear these things better." His sharp tone had the calming effect intended, and the ranks closed again.

The battle was now reaching the climax he had foreseen. While Baird's and Hope's battered divisions continued with their sustained musketry to hold the ridge against frontal attack, the French—deceived by appearances—were pouring into the valley towards Airis and the approaches to Corunna, imagining that they had encircled the British right. They had completely failed to realise that Moore had two unused divisions behind his lines. He now gave the order for the rest of the Reserve to reinforce the 95th and 52nd and expel the intruders and for Major-General Fraser's division, lying back near the port on the Corunna-St. Iago road, to move up in support. At the same time he launched the 4th Foot from the right of the ridge against the flank of the incautious French and sent the 50th and 42nd forward against Elvina.

In the smoke-filled valley on his right everything went as Moore had intended. As Soult's troops surged forward they encountered Paget's advancing line and discovered—for the first time—the real right of the British army. Enraged by the memory

of all they had suffered on the retreat and supported by the enfilading fire and bayonets of the 4th, the veterans of the Reserve
quickly turned the enemy's advance into a rout and, carrying all
before them, surged up the valley towards the great battery itself.
Meanwhile, led by Napier and his young fellow major, Charles
Stanhope—Pitt's nephew—the 50th cleared Elvina and dashed
on in a rough, scrambling fight into the stony lanes and fields
beyond. Owing to a misunderstanding, however, the Black
Watch fell back to replenish their powder; on seeing this the
general rode up to them, exclaiming, "My brave 42nd, if you've
fired your ammunition, you've still your bayonets. Remember
Egypt! Think on Scotland! Come on, my gallant countrymen!"
Then, sending back young George Napier, his aide-de-camp, to
bring up the Guards in support, he remained erect and motionless on his horse, watching the development of the attack on the
French battery. At any moment now the guns would be his;
the 14th Foot on his left had retaken Palavia Abaxo; the discouraged enemy, their ammunition failing, were everywhere
giving ground. Behind them lay the swollen Mero and the
solitary bridge at El Burgo. The experienced eye of the great
Scottish soldier told him that victory was his; the sufferings he
and his men had endured for so long were about to be avenged.

At that moment a cannon-ball from the threatened battery
struck him from his horse, carrying away his left shoulder and
part of his collar-bone, and leaving his lungs exposed and his arm
hanging by a torn string of flesh. For a moment he lay motionless, then raised himself to a sitting position and, with eyes kind-
ling with their habitual brilliance, resumed his gaze on the smoke
and turmoil ahead. So unmoved was his face that those about
him could scarcely realise the deadly nature of his wound.

A little later Commissary Schaumann saw him being borne by
six Highlanders through the streets of Corunna on a bloodstained blanket, with a little group of aides-de-camp and doctors
walking beside. He had refused to be parted from his sword
which he carried out of the field with him like a Spartan his
shield. Though breathing only with intense pain, he repeatedly

made his bearers pause so that he might look back on the battle. "You know," he murmured to his friend, Colonel Anderson, "I have always wished to die this way."

After Moore's departure—for Baird had also had his arm shattered by the great battery's raking fire—the command devolved on a fellow Scot, Sir John Hope. The latter, isolated on the left from the decisive events which had been taking place elsewhere, was unable to follow up the swift succession of blows planned by his fallen chief. The gallantest of men, pottering instinctively—as one of his officers testified—to wherever the fire was hottest, he was a little overawed by the weight of the responsibility that had suddenly fallen on him; England's only army was in his keeping and her fleet was waiting in a perilous anchorage. It was growing dark and, seeing that the French attack was broken, he called off the pursuit and ordered Moore's instructions of the morning to be put into immediate operation. It was certain now that the embarkation would be unmolested.

In darkness and weariness the men marched to the quayside while the rearguard piquets lit bivouac fires on the abandoned ridge. Hollow-eyed and covered with blood and filth, they looked so terrible that the townsfolk crossed themselves as they passed. But the withdrawal was carried out in perfect order, so well had Moore's measures and a brush with the enemy restored the discipline of his tattered troops. Presently, on the dark, tossing water-front they were grasped by the mighty fists of the sailors and pulled into the boats. As they were rowed across the harbour to the waiting ships, their general lay breathing his last on the soil of the land he had come to save. "I hope the people of England will be satisfied," he whispered, "I hope my country will do me justice." He repeatedly enquired after his officers, urging that this one should be recommended for promotion and begging to be remembered to another. "Is Paget in the room?" he asked, "remember me to him, he is a fine fellow." Then, as his wound congealed and grew cold and the agony increased, he became silent lest he should show weakness.

By the morning of the 17th the whole army was on board

except for 1500 troops whom Hope, resolved to depart in dignity, had left under Hill and Beresford to cover the embarkation of the wounded. The Spaniards, stirred by the battle to a sudden ecstasy of generous enthusiasm, had volunteered to defend the ramparts while the fleet got to sea. The whole town, men, women and children had turned out; "everybody commanded, everybody fired, everybody halloed, everybody ordered silence, everybody forbade the fire, everybody thought musketry best and everybody cannon." "Thus, after all," wrote Schaumann, "we became reconciled to the Spanish character." About the same time Napoleon, having threatened to hang the municipality for the murder of a French soldier, was preparing to leave Valladolid for Paris. His eagles had not been planted on the towers of Lisbon after all. Nor had he destroyed the British army. As it began to grow light and the wind in the bay of Corunna freshened, a party of the 9th Foot with a chaplain and a few mournful officers could be seen making their way along the ramparts on the landward bastion of the citadel. They carried the body of their dead commander, wrapped in his military cloak. Presently they committed it to the ground, and "left him alone with his glory."

CHAPTER 8

Waterloo

"The British infantry are the best in the world. Fortunately there are not many of them."

Marshal Bugeaud

DURING THE AFTERNOON OF Sunday, June 18th, 1815, the city of Brussels was in a state of panic. Since three o'clock a stream of fugitives had been pouring in from the plain beyond the forest of Soignes where, twelve miles south of the capital, Wellington, with 21,000 British and 42,000 Germans and Netherlanders, was barring the way of a victorious French army of 70,000 veterans commanded by Napoleon. Most of the English visitors who had invaded the city in the wake of their army had already fled to the north and were crowding the roads and waterways to Antwerp, where, on Wellington's orders, a state of siege had been proclaimed and crowds waited all day in the rain for news. But hundreds more, unable to obtain transport in the panic—for everything on wheels had been requisitioned—remained in the city without hope of escape. Every few minutes fugitives from the battlefield kept galloping into the town shouting that all was lost and that the French were at their heels. Once a whole regiment of Hanoverian cavalry poured in through the Namur gate, with swords drawn and foam-flecked horses, and rode through the town towards the north, upsetting everything in the streets on their way. There were other fugitives with bloody and bandaged heads, and cartloads of wounded, and occasionally, towards evening, an officer of high rank, British or

Belgian, extended upon a bier borne by soldiers. As the dreadful afternoon advanced and the distant cannonade grew in intensity, the rumour spread—possibly circulated by French sympathisers —that Napoleon had promised his soldiery the sack of the city. Every woman knew what that meant. "I never saw such consternation," wrote Fanny Burney. "We could only gaze and tremble, listen and shudder."

Yet three days earlier Brussels had seemed as securely held by British wealth and the power of united Europe as London. For weeks it had been a scene of gaiety and military pageantry, with the brilliant aristocracy of England flooding the city in the wake of her army and spending money with a profusion never matched by its successive Spanish, Austrian, French and, now, Dutch rulers. The nearest French vedettes had been forty miles away beyond the Sambre, and between them and the Belgian capital two great armies had guarded every road on a hundred-mile front, growing daily in strength and commanded by the two most famous soldiers of the European alliance that in the previous year, had defeated and dethroned Napoleon. The Prussian host of around 113,000 men—almost as numerous as the largest striking force Napoleon could raise from an exhausted and divided France after his escape from Elba—had entered Belgium under Blücher to hold the frontier from the Ardennes to Charleroi, while a smaller joint British, Netherlands, Hanoverian and Brunswick army guarded it from Mons to the North Sea, under the Duke of Wellington. Every week the young, under-strength battalions sent out in haste from England were being joined by the veteran regiments which in the five years after Corunna, had driven the French from Spain and which were now returning from America. Elsewhere more than half a million men, mobilised by the sovereigns of Europe, were on the march, their vanguards already closing in on the French frontiers. The danger to Brussels and the Low Countries, so great three months before, seemed to have passed. Though no official state of war existed—Napoleon being merely treated as an outlaw under the new international system of collective security—it had been known that an invasion of France was to begin in July. It had even seemed likely that the French, republicans or royalists, would themselves throw out the usurper and so avoid the necessity of invasion. Napoleon's house, Wellington had told English visitors to the front, was tumbling about his ears.

On the night of Thursday, June 15th, there had been a ball in the city. It had been given by an English milord of fabulous wealth, the Duke of Richmond, and the principal officers of the British and Allied army had attended it, including the Duke of Wellington and the leader of the Netherlands forces, the Prince of Orange, heir to the throne of the new kingdom. But during its course, and even before it had begun, it had become known that something was amiss. Several times Wellington had been interrupted by messages and was seen to write orders, and at an early hour many of his officers took their leave. During the small hours of the 16th the squares and streets of Brussels had filled with troops as trumpets sounded and drums beat to arms. Presently the troops—green-jacketed Riflemen, scarlet-clad infantry of the line and Highlanders, blue-coated Belgians and Brunswickers in black—had moved off, laughing and joking in the early morning sunshine and asking one another what all the fuss was about. The stolid Flemish country folk, rolling into the city in their carts, had watched them with curious eyes as they marched out down the Charleroi road. Everyone in command had seemed very composed and quiet; old Sir Thomas Picton, commander of the British 5th Division, with top hat and reconnoitring glass slung over his shoulder, cheerfully accosted his friends as he rode through the streets.

Elsewhere—at Enghien, Ath, Grammont, Nivelles, Oudenarde and even as far away as Ghent—other troops, British, German and Netherland, roused from their cantonments, had assembled to the sound of trumpets and bugles, and, marching off along the hot, dusty highroads southwards and eastwards, had begun to converge on the assembly point. It had been a day of intense heat. As they emerged from the beech forests on to the great corn plain that fringed the Sambre to the north, the tramping infantrymen and jingling cavalry and gunners heard a dull, sullen sound like distant thunder and saw on the horizon columns of smoke arising.

For on June 15th, after one of his incredibly swift and secret concentrations, Napoleon had sprung like a tiger across the Sambre and driven in the outposts of Blücher's army at the point where its right touched the left of Wellington's equally scattered force. When the first news of the crossing had reached the Prussian and British commanders, they had suspected it to be a feint. The hours Napoleon had thereby gained had given him the chance to drive a wedge between them. With 124,000 men he had placed himself between Blücher's 113,000 Prussians and Wellington's miscellaneous 83,000. His object had been to defeat one or the other before they had time to concentrate and then, forcing both back on their divergent communications, to enter Brussels as a conqueror. Thereafter, he had believed, the Belgian common people would rise against the Dutch, the war-weary French take heart and unite behind him, the Tory Government in London fall, and his Austrian father-in-law, deprived of British subsidies, sue for peace.

All afternoon on the 16th the people of Brussels had heard, through the hot, airless haze, the sound of cannonading from Quatre Bras, where twenty miles to the south Marshal Ney was trying to brush aside a weak Netherlands force from the crossroads which preserved front-line communication between the Prussian and Anglo-Dutch armies. By some miracle of tough, confused fighting, in which Picton's Highlanders had covered themselves with glory and the Duke of Brunswick had fallen, Wellington, reinforced by successive contingents, had held the crossroads and by nightfall assembled 30,000 troops in Ney's path. But owing to the delay in effecting his concentration—the result of faulty staff work—he had failed to join Blücher in battle that day against Napoleon. By nightfall, six miles away at Ligny, 63,000 Frenchmen under the great Emperor had beaten the 80,000 Prussians concentrated against them and inflicted 15,000 casualties. The seventy-two-year-old Prussian marshal had only narrowly escaped capture after being trampled on by French cavalry.

Yet Napoleon's victory had not been as complete as he had thought. Owing to the failure of one of his corps which, through contradictory orders, had marched and countermarched all day between the two battlefields without taking part in either, the Prussians had escaped annihilation and were able to withdraw in tolerable order into the night. Next morning, when the Emperor, detaching 33,000 troops under Marshal Grouchy to pursue them, had thrown the rest of his army against Wellington, the latter had withdrawn in good time up the Charleroi-Brussels highway. And though Napoleon had supposed that he had driven the Prussians back eastwards towards their communications, Blücher had in fact withdrawn northwards towards Wavre on a road parallel to the British only a dozen miles to the east. Unknown to Napoleon, the Allied armies had thus remained in touch and, though the Emperor had reduced their numerical superiority and shaken their morale, he had not, as he supposed, divided them. Nor, though the people of Brussels had expected all day to see the victorious French emerge from the Forest of Soignes, had the British withdrawal towards Brussels been on the whole precipitate. It had been brilliantly covered by Lord Uxbridge's cavalry and horse artillery, and by nightfall Wellington had concentrated his army on the ridge of Mont St. Jean twelve miles south of the city. During the afternoon Napoleon's advance had been increasingly delayed by torrential thunderstorms which had converted the Charleroi *chaussée* and the fields on either side into quagmires. It had seemed, recalled one officer, as if the water was being tumbled out of heaven in tubs.

The two armies had spent an uncomfortable night. The rain fell almost continually, with flashes of lightning and violent gusts of wind. The ground on which the men lay, drenched to the skin and shaking with cold, was sodden with wet crops. A few old campaigners made themselves tolerably comfortable by smearing their blankets with clay and making pillows of straw. Few of the newcomers to war, who in the Allied army far outnumbered the old hands, got any sleep at all.

Dawn on the 18th was cold and cheerless. Everyone was covered in mud from head to foot. Presently the clouds began to lift, and the men managed to get their camp-fires lit and to cook breakfast. Afterwards, on the officers' orders, they dried their ammunition and cleaned their arms. Later, as the sun came out, Wellington rode round the lines, accompanied by his Staff. They looked as gay and unconcerned as if they were riding to a meet in England.

. . . .

The ridge or rather rolling plateau on which the British army had halted was one which the Duke had long marked as a favourable position for the defence of the Belgian capital. It crossed the highroad from Brussels to Charleroi a mile and a half south of the village of Waterloo and the forest of Soignes. It was named after the little village of Mont St. Jean which nestled by the roadside in one of its northern folds. In the course of riding and hunting expeditions Wellington had carefully studied its gentle undulations and contours. It was here that twenty-one years before, when he was a young lieutenant-colonel marching from Ostend to join a hard-pressed and almost identically circumstanced army, his chief, the Duke of York, had urged the Austrian generalissimo, Coburg, to give battle to Jourdan's levies after Fleurus. But Coburg had chosen to fall back eastward on his communications, leaving Brussels to its fate and the British to shift for themselves. It was because, after a generation of disaster and servitude, a Prussian field marshal had learnt the necessity of unselfish co-operation between allies, that Wellington was able to take his stand here. For though his only reliable troops were outnumbered by two to one and though the French had nearly double his weight of artillery, he knew that he had only to hold his ground with one wing of an international army until the other under Blücher could reach the battlefield. Then, on the morrow, the whole mighty force could take the offensive and sweep Napoleon back to France.

Unlike Blücher at Ligny, who, in the normal continental manner, had drawn up his army in view of Napoleon, Wellington—the greatest master of defensive tactics in Europe—had chosen a position where his infantry could inflict the utmost damage on the attackers while suffering the least themselves. Its reverse or northern slope, in whose undulations he concealed his forces, gave him precisely the cover and field of fire needed for an active defence. Behind it lay the forest which, stretching for miles on either side of the Brussels highway, constituted, with its close-growing beeches and freedom from undergrowth, an excellent temporary refuge into which to withdraw inexperienced troops if they proved unable to withstand Napoleon's attack. Once inside it, he remarked, he would have defied the Devil himself to drive him out. But as, like his ally, he was thinking in ultimate terms, not of defence but of offensive action, he gave battle on the open plain where the full strength of the Prussian and British armies could later be brought to bear on Napoleon.

Until then, however, Wellington knew that his rôle must be strictly defensive. At least half the foreign troops under his command could not be trusted to manœuvre. Kincaid drew the picture of a detachment of them at Quatre Bras; whenever, after a careful explanation of their rôle, they were given the word to march, they had started blazing away at the British skirmishers ahead—"we were at last," Kincaid wrote, "obliged to be satisfied with whatever advantages their appearance would give, as even that was of some consequence where troops were so scarce." Later in the day, he admitted, when they got used to the sensation of being fired at, they behaved quite well. Many, however, having fought for Napoleon when Belgium, Holland and Western Germany formed part of his empire, had little stomach for fighting against him. Many more were boys and raw *landwehr*, though, in the case of the Brunswickers, with good officers and N.C.O.s. Few were adequately equipped or trained. Of the 42,000 foreign troops in Wellington's army only the 5500 men of the veteran King's German Legion—an integral part of the British Army—could be described as first-line troops.

Wellington was, therefore, forced to do as he had done in early Peninsular days; to stiffen his foreign formations with redcoats. In the teeth of opposition, particularly from the King of the Netherlands, he had tried to make his force as international in organisation as possible; to this end he habitually wore the national cockades of all the Allies in his hat and forbade the playing of "Rule Britannia" at regimental concerts. As at Talavera, the most immobile troops of all he stationed among buildings and behind walls. Fortunately one of the features of his position was the presence of villages and farms on either flank of his two-and-a-half-mile front—Smohain, Papelotte, La Haye and Frischermont to the east, and Merbe Braine and Braine l'Alleud to the west. In these he placed some rather uncertain Nassauers, who, however, defended them bravely: Chassé's Belgian division and the youthful Brunswickers who had suffered so severely at Quatre Bras. They thus served—an old device of Wellington's—both as flank guards and reserves.

The backbone of his polyglot and what he afterwards described as "infamous army" were its 21,000 British regulars—of whom more than 2000 had arrived from Ostend only that morning—and their comrades of the King's German Legion. Yet of this vital 26,500—a smaller force than any he had commanded since his first Portuguese campaign—only about half had been under fire. Several of its units were weak second-line battalions, scarcely out of the goose-step. Even most of the eighteen infantry battalions that had fought in Spain had been brought up to strength by recruiting from the plough before they left England. Probably not more than 12,000 had served in the incomparable army that had marched from the Douro to Toulouse and been sent in 1814 to America.

Compared with his Peninsular army, Wellington's force was relatively stronger in cavalry than infantry. Its 7000 British and King's German Legion cavalry, though far outnumbered by Napoleon's cuirassiers and lancers, made an imposing spectacle, superbly uniformed and caparisoned—the Prince Regent saw to that—and mounted on the finest horses in the world. They could ride across country like a field of high-metalled foxhunters, for they came from a land where horsemanship was a passion. At a review they left Blücher speechless with admiration. "It did one's heart good," wrote a Rifleman, watching them on the retreat from Quatre Bras, "to see how cordially the Life Guards went at their work; they had no idea of anything but straightforward fighting and sent their opponents flying in all directions." Their chief, the Earl of Uxbridge, was the Lord Paget who had commanded Moore's cavalry so brilliantly during the Corunna campaign, but whose service in the Peninsula had been cut short by an elopement with the wife of Wellington's brother. Apart from his amatory exploits,[1] he was an excellent officer, quiet and incisive, though, like his command, rather too dashing.

What the British cavalry lacked, except for the King's German Legion and a few fine Peninsular regiments like the 23rd Light Dragoons, was experience of war and, in their high-spirited younger officers, discipline. Too many of the latter held their commissions, not because they wanted to be professional soldiers, but because a few years in a crack cavalry mess was a mark of social distinction. Their courage and dash were indisputable; their self-control and staying power less certain. The troopers, splendid fighting material, were what the officers—so much less experienced and realist than their humbler infantry colleagues—made or failed to make of them. The same witness of the Life Guards' charge during the retreat noticed with amusement that, whenever one of them got a roll in the mud, he went off to the rear as no longer fit to appear on parade.

In artillery, though he only acknowledged it sparingly, Wellington was brilliantly served. Its mounted branch was

---

[1] When someone mentioned to Wellington that Lord Uxbridge had the reputation of running away with everybody he could, he replied, "I'll take good care he don't run away with me." In this anecdote, Fraser adds, he was compelled to soften "the vigorous vernacular of the Duke." Sir William Fraser, *Words on Wellington*, 185.

magnificently horsed, and, Horse and Field Artillery alike, officers and men were animated by the highest professional spirit. Only 96 of the 156 guns opposed to Napoleon's 266 pieces were British or King's German Legion, but they were probably better handled than any guns even on a battlefield where one of the commanders was the master gunner of all time. They were lighter metalled than the French guns, many of which were the dreaded twelve-pounders. Yet, thanks to the foresight of Sir Augustus Frazer, three of the seven mounted batteries had recently substituted nine-pounders for the normal six-pounders. There were also some howitzers.

In the last resort, as Wellington well knew, everything depended on his British infantry. There were far too few of them; as he carefully sent them off after Quatre Bras before the rest of his troops, he remarked, "Well, there is the last of the infantry gone, and I don't care now." A few weeks before, Creevey, encountering him in a Brussels square, had asked whether he and Blücher could do the business. "It all depends upon that article there," the Duke had replied pointing at a private of one of the line regiments who was gaping at the statues, "give me enough of it, and I am sure."

He, therefore, placed his thirty-five under-strength British and King's German Legion infantry battalions where he thought the danger was greatest, but left no part of the battlefield without them. He had received in the small hours of the morning, before retiring to sleep, Blücher's assurance that he would join him in the course of the day with not less than two corps—a force as large as his own. His anxiety was, therefore, for his right rather than his left. Believing it to be to Napoleon's interest to shift the battle away from the Prussians' impending flank march, he expected him to incline to the west, possibly even striking as far as the Mons-Brussels road to seize the Belgian capital in his rear and break his communications with England. For this reason he had retained at Hal and Tubize, some ten or twelve miles to the west, 15,000 Dutch and Hanoverian and 3000 British troops to guard the Mons-Brussels road, protect the capital and keep open his lines to Ostend, where more veterans from America were expected. In the event of the battle shifting to the west this force might have an important effect, either against an offensive or in pursuit of a French retreat towards Maubeuge or Lille.

There was a more immediate reason why Wellington felt anxious about his right. The unobtrusive but fine defensive position he had chosen had one flaw—a narrow, winding, shallow depression which, passing under the walls of a country house called Hougoumont in the plain below the ridge, afforded an approach by which a column could climb round the west shoulder of the plateau out of direct gunfire and debouch on to the reverse slope where his army was drawn up. For this reason he placed near the danger spot on the right of his front line the First or Guards Division and behind it, in reserve and *en potence*, Clinton's fine 2nd Division which, with its two brigades of veteran British and King's German Legion infantry, was the nearest he possessed to his old Peninsular Light Division—a force which could manœuvre quickly. Beyond it he stationed at Merbe Braine and Braine l'Alleud his less mobile reserve of Brunswickers and Chassé's Belgians. In addition, since the winding hollow which his experienced eye had perceived could be commanded by musketry fire from Hougoumont, he adopted the unorthodox expedient of fortifying and garrisoning an outpost nearly a quarter of a mile in advance of his main position on the ridge. With its château, barns, orchards, gardens, park and woods, the estate of Hougoumont formed a 500 yards square whose wooded southern border extended almost to the ridge occupied by the French. Without its possession Napoleon could neither move a column up the hollow nor, unless he divided his army in the presence of his enemy's best troops, envelop the Allied right. Wellington, therefore, placed seven hundred Hanoverians and Nassauers in the Hougoumont woods, and four light companies of the Guards, detached from the Guards' Division on the ridge behind, to hold the house, gardens and orchard and command the sunken way. To the west, defending the avenue to the house from the Nivelles road, he stationed Mitchell's British brigade with some light cavalry in rear. Thus garrisoned, the Hougoumont estate outflanked from the west the plain between the rival armies; if it could be held till the Prussians arrived, Napoleon's position would become untenable. In the meantime it would gravely delay and impede his attack.

Having secured his right, Wellington strengthened the remaining two miles of his front in his usual way by placing his formations, except for the guns and skirmishers, on the reverse slope of the ridge. They were thus out of sight, though not out of range, of the enemy's cannon. They were deployed in broken and staggered lines and so disposed as to present single rather than double targets for the enemy's round-shot. The artillery, save for the reserve batteries, Wellington placed along the summit of the ridge, with orders to reserve its fire for the enemies' columns. The skirmishers and riflemen were stationed on the forward or southern slope, concealed, as were all his troops, in the corn which, almost shoulder-high, covered the entire battlefield. By this arrangement the French masses would have to advance through three successive zones of fire—the rifle fire of picked marksmen, the round-shot and grape of the guns, and, as they came over the crest, the musketry volleys of deployed and, till then, invisible infantry.

Apart from Hougoumont on the west, Smohain, Papelotte and La Haye on the east, and the little farm of Mont St. Jean just behind the British lines, there were no buildings on the open ground Wellington had chosen for battle except the farm of La Haye Sainte. This lay a hundred yards or so down the slope on the southern side of the ridge, abutting on to the straight-paved *chaussée* from Charleroi to Brussels which, ascending the hill here through a cutting, intersected it and the British line at right angles. Here, in the centre of his line of skirmishers, Wellington placed a battalion of the King's German Legion under Major Baring. Behind it and at the top of the ridge the Charleroi-Brussels road was crossed at right angles by a sunken lane which following the crest from east to west, joined, north of Hougoumont, another highway that fanned out of the Brussels road at

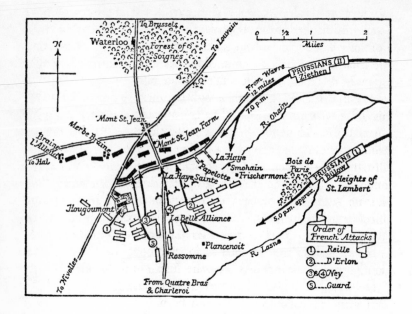

Waterloo

Mont St. Jean and ran through a cutting south-westwards towards Nivelles. This road, like the orchards and woods of Hougoumont, had the effect of constricting the frontage on which the French could assail Wellington's right.

It was generally believed by the British—though not by Wellington, who knew his adversary's overweening confidence and impatience—that there would be no attack that day. But in the course of the morning, it became clear that the enemy advance-guard, which had bivouacked during the night on a parallel ridge three-quarters of a mile to the south, was being joined by the entire French army. Presently the sun came out, and watchers could see the long lines of massed troops, with their glittering helmets, cuirasses and arms, forming a magnificent spectacle, on the ridge of La Belle Alliance—named after the solitary, red-tiled public house of that name. At one time there was a burst of cheering as a grey figure on a white horse, accompanied by a cavalcade, rode down the lines. For the French were not only intending to attack, but, in their resolve to conquer, were partaking of a sacrament. Napoleon might not have France, or even all his anxious generals behind him, but there was no question of the devotion of his fighting men. Between him and his old *moustaches* was a bond to be found in no other army on earth. For all his grandiloquent pretensions, he and they were familiars. Cam Hobhouse, watching him review the Imperial Guard just before the campaign began, was amazed at the way he mingled with his troops, leaving the saluting base and marching in time beside each column; once he went up to a grenadier and affectionately pulled his nose. He might be prodigal of his men's lives, but, unlike Wellington, who was not, he valued his command of their hearts. It was the foundation of his fortunes. At that moment as he rode along the lines amid shouts of "*Vive l'Empereur!*," Leipzig, the retreat from Moscow and the abdication were as though they had never been.

Neither Napoleon nor his men doubted their ability to destroy Wellington's army and reach Brussels by nightfall. Their triumph over the Prussians two days before—achieved against superior numbers—had whetted their appetite for glory. They saw themselves, for all their difficulties, on the verge of a new Marengo. Nor was the urgent victory Napoleon needed the key only to political salvation. It would be a revenge for all the humiliations the English had heaped on him. Wellington was the one commander with a European reputation whom he had never beaten and the British the one army. "Because you have been defeated by Wellington," he told his Chief of Staff, Soult, who dwelt on the British capacity for recoil, "you think him a great general! I tell you that Wellington is a bad general, that the English are bad troops and that this will be a picnic!" His only fear was that they would vanish before he could attack them, as they had done on the previous day at Quatre Bras and seven years earlier under Moore on the Carrion. As, however, they now appeared to be calmly waiting for him, their doom was certain.

"We will sleep to-night," he told his officers, "in Brussels."

Owing to the usual dispersal in search of food and plunder the last of the French only reached their battle stations at midday, three hours after the time originally ordered. Napoleon, however, was not hurrying, since to make full use of his superior artillery and cavalry, he wanted the ground to dry. Despite warnings from those who had fought in Spain, he was quite sure that, once he struck in overpowering force, there would be little need to waste time in manœuvring. Most of Wellington's foreign auxiliaries, he reckoned, would bolt at the start, and the stiff redcoats would then break under the triple shock of his massed bombardment, veteran columns and discharge of grape at close range. "I shall hammer them with my artillery," he announced, "charge them with my cavalry to make them show themselves, and, when I am quite sure where the actual English are, I shall go straight at them with my Old Guard."

As for the Prussians, he was so convinced that they had retreated eastwards, as he wished, that he never considered the possibility of their appearance on the battlefield at all. After the hiding he had given them at Ligny they were manifestly incapable of further fight for the present. Having detached Grouchy to shepherd them out of Flanders, he felt he could discount them. They could be trusted, as in the past, to act selfishly and leave their allies to their fate. It had never been his habit to keep faith with anyone unless it suited him. That a Prussian commander should endanger his army and strain his communications to keep faith with Wellington never occurred to him.

The Emperor, therefore, decided to open his main attack at one o'clock. In the meantime, while he massed eighty field-pieces on a spur of high ground in the middle of the valley opposite and about 600 yards short of the British centre, he ordered the troops on his two flanks to engage the extremities of the defenders' line at Papelotte and Hougoumont in order to distract attention from his impending blow, and probably—though of this there can be no certainty—to clear a way for the use, at the decisive moment, of the sunken hollow leading to the heart of

Wellington's right. In that case, however, he was unfortunate in his adversary.

The first shots of the battle were fired at about half-past eleven in front of Hougoumont. After a short preliminary bombardment, four battalions of Prince Jerome's division advanced against the wood to the south of the château. During the next hour they succeeded in driving out its not very numerous German defenders. But they then went on to attack the gardens and mansion and in doing so came up against a far more formidable adversary, the four light companies of the British Guards under Lord Saltoun. The attackers not only attracted the close attention of Wellington, but brought upon themselves exceedingly heavy casualties—1500 in the first forty minutes, both from the steady aim of the British guardsmen, firing through embrasures in the walls, and from the accurate fire of Bull's howitzer battery stationed on the ridge behind the house. When the Guards counter-attacked and drove them back, Jerome threw another brigade into the assault and tried to gain a lodgment in the courtyard of the château. So furious was his attack that at one moment a detachment of his men broke open the great gate with an axe and swarmed in, only to be surrounded and destroyed inside, while four officers and a sergeant of the Coldstream closed the door behind them by main force. Once again the British counter-attacked with four companies of the Coldstream whom Wellington sent down from the ridge. "There, my lads, in with you," he said as they moved off, "let me see no more of you."

Jerome's answer and that of the commander of the French left, General Reille, was to undertake—a quarter of an hour before Napoleon's main attack on the centre was due to begin—a third attack on Hougoumont with still larger forces. For every regiment they committed, the frugal Wellington staked no more than a company or whatever smaller force was necessary to hold the position. All the while his guns continued to shell the wood with such effect that, as one unending column of fresh attackers poured into it, another—of wounded—as continuously poured out.

So far Napoleon had been only partially successful. His diversion to the east had made little effect on the Netherlanders in Papelotte and La Haye, while the more important one to the west, though occupying Wellington's attention, had failed either to by-pass or capture Hougoumont. It was now one o'clock, the hour at which the bombardment of the Allied centre was due to begin. But before its smoke enveloped the battlefield, Napoleon, watching the preparations from a knoll beside the Brussels road, observed through his telescope a suspicious movement on the high ground towards Wavre five or six miles to the east. It might—at first it seemed to him that it must—be Grouchy, from whom he had just heard that the Prussians were retiring, not on Liége as both men had thought, but on Brussels. Yet this was scarcely likely, as Grouchy in his dispatch, dated at six that morning, had announced his intention of following them northwards on Wavre. And, as Grouchy, like Napoleon, had been wrong once about the Prussians' movements, there was another and less pleasant possibility.

At that moment, this terrifying suspicion was confirmed. For a Prussian hussar, captured by a French vedette to the east of the battlefield, was brought to Napoleon bearing a dispatch from Blücher to Wellington which showed that the troops visible on the heights of St. Lambert were Bülow's corps, advancing from Wavre, and that the rest of the Prussian army had spent the night around that town, only thirteen miles away.

Napoleon, in other words, had been "making pictures"—the crime against which he had always warned his subordinates. He had made his dispositions to fight under conditions that did not exist. Instead of having only the English and their feeble auxiliaries to contend with, he would have, if he proceeded with his attack, to face before nightfall the intervention of another army. The attempt to separate Wellington's and Blücher's forces had failed, at least in any but the most temporary sense. The French must either withdraw—the prudent course—or defeat the British in the next three hours. For after that they would have to contend against two foes.

Being a gambler, and being, both politically and strategically, in desperate need of an immediate victory, Napoleon decided to proceed with the battle. It still seemed unthinkable to him that the breach he was about to blast in the British centre could fail to defeat Wellington, and, with him out of the way, Blücher could be dealt with in turn. Indeed, with Grouchy in his rear and his army committed to the muddy defiles between Wavre and Mont St. Jean, the old Prussian might end the day in an even worse disaster than Ligny. Napoleon, therefore, detached part of his reserve to delay the still distant Prussian advance, and ordered the attack on the British to proceed.

The eighty-gun bombardment, which opened at one o'clock, fully came up to expectations. Twenty-four of the guns were Napoleon's great twelve-pounders, with a 2000 yards range. It took away the breath of Wellington's young recruits and militia men and surprised even Peninsular veterans by its intensity. Captain Mercer, commanding a reserve battery of horse artillery in a hollow several hundred yards to the right and in rear of the British right flank, found, even in that sheltered position, the shot and shell continually plunging around him. One shot completely carried away the lower part of the head of one of his horses. Fortunately the ground was still wet and many shells burst where they fell, while the round-shot, instead of hopping and ricochetting for half a mile or more, frequently became embedded in the mud.

But though very alarming, owing to Wellington's skilful dispositions the bombardment did comparatively little harm except to a brigade of Belgians, whose commander, General Bylandt, misinterpreting his orders, had drawn it up, in the continental manner, on the forward slope of the ridge. During its half-hour of bombardment in this exposed position it lost one man in four, and, had it not been hastily withdrawn to a less conspicuous position, its loss might have been still greater. When, therefore, at half-past one, D'Erlon in charge of the French right moved his corps forward to the attack with all the panoply and terror of a Napoleonic offensive—drums beating at the head of dense columns, bearded grenadiers marching four hundred abreast shouting at the top of their voices, and clouds of *tirailleurs* running and firing ahead—the customary conditions for success seemed to have been ensured. Four divisions of infantry—more than 16,000 men—each moving in close column of battalions at a quarter of a mile's distance, tramped down the slope and up the hill against the British centre and left through clouds of sulphurous smoke. Behind came companies of sappers, ready to turn the village of Mont St. Jean beyond the British centre into a fortress as soon as it was captured.

A hail of shot from the artillery on the crest greeted them. But it did not halt the men who had conquered at Wagram and Friedland. One column, supported by cuirassiers, swept round La Haye Sainte, encircling it and its German defenders and driving back the two companies of the Rifles—the most formidable marksmen in Europe—who were stationed in a sandpit on the opposite side of the *chaussée*. Another, to the west, forced the Dutch out of Papelotte and La Haye and temporarily occupied Smohain. In the centre about 8000 men approached the summit simultaneously. As they did so, Bylandt's Belgians—raw troops who had endured to the limit of their capacity—fired one hysterical volley at the advancing, shouting column and took to their heels, carrying away the gunners of the reserve batteries behind. They never stopped till they reached the Forest of Soignes, where they remained for the rest of the day.[1]

To Napoleon, watching from the knoll near La Belle Alliance, it seemed as though, as at Ligny, his adversary's centre was broken. But it was not a Netherland or even a Prussian army he had to dislodge, but a British. As the French bore down on the gap they had opened, Picton deployed Kempt's reserve brigade in their

[1] "I peeped into the skirts of the forest, and truly felt astonished; entire companies seemed there, with regularly piled arms, fires blazing under cooking kettles, while the men lay about smoking as coolly as if the enemy were within a day's march. . . . General Muffling, in his account of Waterloo, estimates the runaways hidden in the forest at 10,000." Lt.-Col. B. Jackson, *Notes and Reminiscences of a Staff Officer*, 17.

path. It was the familiar story of every battle of the Peninsular War. "The French came on in the old style," said Wellington afterwards, "and we drove them off in the old style." The 28th, 32nd, 79th Highlanders and the 95th Rifles—all veterans of Spain —held their fire till the head of the column was only twenty yards away. Then, from their thin extended line, they poured in a tremendous, disciplined volley, and, as the leading French files tried, too late, to deploy, charged with the bayonet. At the moment of his triumph Picton was struck in the head by a bullet and killed.

Farther to the east, D'Erlon's two other divisions reached the summit. Here, after its heavy losses at Quatre Bras, Pack's brigade—Royals, 44th, 42nd and 92nd Highlanders—could only muster 1400 bayonets. Slowly, against such odds, they began to give ground, while a brigade of French cavalry on their flank, having cut a Hanoverian battalion to pieces, swarmed on to the crest.

At that moment, Lord Uxbridge, waiting behind the British infantry with two brigades of heavy cavalry ready deployed, gave the order to charge. Leading the Household Brigade in person, he drove the astonished French cuirassiers into the ranks of the infantry behind, who, seeing the big, scarlet-coated Life Guardsmen slashing at them, turned and joined in the flight. It was the charge at Salamanca over again. Simultaneously the Union Brigade—consisting of Royal Dragoons, Scots Greys and Inniskillings—swept down on another French column. Within a few minutes the flower of D'Erlon's corps was flying across the plain with 2000 British cavalry after it. "Hundreds of the infantry threw themselves down and pretended to be dead," wrote Kincaid, "while the cavalry galloped over them, and then got up and ran away; I never saw such a scene in all my life." More than 4000 were cut down or taken prisoner. Many did not stop till they reached Genappe.

Unfortunately the pursuers did not stop either. The secret of cavalry is iron discipline. It was a secret that the British cavalry, though superlative in dash, physique and horsemanship, had never wholly mastered. According to Hamilton of Dalzell of the Scots Greys, the troopers had been served with rum before the charge. They followed the French into the heart of Napoleon's position, sabring the gunners of his great battery and riding on to the ridge of La Belle Alliance itself as though they were after a fox. Having charged in the first line, Uxbridge was unable either to stop them or to bring up reserve cavalry in support. When the French cuirassiers and lancers counter-attacked in superior strength, the scattered, breathless men and horses were powerless and became themselves the pursued. The flower of Wellington's cavalry—the striking-force of his tactical reserve—having saved his centre, was itself needlessly destroyed. Sir William Ponsonby was struck down at the head of the Union Brigade, and nearly half the personnel of the six splendid regiments which had smashed D'Erlon's columns were killed or taken prisoner. Vandeleur's brigade, which gallantly tried to cover their retreat, also suffered severely. Those who got back to the British lines were too few to intervene with real effect in the battle again. Some of the weaker brethren never returned to the field at all.

.   .   .   .

But for this unexpected advantage, there would have seemed little object in Napoleon's continuing the battle. It was now three o'clock. Not only had one of his two corps of front-line infantry become heavily committed to an increasingly costly and still unsuccessful struggle in front of Hougoumont, but the British, contrary to expectation, had repulsed and shattered the other which, untouched at either Ligny or Quatre Bras, was to have breached and pinned down Wellington's centre until Lobau's reserve infantry, Ney's cavalry and, at the end of all, the Imperial Guard, had destroyed him. Instead, Napoleon now found himself committed to an impending battle on a second front, to avert or postpone which he was forced to detach, under Lobau, the very reserve of infantry which was to have followed up D'Erlon's expected success. With the Prussians approaching from the other side, he dared not commit this now to a left-hook against the British centre, the vital approach to which was still untaken. Apart from the small portion of Reille's corps still uncommitted to the unending fight around Hougoumont, he had no infantry left for a new attack on the ridge except the twenty-four battalions of the Imperial Guard. And these, in view of the growing threat to his flank and the, to him, unexpected revelation of British defensive striking-power, he was not yet prepared to commit. For the Guard was the last card that stood between him and ruin. He kept it 13,000 strong, the apple of his eye, unused beside him.

For about half an hour there was a pause in the battle, except at Hougoumont, where Jerome and Foy threw ever more troops into the inferno round the blazing but still defiant buildings. Wellington took advantage of the lull to readjust his dispositions. Pack's brigade took the place vacated by Bylandt's Netherlanders, Lambert's brigade came up from the second line to strengthen Picton's battered division, and two more companies of the King's German Legion were thrown into La Haye Sainte. The Prussians were taking far longer to arrive than the British commander had expected. There had been a delay in their start, aggravated by a fire in the narrow streets of Wavre and the fact that Bülow's as yet unused corps had the farthest distance to march. After the rains, the cross-country lanes were almost impassable for transport, and Gneisenau, the Prussian Chief of Staff, was reluctant to attack Napoleon, with Grouchy's troops in his rear, until he knew for certain that Wellington was standing fast. Only Blücher's insistence—for the old man, oblivious of his injuries, was with Bülow's advance guard by midday—carried the tired and hungry troops forward through the soggy defiles of the Lasne and the dense woods that lay between it and the battlefield. "I have promised Wellington," he told them as they dragged the guns axle-deep through mire, "you would not have me break my word!"

Meanwhile, the French gunners had taken up their position again on the central ridge and, soon after three o'clock, reopened their fire. It was more intense than anything the oldest Peninsular veteran had experienced. The range was so accurate that almost every shot told, and after a quarter of an hour Wellington withdrew his infantry a hundred yards farther back from the crest. Under cover of the bombardment, La Haye Sainte in the centre was again surrounded. But Baring's handful of German Legionaries continued to hold the walls, and, with Kempt's and Lambert's men standing firm on the plateau above, D'Erlon's mangled infantry refrained from pressing home their assault. They seemed to fear a renewal of the storm of cavalry that had struck their comrades.

Suddenly the battle took a novel and spectacular form. For, mistaking the partial withdrawal of Wellington's infantry for the beginning of a general retirement, Marshal Ney decided to take a short cut to victory by sweeping the ridge with heavy cavalry. Of these—the finest in the world—his master had almost as many as Wellington's British infantry. He therefore ordered forward 5000 of them, including eight regiments of cuirassiers, drawing them up in the plain immediately to the west of the *chaussée* where the slope was easiest.

Wellington watched the splendid spectacle with amazement. It seemed unbelievable that the French would dare to assail a line of unbroken British infantry with cavalry alone. But such was plainly their intention, and, with his own heavy cavalry too weakened to counter-charge in strength, there was a danger that, if Napoleon was able to bring up infantry and guns behind them, the defenders, forced to remain in square, might be blasted out of existence by case-shot. The two divisions to the west of the Brussels road—the Third and First—were ordered to form battalion squares or oblongs in chequer-wise pattern across the gently swelling, corn-covered plateau. They were aligned so that every face of every square had a field of fire free of the next. Until the attackers appeared over the crest Wellington ordered the men to lie down. Behind the twenty squares his cavalry, including the remnants of the two British heavy brigades, were drawn up in support.

Between and a little in advance of the squares Wellington placed his guns, bringing up his last two reserve batteries of Horse Artillery to inflict the utmost damage on the advancing cavalry. As Mercer's men, on the order, "Left limber up, and as fast as you can!" galloped into the inferno of smoke and heat on the plateau, they heard a humming like the sound of myriads of beetles on a summer's evening. So thick was the hail of balls and bullets, wrote their commander, that it seemed dangerous to extend the arm lest it should be torn off. Their orders, in the event of the enemy charging home, were to run for shelter to the nearest square, taking the near wheel of each gun with them.

Mercer disregarded this order—one that could only have been given to gun detachments of the highest discipline and training —not because he doubted his battery's morale, but because he believed that the young Brunswickers in square on either side of him, who were falling fast, would take to their heels if they saw his men run. As soon as the French appeared out of the smoke a hundred yards away—a long line of cuirasses and helmets glittering like a gigantic wave on the crest of the rye—he ordered his six nine-pounders, doubly loaded with round-shot and case, to open fire. As the case poured into them, the leading ranks went down like grass before a skilled mower. Again and again, when the French charged, the same thing happened, and the Brunswickers, who, before the battery's arrival, had stood like soulless logs in their agony and had only been kept at their posts by the gallantry of their officers, recovered heart.

Elsewhere, where the gunners obeyed Wellington's orders, the French cavalry, crowded in a dense mass into the half-mile gap between Hougoumont and La Haye Sainte, rode over the abandoned guns and swept round the squares beyond. They did not gallop like English foxhunters but came, as was their wont, at a slow, majestic pace and in perfect formation, their horses shaking the earth. As they appeared the British infantry rose at the word of command, their muskets at the ready and their bayonets bristling like massed gigantic *chevaux de frise*. If the

cavalry of the Empire were Atlantic breakers, the British squares
were the rocks of an iron coast. The men, many of them rosy-
faced youngsters from the plough, were much impressed by the
splendid appearance of the hordes of legendary horsemen who
suddenly encircled them and even more by their courage, but
they were not intimidated by them, as Ney had intended. As
their experienced officers and N.C.O.s seemed to regard the newcomers as harmless, in their stolid, unimaginative English way
they did so too. The cuirassiers and lancers made a great deal of
noise and glitter, brandishing their weapons like pantomime
giants and shouting "*Vive l'Empereur,*" but they seemed infinitely
preferable to the continuous hail of shot and shell which
had poured from the French batteries till they arrived on the
ridge.

Short of impaling their horses on the hedges of bayonets,
Ney's cavalry tried every device to break the squares. Occasionally little groups of horsemen, led by frantic officers, would dash
for the face of one, firing off carbines and pistols and hoping to
draw sufficient fire to enable their comrades behind to break in on
a line of unloaded muskets. But the British and Hanoverian
squares preserved perfect discipline, withholding their fire until
they received the word of command and then, with their volleys,
bringing down everything before them. The loss of horses was
prodigious; the poor creatures lay dead or dying in hundreds,
their riders, many of them wounded, making their way in a
continuous stream back down the hill, or sprawling in their
heavy cuirasses in the mud, looking, as Wellington afterwards
recalled, like overturned turtles.[1]

Whenever he judged that the intruders were sufficiently worn
down and wearied, Wellington endeavoured to push them off

[1] Someone once asked him whether the French cuirassiers had not come up
very well at Waterloo. "Yes," he replied, "and they went down very well
too." See Croker, I, 330; Lynedoch, 759; Ellesmere, 98-9, 240; Fortescue, x,
370-6; Fraser, 558-9; Frazer, 559; Gomm, 373; Gronow, I, 69-73, 190-1;
Houssaye, 204-14; Jackson, 48-51; Kennedy, 19, 20, 115-16; Mercer, I, 310-
11; Picton, 81-2, 85-6; Siborne, 1-12; Tomkinson, 305.

the plateau with his cavalry, or, in default, by edging forward his squares in echelon towards the abandoned guns. He did not hurry, for he was playing for time, and he could not afford to let his light British and King's German Legion cavalry encounter the heavier armed cuirassiers until the latter were too exhausted and reduced to retaliate. The foreign Horse which he had brought up from the flanks and reserve to take the place of Ponsonby's and Somerset's lost squadrons proved, most of it, worse than useless, refusing repeated appeals from Uxbridge to charge. One regiment of Hanoverian hussars, led by its colonel, fled as far as Brussels.[1]

Even the British cavalry showed a reluctance at times to charge home in the face of such overwhelming weight and numbers, though several regiments, particularly the 13th Light Dragoons and the 15th Hussars, behaved with the greatest gallantry. The shock felt by men encountering for the first time the sights and sounds of battle—and such a battle—had in the nature of things a more paralysing effect on cavalry than on infantry whose men in square had the close support of officers and comrades. Once Uxbridge, whose energy and initiative throughout this critical time was beyond praise, was driven into exclaiming that he had tried every brigade and could not get one to follow him, and then, as he rode up to the 1st Foot Guards, "Thank God, I am with men who make me not ashamed of being an Englishman." One of the officers recalled how, while Wellington was sheltering in his square, the men were so mortified at seeing the cuirassiers deliberately walking their horses round them that they shouted, "Where are our cavalry? Why

[1] "The Aide-de-Camp . . . seeing that the Hanoverian would not advance, said, 'As you do not attend to the order given, I have another from the Duke of Wellington which is *that you fall back to the rear of the army.*' This the Hanoverian readily complied with, saying it was very considerate of the Duke, when engaged in so much action, to think of his corps with so much care. Accordingly this corps retreated, and it was from them that a report reached Brussels that the French had gained the victory." Farington, VIII, 19-20. See also Hamilton of Dalzell ms., 73; Frazer, 560-1; Siborne, 14, 11-19; Stanhope, 221, Tomkinson, 296.

don't they come and pitch into these French fellows?" Such resentment failed to take into account the hopeless numerical inferiority of the Allied cavalry after its earlier losses, and was based on an incomplete view of the battlefield. All the hard-pressed infantrymen could see, amid clouds of thick, eddying smoke, was the outer face of the square on either side, and the hordes of encircling French horse. They could not realise that the very presence of the decimated English squadrons in their rear helped to sustain the wavering morale of the Netherlanders and Brunswickers, and that the memory of their earlier and heroic onslaught accounted for Napoleon's failure to follow up his cavalry with infantry and subject their squares to case-shot at close range.

Five times in two hours the French horsemen were driven from the plateau; four times, after rallying in the plain, they returned. Whenever they disappeared the British gunners ran out of the squares and reopened fire, while Napoleon's guns resumed their cannonade. Some time after five o'clock Ney brought up the last cavalry from the second line—Kellermann's two divisions of cuirassiers and the heavy squadrons of the Imperial Guard. At one moment more than 9000 horse assailed the ridge in a compact phalanx. This immense body was packed in the 800 yards front between the *chaussée* and the British bastion at Hougoumont, where the ground was a morass piled with dead horses. The front ranks, including most of the senior officers, were completely wiped out by the English batteries, and the weary mounts could only proceed at a walk. Yet they still continued to return.

Throughout this time and during the bombardments which preceded each assault the British infantry patiently endured their fate. They seemed in their steady squares to be rooted to the ground. Though it would have been hazardous in the extreme to have manœuvred with some of the young British second and Hanoverian *landwehr* battalions, they showed themselves, under their fine officers and N.C.O.s, as capable of standing fire as the oldest veterans. Theirs, as Harry Smith said, was no battle of science; it was a stand-up fight between two pugilists, milling away till one or the other was beaten. Inside each suffocating square, reeking with the smell of burnt cartridge and powder, it was like a hospital, the dead and dying strewing the ground. The sufferings of many of the wounded were indescribable; one rifleman had both legs shot off and both arms amputated, but continued to breathe as he lay amid his comrades. Few cried out in their pain, and, when they did so, their officers immediately quieted them; it was a point of pride with Englishmen of all classes to take punishment without murmuring. Their stoicism was equalled by that of the French cavalry, who won the ungrudging admiration of the entire British army.

Nor was less courage shown by the defenders of Hougoumont. The flank companies in the burnt-out mansion among the charred remains of their comrades, the Coldstream lining the hedge and garden wall, the 3rd Guards in the orchard, all lived that day up to the highest tradition of the Brigade of Guards. They had made up their minds to die sooner than yield. Three times the wood was taken and retaken; every tree was riddled with bullets, and in the orchard alone more than two thousand bodies were crowded together. "You may depend upon it," said Wellington, "no troops could have held Hougoumont but British, and only the best of them."

．　．　．　．　．　．　．　．

During the last hour of Ney's cavalry attacks the sound of the Prussian guns had been audible on the British ridge in the lulls of firing, though few yet realised its import. By four o'clock, the two leading divisions of Bülow's corps had reached the western edge of Paris wood, just over two miles east of La Belle Alliance. Half an hour later, in view of the urgency of Wellington's messages, they went into action without waiting for their supports. Soon after five, when they had advanced to within a mile and a half of the Brussels road, Lobau counter-attacked and drove them back. But at six o'clock, two more Prussian divisions having emerged from the wood, Bülow again attacked, striking round Lobau's southern flank at Plancenoit, a village less than a mile from the French lifeline.

The situation was growing grave in the extreme for Napoleon. His troops had been marching and fighting almost continuously for four days; their losses during the afternoon had been heavier than in any engagement of comparable scale in his career. Again and again they had seemed on the point of carrying the ridge and sweeping Wellington's international flotsam and jetsam down the Brussels road. Yet whenever the smoke cleared, the stubborn redcoats were seen to be still standing. The Prussian shot, already playing on the *chaussée*, brought home to the Emperor that, unless he could break Wellington's line in the remaining hours of daylight, his doom was certain.

The Emperor descended from the mound on which he had so long watched the battle. Though, like his adversary, still in his middle forties, he had so far taken little active part in the direction of the assault. After a study of the battlefield in the early hours and the issue of orders for the attack, he had delegated tactical control to Ney. Exhausted by the exertions of the last three days, he had spent part of the afternoon in what seemed to onlookers a coma, and had not even intervened to stay the impetuous marshal's abuse of his cavalry. But he now roused himself, to snatch, as so often in the past, victory from defeat.

He had to fight on two fronts. To the south-east 30,000 Prussians were striking at his communications; to the north 20,000 Britons and as many or more Germans and Netherlanders were still barring the Brussels road. Despite his casualties he still had between 50,000 and 60,000 veteran troops, though of Grouchy's 33,000, wandering somewhere in space to the east, there was no sign. To clear his flank and gain time for a further assault on the British, he dispatched eight young battalions of the Imperial Guard to reinforce Lobau and recover Plancenoit. Simultaneously he gave Ney peremptory orders to throw in infantry and capture La Haye Sainte.

Conscious that the crisis of the battle was at hand and that the interminable and futile attacks of the French cavalry must now be followed up by infantry, Wellington had already reorganised his line. Taking advantage of the lull after the last charge, he had brought up Clinton's division of Peninsular veterans from its place in reserve to a point at which, standing between the defenders of Hougoumont and Maitland's Guards, they could enfilade any attack on his right. Feeling that Hougoumont was now secure and that, as a result, no threat could develop from that quarter, he also summoned Chassé's Netherlanders from Braine L'Alleud and placed them in rear of his centre. Simultaneously, seeing that Ney's force was spent, he deployed his shrunken battalions from square, forming them four-deep instead of in the normal two-rank line, so as to give extended fire-power against infantry while preserving sufficient solidity to repel what remained of the French cavalry.

Soon after six Ney attacked in the centre with two columns of infantry and cavalry. They were driven back by a terrific fire from the British guns. But the French were fighting magnificently and with the recklessness of despair, and the young Prince of Orange, in charge of the defenders at this point, was without experience of command. Repeating a mistake made at Quatre Bras, he ordered one of Ompteda's battalions of the King's German Legion above La Haye Sainte to deploy in the presence of cavalry, with disastrous consequences. Their comrades inside the farmhouse were now down to their last round of ammunition and at about six-thirty the key to the British centre was captured. Baring's remaining forty men fought their way back to the ridge with the bayonet. At about the same time the eight battalions of the Young Guard, sent to Lobau's aid, recovered Plancenoit.

This double success gave the French, at the eleventh hour, a chance of victory. Throwing sharpshooters and guns forward from the captured farm, they established themselves on the ridge and opened a destructive fire on the left of the Third Division and the right of the Fifth. The Prince of Orange, who had by now completely lost his head, deployed another of Ompteda's battalions in the presence of cavalry with the same disastrous result. A few minutes later Ompteda was killed. His shattered brigade and that of Kielmansegge's young Hanoverians had reached the limit of their enduracne and were on the point of breaking. Only the gallantry of the Rifles and a charge by the 3rd Hussars of the Legion prevented immediate disaster.

Had Napoleon been on the spot to exploit the opportunity, he might have turned the gap in the British centre into a chasm. But when, still watching from La Belle Alliance three-quarters of a mile away, he received Ney's urgent appeal for more infantry, he only asked petulantly whether the marshal expected him to make them. At the crisis of his gamble his moral courage faltered; he was not ready to stake everything. And while the twelve remaining battalions of the Imperial Guard waited, unused, Wellington, summoned from his position with the Guards Division above Hougoumont, galloped to the spot, calling up every remaining available unit.

The British commander-in-chief had received the news with his habitual calm and decision. As all the Allied leaders in the centre had by now been killed or wounded, he temporarily took over command there himself. Leading five young Brunswick battalions into the full storm of the French batteries, he rallied them when they broke under the hurricane of shot and brought them steadily back into line. Meanwhile, Vivian, seeing a new force of Prussians moving up from the east, arrived on his own initiative from the left of the ridge. Uxbridge galloped off to fetch Vandeleur's 11th, 12th and 16th Light Dragoons, and Somerset, with the wreck of the Union Brigade extended in single rank to make the utmost show, instilled confidence and pressure from behind into Chassé's Netherlanders.

The bombardment had now reached a new degree of intensity as Napoleon brought up every available gun to reinforce his massed batteries. All along the Allied centre men were going down like ninepins; close by the crossroads 450 of the 700 men of the Twenty-seventh lay in square where they had fallen. In a neighbouring regiment—the 40th—both ensigns and fourteen sergeants had been killed or wounded round the tattered colours. The Fifth Division, 5000 strong when the battle started seemed to have dwindled to a line of skirmishers. Kincaid with the Rifles began to wonder at that moment whether there had ever been a battle in which everyone on both sides had been killed. The stream of wounded and fugitives towards the rear was so great that a Prussian aide-de-camp, who rode up from Ziethen's oncoming corps to investigate, returned with a report that the British were defeated and in retreat. No one knew what was happening outside his own immediate vicinity, for in the wind-less, oven-like, smoke-filled air visibility was reduced to a few yards.

Yet Wellington's grip on the battle never relaxed. Unlike his imperial adversary he was used to commanding comparatively small armies and to attending to every detail himself. In his grey greatcoat with cape, white cravat, Hessian boots, telescope and low cocked-hat, he rode continuously up and down the line, often alone and seemingly oblivious of the storm of shot. He neither avoided nor courted danger, but, knowing that his presence was necessary to keep his young soldiers to the sticking point, showed himself, placid and unconcerned, wherever the fire was hottest. Everywhere he infected men, near the limit of endurance, with courage and confidence. Almost every member of his staff, including De Lancey, his Quartermaster General, had by now fallen, but, though he looked thoughtful and a little pale, he betrayed no sign of anxiety.[1] Once, chatting with the command-ing officer of a square in which he had taken shelter, he was heard to say, "Oh, it will be all right; if the Prussians come up in time we shall have a long peace." But occasionally he looked at his watch.

[1] Afterwards he said that the finger of God had been upon him, adding simply that it was "a near run thing" and that, if he had not been there, he doubted if it could have been done. Lady Shelley, I, 96, 103, 170; Creevey Papers, I, 237; *see* Broughton, I, 103; Castlereagh, x, 383; Ellesmere, 172-3; Farington, VIII, 32; Frazer, 263, 276; Gronow, I, 69-70; Hamilton of Dalzell ms., 56-60; Kennedy, 126-9, 176; Picton, 88-9, 126; Jackson, 42-44; Smith, 271; Stanhope, 183.

THE FIRE AND THE ROSE

"Hard pounding this, gentlemen," he observed, "but we will see who can pound the longest." And when the smoke for a moment drifted away and the scanty lines of red were seen everywhere to be standing, a cheer went up from his tired countrymen that showed him to be justified. The hour for which he had waited had come. For streaming on to the east end of the battlefield from Smohain, driving the French from the environs of Papelotte and La Haye and filling in the two-mile gap between Bülow's men before Plancenoit and the left of the British line, came Ziethen's Prussian corps. Its intervention was far more decisive than Bülow's earlier but more distant attack on Plancenoit. As the Prussian batteries, adding their quota to the inferno on the ridge, began to shell the ground near La Belle Alliance, Napoleon knew that the end was at hand. Already, from his right rear, news had come that the Young Guard had been driven out of Plancenoit. The field was closing in as it had done at Leipzig, and the night was little more than an hour away.

Soon after seven the Emperor took his final resolution. He sent two of the magnificent, untouched battalions of the Old Guard to recapture Plancenoit and prevent encirclement. Then, bidding his aides-de-camp announce that Grouchy had arrived from the west, he ordered a general advance of all units. As its spearhead he brought forward the remaining battalions of the Imperial Guard, keeping only three as a last reserve. With these he descended the plain, marching at their head towards the British ridge. As he did so the French guns again increased their tempo.

The Guard, fresh from its triumph at Ligny two nights before, advanced with a deeply impressive *élan*. Its men were conscious that they bore the destinies of the world. The two veteran battalions who had been sent to recapture Plancenoit did so in twenty minutes without firing a shot. Those of the Middle and Old Guard advancing against the British were inspired by the personal presence of Napoleon. At the foot of the slope, in a sheltered hollow, he halted to let them pass, throwing open his greatcoat to display his medals and repeatedly crying out, "*À*

302

Bruxelles, mes enfants! à Bruxelles!" They answered with shouts of *"Vive l'Empereur!"* and pressed forward with solemn tread and shouldered arms. In front of each regiment rode a general, Marshal Ney—*"le rougeout"*—with powder-blackened face and tattered uniform, directing. Cavalry moved on their flanks, and in the intervals between the battalions came field-pieces loaded with case-shot. Ahead went a cloud of sharpshooters.

The Guard went up the hill in two columns, the one moving obliquely up a spur from the Brussels road towards the centre of the British right, the other using, so far as Wellington's dispositions admitted, the sheltered ground between La Belle Alliance and Hougoumont. True to the tactical conception that had dominated the earlier attacks, the frontal blow was to be clinched by a left hook. But with Hougoumont firmly held and Duplat's Hanoverians and Adam's brigade of Light Infantry deployed across the hollow way between it and the ridge, the front on which the attackers could operate was narrower than ever. And, with his unerring tactical sense, Wellington was waiting at the very spot at which his adversary's knock-out blow was aimed: on the right of the Guards Division where it touched the left battalion—the 95th—of Adam's brigade. Warned of the approach of the Old and Middle Guard by a deserting royalist colonel, he had ordered his men to lie down out of fire of the guns and *tirailleurs* until the French appeared; their long vigil of endurance, he told them, would soon be over.

In the general darkness and confusion, and because of the fire from the guns on the ridge, the leading battalions of the first column struck the British line at two points: where Halkett's battered brigade of the Third Division was drawn up in front of Chassé's Netherlanders, and immediately to the west where Wellington was waiting with Maitland's 1st Guards. As the huge bearskins suddenly loomed out of the darkness, the waiting British sprang to their feet in the corn and poured from their extended line a volley at point-blank range into the head of the advancing columns. The French tried to deploy but too late, and most of their officers were swept down. Then, while they were still in confusion, the British charged, Wellington himself giving the word to the Guards with a quiet, "Now, Maitland, now's your time!"

But though the Imperial Guard recoiled, it did not break. Both parts of the columns re-formed and opened fire on the on-coming British, their guns supporting them with case. To the east the remnants of the 33rd and 69th were driven back and at one moment almost broke, but were rallied by Halkett. A Dutch battery, behaving with great coolness and gallantry, raked the French column, and Chassé's Belgians, 3000 strong, came up in support. Gradually the attackers, isolated and without support behind them, began to give ground. Meanwhile those opposed to the 1st Guards, though driven back for some distance, had also rallied. Maitland ordered his guardsmen back, but his voice could not be heard above the firing, and some of them, mistaking his intention, tried to form square. In the confusion the two British battalions withdrew in disorder, only to re-form at the word of command with their habitual steadiness on regaining their original position.

But before the battle between the rival Guards could be re-sumed, it was decided by the action of the most experienced regiment on the British side. Wellington always maintained that, if he had had at Waterloo the army with which he crossed the Pyrenees, he would have attacked Napoleon without waiting for the Prussians: "I should have swept him off the face of the earth," he said, "in two hours." The first battalion of the 52nd, commanded by John Colborne, afterwards Lord Seaton, had served in John Moore's original Light Brigade; Colborne him-self was Moore's finest living pupil. It had gone into action at Waterloo with more than a thousand bayonets, being one of the very few British battalions which was up to strength—"a regiment," wrote Napier of its Peninsular exploits, "never surpassed in arms since arms were first borne by men." Owing to the skilful way in which Colborne had placed and handled it, its casualties during the French cavalry charges and the long hours of bombardment had been extraordinarily light.

As the second and westernmost column of the Imperial Guard
after passing by Hougoumont pressed up the slope towards
Maitland's unbroken line, the drummers beating the *rummadum,
dummadum, dum,* of the *pas de charge,* Colborne, who was stationed in the centre of Adam's brigade to the right of the Guards,
took a sudden decision. Without orders either from the Duke
or any superior officer, he moved his battalion forward out of
the line for a distance of three hundred yards, and then, as it
drew level with the leading company of the advancing French
column, wheeled it to the left with the order, "Right shoulders
forward." He thus laid it on the flank of the French. By doing
so he took the risk both of leaving a gap in the line behind and
of having his men cut to pieces by cavalry—a fate he had experienced when, as one of Stewart's brigade commanders, he had
moved up the hill at Albuera.

The reward of his daring was decisive. The Imperial Guard,
taken by surprise, halted and poured a volley into the 52nd which
brought down a hundred and forty of its men. But the British
reply of this grave Roman battalion was decisive. It seemed as
though every bullet found its mark. So heavy were the casualties
in the dense, astonished column that the Imperial Guard did not
wait for the 52nd to charge. It broke and fled. As it did so, the
52nd resumed its advance eastwards across, and at right angles to
the British front, with the two other battalions of Adam's brigade
—the 95th and 71st—moving up on Wellington's instructions on
either flank. A few hundred yards on they encountered another
French column re-forming—the first that had attacked—and
dealt it the same treatment and with the same results. Gradually,
as the recoiling units of the French army streamed back across
their path from the impregnable plateau, the British Light Infantry inclined to the right towards La Belle Alliance. Round
them, out of swirling smoke, scattered units of British and French
cavalry appeared in charge and counter-charge.

For from the ridge above them, starting from the right, the
whole British line had begun to advance as Wellington, hat
raised high in air, galloped eastwards from one tattered, enduring

regiment to another. The time for which he and they had waited had come. "Who commands here?" he shouted to Harry Smith, Lambert's brigade major. "Generals Kempt and Lambert, my Lord." "Desire them to form columns of companies and move on immediately." "In what direction, my Lord?" "Right ahead, to be sure."

It was now nearly dusk. But, as the French cannonade ceased and the smoke began to drift from the ridge, the setting sun cast a ray of light along the glinting British line, now motionless no more, and on the accoutrements of the defeated columns in the plain. The whole French army was suddenly dissolving with the landscape: entire regiments leaving their arms piled and taking to their heels. From the east the Prussians were pouring in a great flood across the battlefield, and to the south-east, where the Old and Young Guard were still fighting fiercely to keep Napoleon's life-line open, Bülow's men had swept through Plancenoit and were approaching the *chaussée*. "I have seen nothing like that moment," wrote Frazer of the Artillery, "the sky literally darkened with smoke, the sun just going down and which till then had not for some hours broken through the gloom of a dull day, the indescribable shouts of thousands where it was impossible to distinguish between friends and foe."

In that final advance, with little groups of French gunners and horsemen and the last unbroken squares of the Old Guard fighting gloriously to give their Emperor time to escape, a few score more fell, among them Lord Uxbridge, who, riding forward by the Duke's side, had his leg shattered by a shell. Most of the British regiments were so exhausted that they halted in the plain between the ridges. Only the cavalry and Adam's brigade, following the retreating squares of the Imperial Guard, proceeded through the heart of what had been the French position.

As Ziethen's Prussian cavalry from the east and Vivian's and Vandeleur's British from the north met at La Belle Alliance, the union of the armies, fought for so fiercely during three days and nights, was consummated. Shortly after nine o'clock the two men, whose good faith, constancy and resolution had made it possible, met on the spot where Napoleon had launched his attack. They were both on horseback, but the old Prussian embraced and kissed his English friend, exclaiming, *"Mein lieber Kamerad"* and then, *"Quelle affaire!"* which, as Wellington observed, was about all the French he knew.

Then, in weariness and darkness, Wellington turned his tired horse towards Waterloo and the ridge he had defended. He rode in silence across a battlefield in which 15,000 men of his own army, including a third of the British troops engaged, and more than 30,000 Frenchmen lay dead, dying or wounded. The sound of gunfire had ceased, but, to the south, trumpets could be faintly heard as the tireless Prussian cavalry took up the pursuit of their inexorable enemies. As their infantry, many of whom had marched fifty miles in the past two days, debouched from Plancenoit into the Charleroi highway, where the 52nd, with its tattered colours, was halted by the roadside, they broke into slow time and their bands played "God save the King."

Note on Sources

The original versions of the narrative chapters included in this book will be found in the following volumes: "The Holy Blissful Martyr" from *Makers of the Realm*, [1953]; "The Grey Goose Feather" and "The Hurling Time" from *The Age of Chivalry*, [1963]; "The Miraculous Providence" from *King Charles II*, [1931]; "The Revolt of Tom Bowling" from *The Years of Endurance*, [1942]; "Touch and Take" from *The Years of Endurance*, [1942] and *Years of Victory*, [1944]; "Retreat to Corunna" from *Years of Victory*, [1944]; and "Waterloo" from *The Age of Elegance*, [1950].

Index

INDEX

Foy, Gen. M. S., 291
France, relations with Henry II and
  Becket, 8, 31, 32-3; invasion by
  Edward III, 45-57, 60, 63, 73; *Jacquerie*,
  57, 66, 94; successes in Hundred Years
  War, 60, 61, 68, 72; 18th century naval
  wars with England, 129, 133, 181;
  Revolutionary Wars, 8, 134-5, 138, 140,
  142, 143, 154, 155-83; under Napoleon,
  183 et seq.; Army, 218-19, 232, 282-3
  et seq.; Navy, 129, 156, 168, 174, 181,
  182, 202 et seq.; ships, *Bucentaure*, 208,
  211, 212, 213; *Conquérant*, 177; *Fou-
  gueux*, 208, 210; *Franklin*, 180; *Génér-
  eux*, 181; *Guerrier*, 177; *Guillaume Tell*,
  181; *Heureuse*, 177; *Indomitable*, 210;
  Mercure, 177; *Orient*, 179-80, 181;
  Redoutable, 212, 214; *Spartiate*, 177, 178;
  Tonnant, 178; other references to, 99,
  114, 121, 124, 125
Fraser, Maj-Gen. Alexander Mackenzie,
  247, 266
Frazer, Sir William, 278n
Frazer, Col. Sir Augustus, 279
Frederick I, Barbarossa, emp. 24, 32
Frederick the Great, 218
Fremantle, Capt. (later Vice-Adm. Sir)
  Thomas, 192, 194
Frere, John Hookham, 230, 236, 243, 244
Friedland, 216, 288
Frischermont, 277
Froissart, Jean, 54, 56, 57, 74, 84, 93n

Galicia, 187, 227, 232, 238, 239, 242, 246,
  249
Gamonal, 232, 233, 235
Ganteaume, Vice-Adm. Honoré, Comte,
  162, 197
Gardner, Vice-Adm. (later Adm. Lord)
  A., 142-3
Gardner, Lt. (later Com.) J. A., 131, 142n,
  150
Gascony, 45, 47
Genappe, 289
Genoa, 53, 54, 159, 163, 164, 165
George, Prince of Wales (later Prince
  Regent and George IV), 278
George, Dr., 111-12
George Inn, (Bridport), 117
  (Brighthelmstone), 124
  (Mere), 119
  (Portsmouth), 191
Germany, 24, 53, 189, 216, 219, 231, 242,
  253, 256, 276, 288 (*see also* Brunswick,
  Hanover, Prussia)
Ghent, 52, 66, 272
Gibraltar, 162, 163, 203, 223; Straits of,

135, 166, 195, 196, 197, 198, 200, 201,
  202, 203, 204
Giffard, Charles, 100
Glasgow, 217
Gneisenau, Gen. Count, 291
Gosport, 130, 150
Gounter, Col. George, 121, 122-3, 124-5
  Mrs. Catherine (wife of above), 121
Gower, Com. (later Adm.) Sir E., 151
Gower, John, 63, 76
Graham, Lt. Gen. Thomas (later Gen.
  Lord Lynedoch), 237, 239
Grammont, 272
Gravesend, 71, 72
Gravina, Adm., 215
Greece, 172-3
Greenwich, 78-9
Grey, Gen. Sir Charles (later Earl), 150, 219
Grim, 36
Grindcobbe, William, 92, 93-4
Grouchy, Marshal, 274, 284, 286, 291, 298,
  302
Guadarrama Pass, 243
Guadarrama, Sierra de, 237, 239, 242,
  245
Gwent, 43

Hal, 279
Hales, Sir Robert, 69, 71, 75, 77, 83, 84-5
Halidon Hill, 43-5, 51
Halkett, Maj-Gen. Sir Colin, 304
Hallowell, Capt. (later Adm. Sir) Ben-
  jamin, 136, 179, 180
Halsenoth, Joan, 115
Hambledon, 121-3
Hamilton, Archibald James, 290
Hamilton, Emma, Lady, 171, 184, 190,
  191, 192, 193, 195, 207, 214
Hamilton, Sir William, 165, 171
Hampshire, 119, 121-3, 191
Hanoverians, 249, 270, 271, 277, 278, 279,
  280, 281, 289, 292, 295, 296, 299, 300
Harcourt, Godfrey de, 55
Hardy, Capt. (later Adm. Sir), T., 135, 160,
  163, 207, 212-13, 214
Hardy, Thomas, 191
Harmsworth, 66
Harris, Rifleman, 229, 241, 257
Harvey, Capt., 207
Hastings, battle of, 52
Haydon, Benjamin Robert, 190
Heale House (Wilts), 119, 120-1
Helder, the, 157
Henchman, Dr. Humphrey (Bishop of
  London), 120
Henrietta Maria, q. 125
Henry I, k., 24, 25

313

INDEX

Thomas of Woodstock, Earl of Buckingham, 72
Thouars, Capt. Dupetit, 178
Thugut, Baron Franz, 157
Thursfield, J. R., 199
Times, The, 159, 224, 263
Tippoo Sahib, Sultan of Mysore, 156, 166
Tomes, John, 111
Tong, 106
Tordesillas, 241, 242, 247
Toro, 241
Toulon, 156, 158, 159, 162, 163, 164, 182, 183, 184, 188
Toulouse, 277
Tracey, William de, 34
Trafalgar, Cape, 168, 204; battle of, 204–15, 216, 245
Trent, 114, 115, 119
Troubridge, Capt. (later Rear-Adm. Sir) T., 164, 170, 178
Tryvet, Sir Thomas, 76
Tubize, 279
Tudela, 235
Turkey, 156, 182, 253
Twyford, 121
Tyler, Wat, 73, 75, 76, 77, 78, 80, 84, 85, 88, 89, 90, 91, 92, 93
Tytherley, 121

United States of America, 271, 277, 280; War of Independence, 129, 160
Ushant, 187
Uxbridge, Gen. Earl of (later 1st Marquis of Anglesey), 217, 233, 241, 247, 249, 250, 274, 278, 289, 295, 300, 306

Valderas, 249
Valencia, 238
Valetta, 167
Valladolid, 227, 232, 233, 235, 240, 242, 243, 253, 269
Vandeleur, Maj.-Gen. (later Gen.) Sir John, 290, 300, 306
Vandyke, Sir Anthony, 101
Venetian Republic, 156
Venice, 189
Vienna, 147, 189
Vigo, 251, 255, 256, 259
Villacastin, 236, 243
Villafranca, 250, 251, 254, 255, 256
Villeneuve, Adm. P.-C. J.-B.-S. de, 162, 180, 183, 184, 185, 186, 187, 188, 189, 196, 197, 198, 202, 203, 204, 207, 211, 213
Vimiero, 222, 245
Vinegar Hill, 164, 171

Vire, R., 45
Vittoria, 224, 232
Vivian, Maj.-Gen. (later Lt.-Gen.) Sir Richard, 300, 306

Wadicourt, 50
Wales, 41, 42, 44, 102, 105, 111
Walsall, 109
Walsingham chronicler, 67
Waltham, 95
Walworth, Sir William, 77, 82, 87, 89, 91, 92
Warnford, 121, 122
Warwick, e. of, *see* Beauchamp
Warwickshire, 101
Waterloo, battle of, 275–307; references to, 167–8
Wavre, 274, 286, 287, 291
Wellesley, Sir Arthur, *see* Wellington
Wellesley, Richard, 1st Marquis, 185
Wellington, Viscount (Field-Marshal and 1st Duke of), returns from India, 185; meeting with Nelson, 190; drives French from Portugal, 222, 277; in command in Belgium, 270–2; at Quatre Bras, 273; withdraws to Waterloo, 274; directs battle of Waterloo, 275–87, 290–307
Wesley, Rev. Benjamin, 117n
Rev. John, 117n
Western Approaches, 183, 184, 185
West Indies, 183, 185, 186, 217
Westminster, 23, 24, 80, 81, 87, 101; Abbey, 87; St. Stephen's Chapel, 87
Wexford, 159
Whiteladies, 100, 101, 104
Whitgreave, Thomas, 104, 106, 107, 108
Mrs. (mother of above), 108, 109
Wight, Isle of, 125
Willenhall, 109
William I, k. of the Netherlands, 277
William, Prince of Orange, 272, 299
Williton, 34
Wilmot, Henry, Lord (1st Earl of Rochester), 100, 104, 106, 107, 109, 114, 116, 117, 118, 123, 124, 125
Wilton, 120
Wilton Diptych, 87
Wincanton, 119
Winchester, 88, 121
Windham, William, 142, 147
Windsor, 77, 143, 219
Withers, Eleanor, 115
Wolfe, Rev. Charles, 216
Wolfe, Francis, 103, 104
Mrs. Mary (wife of above), 104
Anne, (daughter of above), 104
Wolverhampton, 106

INDEX